Preface Books

A series of scholarly and critical studies of major writers, intended for those needing modern and authoritative guidance through the characteristic difficulties of their work to reach an intelligent understanding and enjoyment of it.

General Editor: MAURICE HUSSEY

A Preface to James Joyce

Sydney Bolt

Longman London and New York

LONGMAN GROUP LIMITED
Longman House
Burnt Mill, Harlow, Essex

Published in the United States of
America by Longman Inc. New York

First published 1981

Library of Congress Cataloging in Publication Data

Bolt, Sydney
  A Preface to James Joyce – (Preface books)
  1. Joyce, James, b.1882 – Criticism and
  interpretation
  I. Title II. Series
  823'.9'12   PR6019.09Z/   79-41169

ISBN 0 582 35194 4 cased
    0 582 35195 2 paper

Printed in Hong Kong by
Wing Tai Cheung Printing Co Ltd

SYDNEY BOLT is Head of the Department of English and General Studies
at the Cambridgeshire College of Arts and Technology and a member of
the Council for National Academic Awards. His previous books include
The Right Response, Poetry of the 1920s and *Twentieth Century Love Poetry.*

62883

Contents

Note

Throughout this book, all quotations are given two page references, e.g. 229/224. The first is that of the page in the edition named in the bibliography, the second that of the page in the Penguin edition.

List of illustrations and tables

Foreword

One of the most attractive topics presented in this book is Joyce's dedication, though a perpetual exile, to his old Irish life. Epic books, like football teams, need homecomings, and a study of this writer has to acknowledge his tenacious memory and disciplined imagination which kept a firm grip on every street of his native city, sending the reader to a city map as on p. 174 to substantiate the author's massive narrations and meditation.

Many of our readers will turn first to Mr Bolt's elegant discussion of *A Portrait*, Joyce's most widely appreciated book. Clear topic outlines and a wealth of significant detail mark the explications below and must prompt the reader towards an appreciation of the aesthetic and linguistic forms created by Joyce's massive wit. Formidable though the later work of Joyce is, the adventurous reader is drawn towards *Ulysses* and will then explore the appropriate section of this critique organized again under similar headings, its material codified and classified into intriguing tables, as on pp. oo and oo. Indeed, as far as I am aware most of the material in this book is unsurpassed in any other introductory monograph of this size and scope.

Paradoxically, Joyce's books are the work of a master of the modern movement and an heir of medieval traditions at the same time. In fact, he seems to have synthesized in them the Irish literary consciousness as a whole. I'm not thinking only of the admired Irish Renaissance with its tiny dynamic Abbey Theatre but of the comic spirit that Swift, Sheridan, Wilde and Shaw exploited in different ways. Further back too I am thinking of Celtic legend and the country's medieval heritage of medieval manuscripts whose skilled penmanship created the free-ranging design and fantasy embodied in the Book of Kells in Dublin's Trinity College. Joyce's pages may be interpreted as the creation of a series of central issues packed in between the lines and interlaces with all manner of bizarre materials in much the same way. Medieval readers were accustomed to universal and encyclopaedic scholars. Isn't this what we have in Joyce also? Having identified, for instance, the Homeric parallels in *Ulysses* we should find it entirely natural to discover other hidden schemes built into the text. Medieval scholars delighted in the hidden web of correspondences that encircles all known aspects of reality and emanates from God the Creator. Such thinking was a most acceptable precursor for Joyce's own, and the Irish literary tradition provided it for him.

To start reading Joyce as he himself wanted is a task that never quite leaves off, and this book has been designed for this series in a learned and quietly persuasive manner by Sydney Bolt, a guide who has long learned how to identify and evaluate both the wood and the trees in the forest of Joyce's unique sensibility.

MAURICE HUSSEY General Editor

Introduction

During the years between the two world wars, for most of which he was living in Paris, James Joyce was an international symbol of modernity. The reputation of his novel *Ulysses*—at that time unobtainable in most countries where it was admired—ensured him that status. Even those who had read the book were not quite certain where its modernity lay but one thing was certain. Considered as a product of technology it challenged comparison with the latest developments in engineering. Only specialists could understand how it was constructed. It was a triumph of remote expertise.

The image of Joyce as the infallible inventor is unequivocally presented in Wyndham Lewis's portrait of him (p. xii). Compare this with a typical portrait of W. B. Yeats, and the peculiar impersonality of Joyce's art is immediately made manifest. Yeats personifies the artist as seer: Joyce looks like an engineer. He has the inhuman look of a man whose glances are not to be returned, because his eyes are devoted to the examination of mechanisms. Indeed, his eyes are not even represented. The direction of his spectacle lenses tells us all we need to know about his vision. They are not aimed outwards, at us, but focussed intently downwards, as if upon some technical problem, laid out for solution on a drawing-board or work bench. The expression of the face is concentrated but in no way tense. On the contrary, there is an air of comfort, almost of complacency, as of the star performer whose appreciation of the difficulty of his task serves only to enhance his sense of mastery.

This is the face of the master, whom a young man stopped in the street, requesting permission to kiss the hand that wrote *Ulysses*. It is not, however, the face of the man who withdrew that hand and advised against kissing it, because it had done other things too. James Joyce was not merely the vehicle of his art, and was capable of distinguishing his powers as an artist from his weaknesses as a man. *Ulysses*, he once stated, was a wise book written by a foolish man. In so far as the foolish man was a great artist he was uncompromising, firm and patient—as well as prickly, vain, suspicious, stuffy and unscrupulous. But the foolish man was also many other things—playful, high-spirited, imprudent, improvident and silly, a boon companion and above all else a family man.

It was this foolish man who provided the material for the infallible artist to scrutinise, and the older he grew the more scrutiny revealed this material to be comic and commonplace. To celebrate his fiftieth birthday he arranged for a caricature to be published, in which he appeared as a clown, as is symbolised by the star stuck on his nose

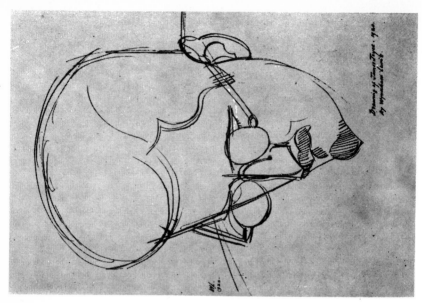

left *César Abin's caricature of Joyce, published in transition, 1932*

right *James Joyce in 1920, drawing by Wyndham Lewis*

(p. xii). The only allusion to art is the song sheet in his pocket, 'Let Me Like A Soldier Fall' Appropriately this is a piece bristling with tests of the singer's technique (as Browne mentions in 'The Dead'), and its theme of the falling hero is that of *Finnegans Wake*, which he was then at work on. The song's heroic proclamation, however, serves only to mock the unheroic, harassed and shabby genteel condition of the clown who carries it. He stoops and wavers, so that his doubtful figure forms an agitated question-mark. The impenetrable spectacles this time suggest not impersonality but blindness, while festoons of cobwebs imply obsolescence, not modern technical efficiency. Parochialism is indicated by the globe: Ireland is the whole world for this pathetic creature, who, as his black hat shows, has also suffered a bereavement. He is in mourning for his father, for, to repeat, the foolish man was above all a family man.

Part One
The Writer and His Setting

Chronological table

	JOYCE'S LIFE	BACKGROUND EVENTS
1882	Born Dublin	Henrik Ibsen, *An Enemy of the People*
1884	Birth of Stanislaus Joyce	Mark Twain, *Huckleberry Finn*
1885		Emile Zola, *Germinal* Walter Pater, *Marius the Epicurean*
1886		A. Rimbaud, *Les Illuminations*
1888	Enrolled in Clongowes Wood College	Death of Matthew Arnold
1890		Fall of Parnell
1891	Withdrawn from Clongowes Wood	Gauguin settles in Tahiti
1892		Death of Tennyson
1893	Joyce family moves to Dublin	
1894		George Moore, *Esther Waters*
1895		W. B. Yeats, *Poems*
1896		Thomas Hardy, *Jude the Obscure*
1898	Enters University College, Dublin	Death of Stéphane Mallarmé
1899		The Boer War
1900	Article, 'Ibsen's New Drama', in the *Fortnightly Review*	Sigmund Freud, *The Interpretation of Dreams* Death of Oscar Wilde

1901	'The Day of the Rabblement'	W. B. Yeats, George Russell *et al.*, *Ideals in Ireland* Death of Queen Victoria
1902	Goes to study in Paris	End of the Boer War André Gide, *L'Immoraliste*
1903	Returns to Dublin Death of his mother	Samuel Butler, *The Way of All Flesh* Henry James, *The Ambassadors* G. B. Shaw, *Man and Superman*
1904	*The Holy Office* Elopement to Europe with Nora Barnacle	Joseph Conrad, *Nostromo* Anton Chekhov, *The Cherry Orchard* Abbey Theatre founded
1905	Moves to Trieste Joined by Stanislaus Birth of son, George (Giorgio)	H. G. Wells, *Kipps*
1906	Moves to Rome	
1907	Returns to Trieste *Chamber Music* published	Synge, *The Playboy of the Western World* Cubist Exhibition in Paris
1908	Birth of daughter, Lucia Anna	Arnold Bennett, *The Old Wives' Tale*
1909	Visits Dublin twice	
1910	Returns to Trieste	The Futurist Manifesto
1912	Last visit to Dublin *Gas from a Burner*	
1913	Contacted by Ezra Pound	Marcel Proust, *Du côté de chez Swann* D. H. Lawrence, *Sons and Lovers*

1914	*A Portrait of the Artist as a Young Man* begins serial publication in *The Egoist* *Dubliners* published Work started on *Ulysses*	Outbreak of First World War
1915	Moves to Zürich	Ezra Pound, *Cathay*
1916	Publication of *A Portrait of the Artist as a Young Man*	Dadaist movement started in Zürich
1917	First eye operation	The Russian Revolution T. S. Eliot, *Prufrock and Other Observations*
1918	*Exiles* published *Ulysses* starts serialisation in the *Little Review*	The Armistice Luigi Pirandello, *Six Characters in Search of an Author*
1919	Returns to Trieste	
1920	Moves to Paris *Little Review* restrained from publishing *Ulysses*	Paul Valéry, *Le Cimetière Marin*
1922	*Ulysses* published in Paris	T. S. Eliot, *The Waste Land*
1923		R. M. Rilke, *The Duino Elegies*
1924		E. M. Forster, *A Passage to India* André Breton, *The Surrealist Manifesto* Thomas Mann, *The Magic Mountain*
1925		F. Scott Fitzgerald, *The Great Gatsby* Franz Kafka, *The Trial* Sean O'Casey, *Juno and the Paycock* J. Dos Passos, *Manhattan Transfer* Virginia Woolf, *Mrs Dalloway*

1926		T. Dreiser, *An American Tragedy*
1927	*transition* begins serial publication of *Work in Progress* *Pomes Penyeach*	
1928		Death of Thomas Hardy W. B. Yeats, *The Tower*
1929	*Our Exagmination round his Factification for Incamination of Work in Progress*	William Faulkner, *The Sound and the Fury* Ernest Hemingway, *A Farewell to Arms*
1930	Stuart Gilbert, *James Joyce's 'Ulysses'*	Death of D. H. Lawrence
1931	Marriage Death of his father	
1932	Birth of his grandson	W. H. Auden, *The Orators* W. B. Yeats, *The Winding Stair*
1933	*Ulysses* permitted publication in USA	
1934	Frank Budgen, *James Joyce and the Making of 'Ulysses'*	
1935		Christopher Isherwood, *Mr Norris Changes Trains*
1937		Jean-Paul Sartre, *La Nausée*
1939	*Finnegans Wake* published	Outbreak of Second World War Death of W. B. Yeats
1940	Moves to Zürich	
1941	Death in Zürich	

1 Biographical background

Family

For the harassed individual James Joyce, art supplied a means of getting outside himself. After a placid early childhood he had to learn to escape distress by the deliberate employment of detachment. Distress entered his life in 1891, when he was nine years old and his father removed him from the expensive boarding school of Clongowes Wood. The following year, as a further economy, the family moved from the fashionable neighbourhood of Bray, where they had been living comfortably, into Dublin, where they were to live in increasing squalor. This was only the first of many such moves, each marking in its turn a further descent. The descent, however, was never regarded by John Joyce, the father, as social. He never ceased to have a high regard for himself as a gentleman, and James, his eldest son, inherited this hauteur.

Furthermore, the decline of the family fortunes was incorporated into the myth of Parnell, the haughty national leader with whose downfall it coincided. John Joyce had considerable private means, but the bulk of his income had been his salary from a lucrative although undemanding post in local government to which he had been appointed in 1880 in recognition of services to the Liberal Party. It was as a nationalist that he had rendered these services, and when his post was abolished he found it natural to associate his misfortune with the simultaneous martyrdom of Parnell.

John Joyce remained a staunch supporter of Parnell when the scandal of the leader's adultery with Kitty O'Shea lost him the support of most of his followers. The theme of betrayal was thus frequently sounded in the Joyce household. Young James himself wrote a poem on the subject—'Et tu Healey'—and did not fail to learn the lesson that heroes are stabbed in the back, a fate which he was too apt, if not even eager, himself to expect in later life. But he also derived from the same experience the more fruitful lesson that heroes have clay feet. The heroes of his fiction are anti-heroes, even when they are modelled on himself.

From then on the family atmosphere was clouded by anxieties about rents, loans, mortgages, sales and repayments; chilled by poverty; and poisoned by the moody temper of the father whose awareness of his family responsibilities led him to resent them rather than fulfil them. Never again to be permanently employed, he was still always ready to buy a drink. On one memorable occasion when his father came home drunk, James had to jump on his back to prevent him from attacking his mother. The latter's patient suffering affected the boy ambiguously. It fostered distrust of the religion which demanded such self-sacrifice. It also fostered a belief that women were purer than men—or at least could be expected to be so. This latter belief proved perfectly compatible with a belief in male superiority, as also in the existence of a totally different sort of female, the faithless temptress. This view of the untrustworthiness of women may have originated in the experience of a first-born who found his position as mother's darling usurped by no less than nine successors (not counting three miscarriages).

Despite this early invitation to self-pity and misery, Joyce's ultimate view of the general process of decline and fall was comic. That this was so was due to the strange conjunction in his temperament of vitality with equanimity. His family nickname was 'Sunny Jim', and he had little (although he did have some) of the priggishness with which he endowed his fictional representative, Stephen Dedalus. The inflexibility belonged rather to his younger brother, Stanislaus, whose moral view was consistently black and white. 'I wish I could see now, or could have seen then,' Stanislaus later protested, in *My Brother's Keeper*, 'the funny side of such happenings, as my brother did.' (The happening in this instance was their father stopping on his drunken way home to play a barrel-organ in the street, an incident which James found entertaining.) Although noted for his aloof coldness, Joyce was popular at school and college, where he played a prominent role. His detachment did not quell his high spirits. Here again a comparison with Stephen in *A Portrait* is surprising. In the second chapter of the novel, a cunning schoolfellow tries to lure Stephen into mimicking the headmaster in the school play. In real life the young James Joyce seized the opportunity to do just that, as was afterwards recalled by one of those present.

> Joyce, who was cast for the part of a master in the school play, ignored the role allotted to him and impersonated Father Henry. He carried on, often for five minutes at a time, with the pet sayings of the Rector, imitating his gestures and mannerisms. The other members of the cast collapsed with laughter on the stage— completely missing their cues and forgetting their parts—and the schoolboy audience received the performance with hysterical glee.

(U. O'Connor (ed.) *The Joyce We Knew*, Mercier 1967)

His uproarious laughter was notorious, and he was in demand at parties for his songs and his clowning.

Nor did he view his father simply as a figure of fun, much less as an object of contempt, as Stephen Dedalus regards his father in the novel. Once again, in this respect he has endowed his fictional counterpart with his brother's traits. The scapegrace father was also a wit, a gifted storyteller and a singer. His eldest son appreciated these accomplishments no less than his cronies did in Dublin bars. To those who might censure him in his reduced circumstances John Joyce's response was ironical mockery which reduced them in their turn. His stance was that of one who, having lived among heroes, was in a position to give you the lowdown on their puny successors. This view—that to get at the truth means to expose a sham—was central to the literary art of his son. Hostility to the smug, contempt for the respected, and a sceptical realism are postures readily adopted in a family that has come down in the world. In Stanislaus this attitude led to aggressive anti-clericalism and radicalism. As regards politics, James retained an interest in socialism at least until the 1914 war, but his fundamental principle was one of self-centredness. He was interested in the truth more because he believed it would set his mind free, than because it could be used as a weapon against the enemies of the people. As for Christianity and the Church, his attitude to both was always more appreciative than hostile, although totally sceptical—in keeping, indeed, with his attitude to most things. (The youthful refusal to go to Mass at Easter, attributed to Stephen in *A Portrait*, was in fact a gesture of Stanislaus, which his elder brother advised against in the interest of peace and quiet.)

The most marked characteristic of Stephen Dedalus in *A Portrait* is his isolation. Self-centred though he undoubtedly was, Joyce himself was well supplied with companions, both as a boy and as a young man, and his family was not excluded from intimacy with him. It is impossible to imagine the young man in the novel trying to share his literary enthusiasms with his mother, or submitting a play he had written to his father's approval, but Joyce did both. Stanislaus was an eager participant in his development, half proud, half resentful of his role as 'whetstone', on which the elder brother (whom he already admired as a genius), sharpened new ideas before using them to dazzle peers and rivals. Although he feared it, Joyce's sense of the family bond was deep and keen. In 1902 he broke free and went to Paris, only to rush home the following year at the news of his mother's fatal illness. Beside the deathbed, when she was already unconscious, James and his brother refused to obey a command to kneel, but another incident shows that his heart was too tender to put principle before sympathy. Finding his nine-year-old sister in tears he sat on the stairs with his arm round her, and told her that as their mother was now in heaven watching them it was a mistake to spoil her happiness by crying, while it would please her if one prayed.

If Joyce failed the family he was born into, it was not in feeling but in action. As the eldest son and brightest hope, he might have been expected to shoulder the responsibilities his father could not bear. For several years, however, it had become increasingly clear that he was not aiming at a recognised career. At school he had been a prize pupil, but at university, although he did not fail his courses, he concentrated his studies on those writers—some modern and little known, others ancient and barely remembered—who served his idiosyncratic interests. When he left university as a poet, author of several prose pieces, and inventor of an aesthetic theory, he had already decided that his sole duty was to his art. In 1904, at the age of 22, he again left Ireland and this time, except for three brief and unsatisfactory interludes, his exile was to be permanent. Even so, the break with the family was more apparent then real. Before long he sent for Stanislaus to join him, and, a little later, invited a sister as well.

More significantly, he had abandoned one family only to set up another, which he was to fail neither in feeling nor responsibility for the rest of his life. When he left Dublin, Nora Barnacle, a country girl working in Dublin as a maid in a hotel, intrepidly agreed to accompany him although the young artist's egotistical principles would not even allow him to admit he loved her, let alone propose marriage. Nevertheless, she did not find it hard to convert him into a quite ordinary husband, a position legalised when, in 1931, they at last got married to safeguard the status of their children. In a relationship which had its initial ups and downs, he tried at first to fit her into the role of pastoral innocent or, alternatively, bestial temptress. Happy-go-lucky and down-to-earth, she indulged his fancies as far as she could without unduly putting herself out. The one role she would not play was Galatea to his Pygmalion. She would stand no nonsense. He said she made a man of him, and certainly she made it impossible for him to see himself as a hero. Even at the height of his fame in Paris, she was known to observe to startled devotees that it was a pity her husband, who had once sung on the same platform as John McCormack, had abandoned his singing, and taken up writing instead.

The Irish question

A memorable feature of the *Portrait* is the melancholy family sing-song which confirms Stephen in his rejection of the priesthood, and song recitals by Giorgio, Marie Jolas, and Joyce himself, were a notable feature of the parties he gave in Paris to intimate friends. His family had a long musical tradition, perhaps most strikingly exemplified when his grandfather on his deathbed urged his only son not to miss the opera by hanging about waiting for his last breath. His father was a noted singer, and almost became a professional. The same career was open to Joyce, and for a time he seriously contemplated it, spending some of his scanty cash on training his faint but appealing tenor voice. He sang professionally at concerts (thus gathering material for 'A Mother'), and almost won a gold medal at a festival of music—his failure being due to his inability to sing at sight which he converted into a refusal on artistic principle. In 1904 he toyed with the idea of touring the south coast of England, singing old English songs to the accompaniment of a lute.

Although literature was his chosen art, music made a continuous contribution to his writing, not only in the many scenes of musical performance and discussion, but in the delicately modulated cadences of his sentences. His taste was characteristically comprehensive, ranging from street ballads and music-hall songs to opera, and provided him with a wide field of reference which he drew upon in his work from first to last. As Matthew Hodgart has demonstrated, the reader who comes to Joyce with a familiar knowledge of the *Irish Melodies* of Tom Moore, or the works of Wagner, will earn his reward.

This musical skill and passion constituted his most sympathetic link with his fellow Dubliners, for musical events provided one of the chief sources of social life there, and famous singers rivalled national leaders in their popularity. To tell the truth, at the time when Joyce came to manhood in Ireland political heroes were hard to find. It is hard to dissent from Joyce's view that when they rejected Parnell in 1890 the Irish had shown their preference for respectability over genius. Right up to 1912, when he left Ireland for the last time, nothing seemed less likely than that the country would shortly be a scene of revolution. Even Home Rule, which had been Parnell's objective, was hardly a revolutionary aim. It was not, for example, inspired by republican feelings. Its objective was simply to restore the government of the nation to an independent parliament. This was to be achieved by parliamentary means. Parnell's success had been due to his ability to win elections, and to his adroit leadership of the Irish members in an evenly divided House of Commons. Although his disappearance from the scene was a set-back, it was nevertheless still obvious that it was only a matter of time for Home Rule to be granted by the London government without a struggle.

The small bands of young people—male and female—who trained and drilled themselves in readiness for an uprising (like Davin, in *A Portrait*) were regarded as lovable idealists, not to be taken seriously. The most serious challenge to the tameness of Home Rule at this period seemed to come from the Sinn Fein movement, founded by Arthur Griffith, which demanded a more radical break in the form of a dual monarchy on the model of Austria-Hungary. This difference was hardly deep, although it was accompanied by a clearer understanding (shared by Joyce) of the economic nature of Ireland's dependence on England. No major political group made a bid for the national imagination. A cluster of professional politicians jockeyed for position.

This development was fostered by very real changes which had been already instituted by the London government. In the sphere of local government power was passed from the hands of the propertied classes into those of elected representatives. At the same time, thanks to social reforms, the peasants were acquiring the land they tilled, becoming proprietors instead of tenants, and taking to the co-operative movement (founded by Sir Horace Plunkett in 1893) to gain the maximum advantage from their new rights. In the towns industrial development was similarly bringing increased prosperity, together with trades unions and a new, industrial form of unrest. Everything seemed set for Ireland painlessly to take her place among the mild bourgeois democracies of Northern Europe. Those who sought a more radical break with the past were seen as amiable hotheads, with whom it was as impossible to associate in practice as it was impossible not to sympathise.

In this connection it is interesting to note (as Joyce noted) that nationalism, no less than Catholicism, operated as a conservative social force, deprecating the development of class consciousness as a threat to national unity. It was no less conservative in its general cultural effects. One of its most characteristic features was its stress on moral purity, attributing to the Irish people a peculiar innocence, and harking back nostalgically to the Dark Ages, when Ireland had been famous for her saints and sages. Patriotism was essentially a backward-looking, not a forward-looking, force. Traditional Irish pastimes were resurrected by the Gaelic Athletic Association, while si-multaneously the Gaelic League was resurrecting the native language and making available translations of ancient Irish texts which offered mythological heroes as a new source of national pride. (Both tenden-cies are satirised in the 'Cyclops' chapter of *Ulysses*, where the character of 'the Citizen' is based on Michael Cusack, the Athletic Association's founder.) Folklore became the object of earnest study (to the disgust of the cosmopolitan Joyce), and the peasant became the moral hero of the urban intellectual. A new diction, the product of a combination of rural dialect with the peculiar phrasing of translations from ancient Gaelic, came to decorate literature. Racial feelings, too, were roused. The term 'West Briton' (used to insult Gabriel in 'The Dead') began to be applied with opprobrium to citizens who did not stem from the pure native stock but were descended from Scottish or Saxon immigrants.

There were obviously silly and sinister aspects to all this, as Joyce saw to his credit, but the swell of feeling also served as soil to a flourishing literary movement which numbered among its ranks many writers of distinction, such as W.B. Yeats, John Millington Synge, Lady Gregory, AE (George Russell) and, for a time, George Moore. Most notable were the developments in the fields of poetry and drama. In poetry the doctrines of Symbolism then current in Europe blended with the fashionable mysticism of Theosophy and the cult of an idyllic peasant wisdom. In drama the movement initiated in 1899 by the Irish Literary Theatre found a home in the Abbey Theatre, opened in 1904. The aim being to produce Irish plays by Irish writers, talent was in demand. It was sought out, instead of having to fight for recognition. The first sign of promise in a young man like Padraic Colum made him a person of note in a city which was still small enough, despite its national role, for everybody to meet everybody else at regular evenings, at-homes, recitals and study groups. In the midst of this excited and expectant little world, the young James Joyce contemptuously announced that he distrusted all enthusiasms.

Dublin

As César Abin's caricature illustrates, it was as impossible for Joyce to break with nation as with family. His self-imposed exile was only to afford him the observation post from which to contemplate an incurable involvement. Exile was itself a well-established feature of the Irish tradition of rebellion. The wild goose flew abroad to escape captivity in the English net. Joyce's case was different. It was the Irish, rather than the English, whose oppression he fled from. The struggle for Irish independence did not of course leave him unmoved. He held decided views on the major issues involved, and even after his departure continued to follow political developments with interest in the nationalist press. But his conception of national enslavement was deeper and subtler than that of the patriots. He believed that the condition of slavery had produced a slavish mentality in Ireland.

It was not only that, like his father, he maintained the Church had contributed as much as the State to the subjection of his people. It was the more unpopular belief that their subjection had diminished them. Taking such a view, he was unable to share in their national pride. Seeing Ireland as a case for treatment, he was not prepared to treat her as a damsel in distress. Dublin in his view was a musty sick-room, in which everybody conspired to keep the windows shut, instead of letting in the fresh air of truth. This image of letting in fresh air was borrowed from Ibsen by Joyce himself, as a youthful seventeen-year-old, in an essay read to his college Literary and Historical Society on the subject of 'Drama and Life'.

> The sooner we understand our true position, the better; and the sooner then will we be up and doing on our way. In the meantime, art, and chiefly drama, may help us to make our resting places with a greater insight and a greater foresight, that the stones of them may be bravely builded, and the windows goodly and fair. ' ... what will you do in our Society, Miss Hessel?' asks Rörlund— 'I will let in fresh air, Pastor'—answered Lona.

In his view what was required for the liberation of Ireland was an expansion of consciousness, which it was the duty of her artists to achieve. When he looked at the writers of the contemporary Irish Movement, however, the young Joyce found them incapable of the insight and foresight called for, because they were blinded by a mendacious patriotism, which led them to glorify ridiculous myths, together with a foggy otherworldliness, that distracted their attention from the here and now. 'We were the last Romantics', W.B. Yeats wrote later of the movement whose most distinguished member he had been, 'Chose as theme/Traditional sanctity and loveliness'. For the young Joyce, on the other hand, late Romantics were artists who misdirected their attentions to imagined worlds instead of concentrating on the actual; sanctity was a form of concealment; and beauty was to be sought in the future, not in the past. In any case, as far as tradition was concerned, he found the Irish literary traditions which, as he remarked, had not advanced as far as the miracle play, too rudimentary to command respect. The way to expand the insular mentality of the Irish was not to flatter them, but to offer them a picture of themselves seen from a European viewpoint.

While he admired Yeats, therefore, he could not see him, or any other Irish writer of the time, as uttering the truths the nation needed to hear, a judgement he made clear, as a student, in an article which the college magazine refused to publish. Joyce therefore arranged for its private publication as *The Day of the Rabblement*. What was found most offensive in this piece was not the criticism of Yeats. All the students (except Joyce himself) had already united in protest against Yeats's *The Countess Cathleen*, as an insult to the Irish people. But Joyce's broadside was interpreted as another such insult, opening as it did with the words: 'No man, said the Nolan, can be a lover of the true or the good unless he abhors the multitude; and the artist, though he may employ the crowd, is very careful to isolate himself.'

The writer Ireland needed, Joyce proclaimed, was another Ibsen. Ibsen was now dying, but already one successor had been found in Hauptmann—'and the third minister will not be wanting when his hour comes. Even now that hour may be standing by the door.' The man of the hour, clearly, was none other than Joyce himself. In addition to the hostility his criticisms provoked, Joyce's sense of personal destiny also invited ridicule, which became more exasperated and less good-natured between 1901, when *The Day of the Rabblement* was published, and 1904, when he went abroad for the second time. His pretensions appeared so much greater than his achievements warranted.

Distinguishing the foolish man from the infallible artist, it seems fair to say that at this stage of his life Joyce treated his friends to a good deal of the former masquerading as the latter. Their reactions led the foolish man to see them as enemies in disguise. In fact, although he was inevitably the victim of some malice, he was not unlucky in his friends. He was to count on some of them for help years later, after long absence. But he had become a figure to provoke irritation as well as admiration. Besides being a witty companion he was also an inveterate borrower, extracting loans as if they were his due. He was also frequently drunk. Moreover his wit was accompanied by an air of superiority: it was known that he made notes of his friends' sayings and doings not to record their gifts for posterity, but rather their deficiencies. In short, he was the kind of brilliant friend who is welcomed with reservations. These reservations, of which he was acutely conscious, Joyce interpreted as signs of enmity.

He thus had personal reasons for his departure, quite apart from the need for a fresh background for his new life with Nora Barnacle. But, as an artist, he had an even deeper need of exile. By cutting himself off, he was isolating himself from the crowd, following directly in the footsteps of Ibsen, who had done the same thing.

Although their works were very different, the comparison between Ibsen and Joyce is remarkably close, quite apart from the fact that Joyce created similarities by imitation. Norway, Ibsen's homeland, had been subjugated by Denmark, just as Ireland was by England, and with parallel consequences. In the words of B.J. Tysdahl: 'Like Ireland, his [Ibsen's] Norway was an outlying province of Europe. Like Ireland it was vacuous and criss-crossed with parlour-bourgeois suspicion. Like Ireland, it was sustained by prohibitions rather than customs. Like Ireland, it brooded on an epic past. . . . Both Joyce and Ibsen wrote in a conqueror's tongue, while dialects of the autochthonous language continued to be spoken in the countryside. (*Joyce and Ibsen*, Norwegian University Press, 1968, p. 73.) By distancing these limitations, Ibsen had converted them into sources of strength, and the isolation of exile had been essential to this process. So it was for Joyce.

Exile

A remarkable result of Joyce's devotion to Ibsen had been his success, at the age of eighteen, in publishing a piece about *When We Dead Awaken* in the *Fortnightly Review*, which earned him a personal message of appreciation from his chosen master. His ardent letter of reply included a passage of deep personal significance. After relating how he had championed Ibsen in the college, he continued. 'I did not tell them what bound me closest to you. I did not say how what I could discern dimly of your life was my pride to see, how your battles inspired me—not the obvious material battles but those that were fought and won behind your forehead, how your wilful resolution to wrest the secret from life gave me heart and how in your absolute indifference to public canons of art, friends and shibboleths you walked in the light of your inward heroism.'

In other words, the impersonal truthfulness which Joyce admired in Ibsen's drama was not a mere literary device, to be switched off and on. It was the product of a freedom of mind that could not be won without an inward struggle. In 1904, when he left Ireland, he seems to have been satisfied that, in his own case, this battle had already been fought and won. In his own eyes he, unlike his fellow Dubliners, was already a free spirit, which was why there was such a difference in his writings between his treatment of himself and his treatment of them. His treatment of them, in the stories to be collected as *Dubliners*, was clinical: his treatment of himself, in *Stephen Hero*, was almost hagiographical. Stephen, his fictional counterpart, was a hero pure and simple, who 'wished to express his nature freely and fully for the benefit of a society which he could enrich'.

In 1907, however, he created a fictional counterpart of himself to join the cripples in *Dubliners*, to which collection the new story 'The Dead' was added. In the same year he abandoned *Stephen Hero* and set to work on *A Portrait of the Artist as a Young Man*, a piece of autobiographical fiction in which the unhappy Stephen was subjected to such ironical treatment that Joyce was to observe that perhaps he had been too hard on him. He had learnt, since leaving Ireland, that mental freedom called for more than his undeniable indifference to ideologies. It required self-knowledge. In order to expose the motes in his fellow-citizens' eyes it was not merely proper but also artistically necessary for the artist to first see the beam in his own.

And indeed, although he still protested, experience had taught him painfully that he was not very different from other men in his susceptibility to anxiety, jealousy and indignity. Anxiety naturally beset the father of a family, living from hand to mouth on the income of a language teacher, only too happy if he could eke out his regular salary with private lessons that further reduced his time for writing, yet still always needing more than he could earn by any means and consequently in search of advances and loans. Jealousy stabbed him more than once, notably on his second return to Dublin, when a lying friend confided to him that he had secretly shared Nora's favours with him in the old days. The emotional storm which burst in his subsequent letter to her was far removed in tone from his earlier lofty reply to the question whether he loved her—'if to desire a person wholly, to admire and honour that person deeply, and to seek to procure that person's happiness in every way is to "love" them then perhaps my affection for you is a kind of love.' (Letter to Nora Barnacle, 19 September 1904) Indignities beset him not only as the fruits of intemperate drinking but also as the inevitable products of insolvency, as when, during an interval from teaching, he officiated in a bank in a summer in Rome wearing a frock-coat to conceal patches on the seat of his one pair of trousers.

While he was thus qualifying as a 'foolish man', however, he was simultaneously proving his heroism by uncompromising devotion to his art. His patient concentration on his stories and his novel, in the midst of so much harassment, would be enough to establish this. So would the abandonment of four years' work, when he decided that *Stephen Hero* would not do. But worst of all was the apparent impossibility of presenting his work to the world, even when it was finished. 'If Mr. Joyce thinks that the artist must stand apart from the multitude ... we prophesy but ill success', the college magazine had warned him when he was still a student. In the early years of his exile, this prophecy seemed accurate.

His experience was more disappointing than one of continuous rejection. In 1906 an English publisher, Grant Richards, accepted *Dubliners*, only to become increasingly alarmed by the possibility of criminal prosecution for objectionable material contained in the stories, such as the word 'bloody', and a reference to a woman's frequently changing the position of her legs. Joyce tried to meet his requirements, but refused to make any alterations which would substantially alter his work. The argument lasted for almost a year. In the end Grant Richards went back on his offer, and Joyce had to find another taker.

On his second return to Dublin he did so, only to be disappointed once again, and in a more excruciating fashion, because the book was actually printed, yet never appeared. The argument with Maunsell and Co., the Dublin publishers involved in the second fiasco, lasted from 1909 to 1912. In the course of it, Joyce wrote a letter to the press, relating the history of his difficulties as a sign of 'the present condition of authorship in England and Ireland'. He also wrote to George V, to enquire whether he thought that an allegedly offensive reference to royalty should be denied publication. The monarch, through his secretary, declined to express an opinion. In the end Joyce agreed to omit potentially libellous references, dubious passages, and even an entire story, provided the book contained a notice to the reader that essential parts of the work were missing. The publishers, however, continued to prevaricate, and in the end the printers put an end to the business by destroying the sheets. It was now seven years since Joyce had first approached Grant Richards, and he was no nearer to publication. Of Maunsell and Co., he wrote: 'I find it difficult to come to any other conclusion but this—that the intention was to weary me out and if possible strangle me once and for all.' A racy broadside, *Gas from a Burner*, signalled his final departure from Dublin, and he took care that copies were individually distributed to those liable to be affronted by it. His treatment, he argued, was exactly what a distinguished Irishman had to expect from his fellow countrymen.

> This lovely land that always sent
> Her writers and artists to banishment
> And in a spirit of Irish fun
> Betrayed her own leaders, one by one.
> 'Twas Irish humour, wet and dry,
> Flung quicklime into Parnell's eye.

Undaunted, he went on to complete *A Portrait of the Artist as a Young Man* which, in the event, was to be published before *Dubliners*. The only book by Joyce to be published before 1914 was *Chamber Music*, a collection of poems. As they had been written before the direction of his art had become clear to him, he found little satisfaction in their appearance. 'It is a young man's book', he commented. 'I felt like that.' (He was only twenty-five at the time, but about to start work on 'The Dead'.)

Throughout this decade of frustration, he was sustained by his brother Stanislaus. They were together in Trieste for much of the time—the younger helping to support the elder's growing family, and trying to bully him into behaving less like his father. In 1905 they were separated when James went to work in a bank in Rome: towards the middle of each month he wrote a letter to Stanislaus back in Trieste, demanding an urgent remittance to see him through to the end of it. They were also separated on the three occasions when James re-visited Dublin, on two of which he left his family back in Trieste, for Stanislaus to take care of. Returning from one of these visits, James presented Nora with a necklace and pendant inscribed: 'Love is unhappy when love is away'. 'So is love's brother', Stanislaus commented. Relations between them were often strained. Nevertheless, his interest in his brother's art was second only to that of the artist himself, and no less welcome than his money. Despite his creed of indifference, when he was at work on a book Joyce always needed a sympathetic critic to whom to report work in progress. This had been Stanislaus's role as a schoolboy, and he continued to perform it until *A Portrait of the Artist* was complete.

Another friendly critic was Ettore Schmitz, a middle-aged businessman and unsuccessful novelist, who was one of Joyce's pupils at Trieste. Lest the tale of Joyce's misfortunes on his first ten years abroad should read like an unmitigated tale of woe, it is worth quoting from one of the exercises Joyce set this pupil—namely, a written description of his teacher. In this piece, after mentioning that life had not been kind to his subject, Schmitz continues: 'It could have been worst [sic] and all the same Mr James Joyce would have kept his appearance of a man who considers things as points breaking the light for his amusement.' (Ellmann, p. 281)

Stanislaus Joyce in Trieste
inset *James Joyce in Trieste*

The year 1914, when Joyce began work on *Ulysses*, was the year when things began to go right for him. Among those whom Joyce had acquainted with his difficulties was W. B. Yeats. In 1913 Yeats mentioned his name to Ezra Pound, who at once asked him to send him some of his work. That was in December. Pound was enthusiastic, and wasted no time. On February 2nd (Joyce's birthday) of the following year, *A Portrait of the Artist as a Young Man* began to appear in serial form in the *Egoist*, an avant-garde review with which Pound, T. S. Eliot, and other new writers were associated. *Dubliners* was at last published by Grant Richards, also in 1914.

The income from his writing was never enough to support Joyce and his family, but from the time of his arrival in Zürich, although he still needed to give private language lessons, solutions to his financial problems also began to appear in the form of regular remittances from an uncle of Nora's and an American millionairess, grants from literary funds (instigated by Yeats), and finally a settled income bestowed on him by Harriet Weaver, a high-minded, free-thinking, unselfish young woman of Evangelical stock, who edited the *Egoist*, and admired the truthfulness of his work.

The move to Zürich was made in 1915. As a British citizen his position in Trieste was that of an enemy alien, when war broke out in 1914. Stanislaus, who had provoked the authorities, was interned, but James was permitted to take his family to neutral Switzerland, in return for an undertaking to refrain from war activities. Nothing could have been more in keeping with Joyce's attitude than such a promise. He was a natural pacifist, alarmed and revolted by violence, hating and despising coercion—and terrified by thunder. His aggressive impulses went into mental strife.

Any surplus energy was liberally spent in eating, talking and drinking, and in Zürich he could afford to exchange the cheap bars and bistros which, to his brother's disgust, he had frequented in Trieste, for more fashionable restaurants where he became a familiar figure. Here he came into contact with artists from all over Europe. Meanwhile, in England and America, he was becoming famous, a process which was accelerated in 1918, when serial publication of *Ulysses* began. Joyce himself also, from this time on, took carefully calculated steps to nurture his reputation, writing to distinguished figures who expressed an interest, nudging critics into writing opportune articles, and helping along the process of translation.

Notice gratified him even when it was unfavourable. This was just as well. When Miss Weaver decided to publish *A Portrait* in book form (in 1915), seven printers in succession refused to set up the type. When it did appear, the support of Pound and others assured it wide attention, but much of the comment was censorious, some of it savage. The *Irish Book Lover*, for example, warned the author that it was unwise 'to dissipate one's talents on a book which can only attain a limited circulation', and warned the reader that, 'no cleanminded person could possibly allow it to remain within reach of his wife, his sons or daughters'. Serial publication of *Ulysses* could be completed neither in England (owing to the refusal of printers), nor in America, where the *Little Review* was prosecuted for publishing the Nausicaa episode, on a complaint from the Society for the Prevention of Vice.

This notoriety and persecution had the effect of making Joyce's name a watchword. In a contemptuous article in the *Egoist*, commenting on American censorship, T. S. Eliot stated that *Ulysses* was a terrifying book, and went on: 'This is the test of a new work of art—when a work of art no longer terrifies us we may know that we were mistaken, or that our senses are dulled: we ought still to find Othello or Lear frightful.'

The writing of *Ulysses* took seven years. Before the work was finished, he had been installed in Paris as an international celebrity. When he began it he was still in Trieste, with Stanislaus as his chief confidant. The separation from his brother was, of course, involuntary—an accident of war. It was nevertheless also essential to the development of his novel, which as it progressed became less and less like anything he—or anyone else—had written before. When it was finished, while approving the minutely specific truth to life which had won his admiration in his brother's earlier writing, Stanislaus condemned the novelty, artifice and farce which he also found in it, and did so with characteristic frankness. 'There is many a laugh, but hardly one happy impression. Everything is undeniably as it is represented, yet the "cumulative effect" as Grant Richards would say, makes him (the reader) doubt truth to be a liar . . . .' It is easy to see how helpful such shrewd common sense had been to Joyce in his early work, and also how irrelevant it is to the fundamental scepticism of his later work.

In Zürich he had a wide circle of acquaintance, but his favourite companion—probably the closest friend he ever had—was Frank Budgen, an English ex-seaman who had become a painter and moved from Paris to Zürich at the outbreak of war. In him Joyce found a convivial fellow-drinker—who, for example, could perform a belly dance as an accompaniment to the long-legged spider dance with which Joyce, on festive occasions, entertained his inner circle. But Budgen also served at least as a partial substitute for Stanislaus, as the confidant with whom he could discuss his writing as it progressed.

Budgen wrote an account of these discussions—*James Joyce and the Writing of "Ulysses"*—valuable for its insight into the novel, no less pleasing for the picture it paints of Joyce at the height of his powers—enthusiastic, witty, confident, vigorous, enjoying the consciousness of his proved and tested strength, and working hard. But, as ever, Joyce also found time for some foolishness, most notably a quarrel which blossomed into a legal battle, involving the British Consulate in Zürich and even the British Minister in Berne, about who should pay the price of a suit procured by a consular official to wear when acting, as an amateur, in a production of *The Importance of Being Earnest*. By and large Joyce emerged from this fracas as victor, finally rounding the thing off by allotting the names of his opponents to unpleasing minor characters in his novel.

Another episode which provided material for *Ulysses*—the minor infidelities of Mr Bloom—was a minor infidelity of the author himself which began when he was struck by the resemblance between Marthe Fleischmann, a young woman who caught his eye in a Zürich street, and the girl whom he had seen wading by the shore, when he was a boy in Dublin (an experience he had already re-captured at the end of the fourth chapter of *A Portrait*). The young woman was the mistress of a successful engineer, and intended to remain so, but seems to have quickly understood that her new admirer was not dangerous. As a result, for a time she permitted an affair, or rather a game, which was confined from the start by the tacit understanding that nothing would come of it. She was content to enjoy his homage and he to enjoy her charms—at a slight but crucial distance. If the relationship did neither of them credit, it did neither of them any damage, and Joyce could still have described himself as in 1912 he had done to Ettore Schmitz: 'I, who am a real monogamist and have never loved but one in my life'.

Fame

When Joyce arrived in Paris in 1920, a welcome was ready for him. He was already admired in Ezra Pound's circle, and the range of his contacts was quickly extended to include most of the gifted writers working in Paris at a time when it was the literary capital of the world. He became an object of pilgrimage. No young writer felt his visit to Paris was complete until he had paid homage to the master. When Scott Fitzgerald paid his visit, he offered to leap suicidally out of the window into the street as a sign of his devotion.

Those tourists whose interest in literature was confined to reading it paid their tribute in Paris by buying *Ulysses* there. As publication was impossible in America and England, the novel was eventually published in Paris by Sylvia Beach, the owner of Shakespeare and Company, an avant-garde bookshop. The coincidence which in the case of *A Portrait* had befallen fortuitously was carefully contrived for its successor: it made its appearance, in 1922, on the author's birthday—no mean achievement in view of his endless amendments to the proofs. Many knowledgeable readers had already encountered those episodes of the novel which had been serialised. The book was already talked about. But now Joyce set in train arrangements for its reception by a wider public, by prompting critics in advance, most notably Valéry Larbaud. The spontaneous admiration of this distinguished French writer was first tutored and then canalised into a rehearsed lecture which was then received as orthodox doctrine.

In the same way Joyce later supervised the writing of an official biography (Herbert Gorman, *James Joyce—A Definitive Biography*, John Lane, 1941), in an attempt to control posterity's view of him by ensuring certain concealments. In view of the way in which he had himself already dramatised his weaknesses in his fiction, this was a silly undertaking—one more example of the separation of the man from the artist. Another product of this promotion campaign was Stuart Gilbert's book on *Ulysses* which, principally as a result of tips supplied by Joyce, extended the doctrine promulgated by Larbaud by explaining the systematic correspondences and esoteric references which had been worked into the text.

Gilbert was one of a group of minor writers who subscribed to what they called 'The Revolution of the Word', a literary movement whose proclaimed aim was the transformation of experience by means of verbal experiment. Joyce's next work, a dream book in which words were remoulded to express a mixture of myth, philosophy, nonsense and history, was exactly what their programme seemed to require. It became their central text, appearing serially in their organ *transition* under the title *Work in Progress*. This group, with due prompting and assistance, also produced a symposium on this new work, under a title which Joyce himself had suggested, *Our Exagmination round his Factification for Incamination of Work in Progress*.

The tone of this book was adulatory, and Joyce might well be accused of surrounding himself with sycophants in the last years of his life. On the other hand, the work on which he was then engaged was so unorthodox that he looked in vain for support where he had previously received it. Miss Weaver's loyalty never faltered, but, while he wrote to her continually explaining in detail what he was about, he knew that she remained doubtful of its value. Pound, who had expressed reservations about the later, more experimental sections of *Ulysses,* was totally dismissive of the new work. Even Nora caught the general tone, and demanded to know why he could not write sensible books, like other people. Joyce, as always, needed to be reassured about the value of what he was doing, even if his supporters (with the notable exception of Samuel Beckett) were second-rate.

He also needed their assistance in the research required by his new 'universal history', as he was practically blind. This affliction was more than a handicap. It was also a source of frequent, lengthy and acute bouts of pain. The trouble had started in Zürich where, before coming to Paris, he had already undergone eye surgery. During the writing of *Finnegans Wake* (the title under which *Work in Progress* finally appeared on his birthday in 1939), he underwent ten more operations, and he had other painful illnesses to contend with. His family, too, was a source of constant anxiety. His son Giorgio was unlucky in his chosen career as a singer and in his marriage. His daughter Lucia showed increasing signs of mental illness as she matured. He struggled not to recognise this, but eventually had to agree to her confinement in a hospital. Sick and worried, frequently exhausted or in agony, he began to present a woebegone figure, touchy, fussy, and frequently tipsy, whose agile jocularity sounded forced. The days of his week, he informed a friend, were now 'Moansday, Tearsday, Wailsday, Thumpsday, Frightday, Shatterday'.

But he still retained his unpredictable, jack-in-the-box quality. In 1930, for example, at a performance of the opera *Guillaume Tell*, 'the audience', according to a newspaper report, 'were witnesses of a dramatic scene which exceeded in intensity the drama being played on the stage. . . . A sudden hush fell . . . when a man in one of the boxes, whom many recognised as James Joyce, the Irish novelist and poet, dramatically leaned forward, raised a pair of heavy dark glasses from his eyes, and exclaimed: "Thanks be to God for this miracle! After twenty years I once more see the light." ' He had prepared this ludicrous demonstration with care, concealing the success of an operation he had undergone a month before so that he could spring a surprise. All this was to secure publicity for John Sullivan, the Irish tenor who was performing in the opera, and who in Joyce's opinion was suffering from unwarranted neglect.

Sullivan was not the only neglected artist for whom he sought acclaim. Ettore Schmitz received, thanks to Joyce, belated recognition for the work of his youth. Although quick to suspect his friends and quarrel with them, Joyce also knew how to stand by them. During the thirties he was instrumental in arranging the escape of Jewish friends from Nazi Germany. Nor was he slow to recognise his debt to friends like Valéry Larbaud, and Huebsch, the publisher who had championed him in America.

Above all, despite the grief and anxiety they cost, he remained acutely responsive to every family tie. Despite their estrangement, one of the last items in his correspondence is a postcard to Stanislaus, giving the names of people who could help him in his troubles with the Italian authorities following the outbreak of war. The most important event of 1932, for him, was the birth of his grandson

Stephen and when a youthful admirer expressed surprise that he should make so much of such a trivial event he told him that such events were the only important ones. Above all, the older he grew the more he relied on his wife as a mainstay, even though he dodged the restraints she tried to place upon his drinking. When she went into hospital with suspected cancer he went in with her, arranging to have a bed set up for him in her room; and when the time came for him to die in a Zürich hospital in 1941, he asked that she, in her turn, might pass the night in a bed next to his. (The doctor was against this, and he died alone.)

As for his self-imposed exile, although he took every possible measure to stay in touch with Dublin, he never went back. His visit in 1912 proved his last. A visit by Nora and Giorgio in 1922, during the troubles, confirmed all his suspicions. They came under fire on a railway journey, and he was convinced that this proved there was a conspiracy against him. He never saw his father again, a failure which tormented him when the old man died. 'I kept him constantly under the illusion that I would come and was always in correspondence with him,' he told T.S. Eliot, 'but an instinct which I believed in held me back from going, much as I longed to.' His most alienating gesture to Ireland was the one he made when W. B. Yeats wrote to him, inviting him to become a founder member of the Academy of Irish Letters, in the most flattering terms. 'Of

Joyce in Zürich after his ninth eye operation. On his right (left to right) his daughter-in-law Helen, his son Giorgio, and his wife.

Nora Joyce in 1920

course the first name that seemed essential both to Shaw and myself was your own, indeed you might say of yourself as Dante said "If I stay who goes, if I go who stays?" Which means that if you go out of our list it is an empty sack indeed.' The comparison with Dante was not one that Joyce would have rejected, but he had no hesitation about the proposed honour. Politely but coldly he observed: 'I see no reason why my name should have arisen at all in connection with such an academy.'

Finally in 1940, caught in defeated France, Joyce refused to exchange his embarrassing British passport for an Irish one, even though this would have removed the obstacles he was encountering in escaping once again to neutral Switzerland. In the event he was lucky, and it was in Zürich that he died the following January, still worrying about who would pay the bill. Appropriately his funeral expenses were paid by Harriet Weaver, who during their relationship failed him in only one particular—she could not trace a drop of Irish blood in her ancestry.

Conclusion

The 'foolish man' was buried at Zürich, in the Fluntern cemetery. What he had contributed to the works of the fabulous artificer, in addition to their main character, had been a distinct sense of what it means to be alive. 'Welcome, O life!', begins the concluding passage of *A Portrait of the Artist as a Young Man*. 'I said yes Yes I will' are the words with which Molly Bloom ends *Ulysses*. *Finnegans Wake*'s last chosen word is 'the', chosen because it is the most promising of all words.

These affirmations are not mere flourishes of exuberance, such as led W. B. Yeats to compare the youthful Joyce with William Morris, for his vitality. Nor are they expressions of optimism. What they express is the readiness to continue with something against the odds, the will to survive, the irrepressible resilience that carried Joyce through his later years of labour, making nonsense of his bouts of self-pity. His vitality was not that of a cheer leader, but the more surprising energy of a man who, like the hero Finnegan, will not lie down even when he is dead. As a student, he had thanked Ibsen for his 'wilful resolution to wrest the secret from life'. The secret he himself discovered was survival, the operation of an irresistible energy too deep to be inhibited by experience, so that the only effect of calamity upon it was to increase the supply. Survival in this sense—the cycle of rising, falling, and rising again revitalised and nourished by the fall—is an explicit theme in *A Portrait*, the basis of Mr Bloom's claim to heroism in *Ulysses*, the endlessly repeated figure of *Finnegans Wake*.

2 Cultural background

Aestheticism

In 1903, in his *Paris Notebook*, Joyce defined art as 'the human disposition of sensible or intelligible matter for an aesthetic end'. At that time his aesthetic theories had little practice behind them, but in the event the question of disposition—construction as distinct from invention—proved to be his central preoccupation as a novelist. This early definition of art's purpose is also instructive because it reveals the influence upon his thought of the late nineteenth-century Aesthetic Movement. Walter Pater had been the object of one of his schoolboy enthusiasms.

Ezra Pound and T. S. Eliot, with whom he became associated when *A Portrait of the Artist as a Young Man* was serialised in the *Egoist*, were also heirs of the Aesthetic Movement. Not that they believed in 'Art for Art's sake'. On the contrary, they maintained that art performed a valuable public service. When the *Portrait* appeared in book form, in 1915, Ezra Pound, in praising Joyce's 'hard, clear prose' went so far as to suggest that there would have been no war, if only such an accurate instrument of thought had been available in Imperial Germany. More generally, as regards the value of literature, they can all be regarded as subscribing to the claim for poetry made by T. S. Eliot.

> Poetry may make us from time to time a little more aware of the deeper, unnamed feelings which form the substratum of our being, to which we rarely penetrate; for our lives are mostly a constant evasion of ourselves, and an evasion of the visible and sensible world.
>
> (*The Use of Poetry*, Faber 1933)

Joyce shared this belief that literature was an instrument to promote awareness, and the subject of *Dubliners* was precisely the constant evasion of themselves and the world they lived in practised by his fellow citizens, an affliction which he diagnosed as 'paralysis' or 'hemiplegia of the will'. But their aesthetic inheritance was useful to these new writers because it enabled them to insist that art must be independent of other disciplines. A work of literature must not be judged as a philosophical or ethical statement. Its value lay in the perspicuous representation of human experience. The artist's job was not to tell people what to believe, but to make them see things.

For this reason, a work of art must be impersonal. A work of

27

literature was not a message, and the writer who made a novel or a poem into a vehicle for personal communications was abusing his readers. Thus, criticising a contemporary poet, T. S. Eliot complained of receiving 'the disagreeable impression of being personally addressed'. This was a far cry from Wordsworth's definition of the poet as a man speaking to men. The new view of the poet was that he was not a speaker but a maker. His task was to construct a self-contained pattern of meanings which explained itself. And the novel, now raised to equal status with the poem, must be equally impersonal, as Flaubert had demonstrated. It was from Flaubert that Stephen Dedalus derived his concept of 'the indifferent artist', standing aside, aloofly paring his fingernails, while he leaves it to the reader to get on with the task of appreciating what has been offered to him, without assistance. The opposite of the indifferent artist, of course, was a novelist like Thackeray, always ready to abandon his narrative to discuss the trials and tribulations of his characters in the light of common sense.

To possess this self-evidence the work of art must contain within itself the reason why it was what it was and not another thing. It was Coleridge who had already stated the requirement in those terms, a century earlier. Joyce had recourse to his Jesuit education to find terms to formulate it. A work of art must have what Thomas Aquinas called 'wholeness' and 'harmony'. In other words, it must be a complete whole, requiring no support from elements outside itself, and the elements inside it must be so arranged that they could all be seen to fit together. Given wholeness and harmony, the work was also endowed with the illuminating power which he called 'radiance'. There is clearly nothing very new in this and other similar statements. Jane Austen, for example, would not have been surprised by Conrad's opening statement in his introduction to *The Nigger of the 'Narcissus'* (1898), that every line in a novel must justify its presence there. She had no room, in a novel like *Persuasion*, for elements of experience which were irrelevant to the theme announced by her title. What might have surprised her, however, is the range of the elements of experience which Conrad considers might be justifiably present in a novel, whose appeal, he declares

> to be effective must be an impression conveyed through the senses; and, in fact, it cannot be made in any other way, because temperament, whether individual or collective, is not amenable to persuasion. All art, therefore, appeals primarily to the senses, and the artistic aim when expressing itself in written words must also make its appeal through the senses .... It must strenuously aspire to the plasticity of sculpture, to the colour of painting, and to the magic suggestiveness of music—which is the art of arts.

Jane Austen's art does not appeal primarily to the sense. She does not find it significant to inform the reader of such physical details as the way in which a character twisted her neck when she was annoyed, as George Eliot does in the case of Rosamond Vincy. But, as the nineteenth century progresses, physical details had been crowding into narrative. The range of material which the novel had to bring to wholeness was continuously expanding.

The richer the material, the harder it is to harmonise, as Pater explained, using painting as his example:

> And hence the superiority, for most conditions of the picturesque, of a river-side in France to a Swiss valley, because, on the French river-side mere topography, the simple material, counts for so little, and, all being so pure, untouched and tranquil in itself, mere light and shade have such easy work in modulating it to one dominant tone. The Venetian landscape, on the other hand, has in its material conditions much which is hard, or harshly definite; but the masters of the Venetian school have shown themselves little burdened by them. Of its Alpine background they retain certain abstracted elements only, of cool colour and tranquilising line; and they use its actual details, the brown windy turrets, the straw-coloured fields, the forest arabesques, but as the notes of a music which duly accompanies the presence of their men and women, presenting us with the spirit or essence only of a certain sort of landscape—a country of the pure reason or half-imaginative memory.
>
> (*The Renaissance: Studies in Art and Poetry*, 1888)

This passage, applied to the writers of the Irish Movement, explains their preference, when dealing with a contemporary subject, of the topography of the remoter country parts of Ireland to that of Dublin as a background. The basis of Joyce's hostility to them was certainly his contempt for 'a country of the pure reason or half-imaginative memory'. His aim was to write fiction that found room for everything which was actual. He eventually achieved this in *Ulysses*, a full account of a day in the life of two characters, including everyday details which all previous novelists had treated as refuse, the scraps which the form of the novel as they conceived it could not digest.

To do this he had to devise a fictional form that was omnivorous, proliferating, and above all simultaneously flexible and exact. Meanwhile Ezra Pound and T. S. Eliot were engaged on a similar task for poetry. Adopting Pater's strategy, the poets of the nineties had contrived a 'dominant tone' by using constricting verse forms, such as the villanelle, to present attenuated and monotonous feelings. A poetry which was to effect the revelations desired by T. S. Eliot would have to devise quite different methods, and the lines along which he and Ezra Pound were working were remarkably similar to those Joyce had been developing at the time when he joined them. In *A Portrait of the Artist as a Young Man* he had employed them with revolutionary results but he first brought them to fruition in *Dubliners*, on which he was at work from 1904 to 1907.

One of these devices was what Pound called 'the ideogrammatic method', as a result of his study of the Chinese written character. In Chinese writing the sounds of words are not spelt out in letters. Instead each word has its own sign, or ideogram, which when the word stands for a simple object, like a flamingo, is a conventionalised picture of that object. Pound maintained that the Chinese ideograms for common properties were patterns, combining the ideograms for objects which possessed the property in question. Thus the sign for 'red' was a combination of the ideograms of rose, cherry, iron rust and flamingo. In this way, by being combined, these ideograms of objects made manifest a meaning which had only been latent in them. In the same way a poet could combine images so that his reader, comparing or contrasting them, would discover a meaning which they would not otherwise have generated.

A typical example of this process is the following quatrain of T. S. Eliot:

> The couched Brazilian jaguar
> Compels the scampering marmoset
> With subtle effluence of cat;
> Grishkin has a maisonnette.

> ('Whispers of Immortality')

The same device is used in films; a director might produce a similar effect to Eliot's by following a shot of a jaguar, yawning in its lair, with one of a woman, yawning in her boudoir. In fact, after Joyce went to Paris, where he became acquainted with the Russian director and theorist of the cinema, Eisenstein, he took an interest in cinematic technique, and encouraged an abortive project to film a section of *Finnegans Wake*. His early development of this device was, however, based on his knowledge of musical composition. Concern for matching relationships led him to arrange the poems of *Chamber Music* into groups. Similarly the stories in *Dubliners* are arranged in a cumulative sequence—stories of childhood, adolescence, maturity, public life, and finally 'The Dead'.

A similar process operates within each individual story. Elements are offered for comparison and contrast. In 'The Boarding House', the picture of Mr Doran in his bedroom, agitatedly preparing himself for his interview with Mrs Mooney, contrasts with the picture of Polly Mooney, in her bedroom, complacently awaiting that interview's results. In 'An Encounter' the 'spirit of unruliness' that moves the boy to play truant is illuminated by comparing his expectation of seeing a green-eyed foreign sailor with the green eyes which he actually does find in the pervert who bothers him in the field. (He had, he tells us, 'some confused notion' about green eyes.) In 'Counterparts' (a title which points the comparison), Farrington's resentment of his employer's power over him is matched by his abuse of his own power over his child at the end of the story. In 'The Dead', Lily complains bitterly at the beginning: 'The men that is now is only all palaver and what they can get out of you', implying an unfavourable comparison with the men that are no more. In the end, Gabriel realises that compared with the dead Michael Furey he is indeed inferior. One of many matching details enforcing that comparison is that while Gabriel takes great care to protect himself from the cold, Michael Furey had been prepared to stand shivering in the rain for love of the woman Gabriel married. The same story has two contrasting climaxes of recognition—one, in the middle, the social recognition of Gabriel's aunts, when the guests sing 'For they are jolly gay fellows'; the other, at the end, Gabriel's lonely recognition of his personal insignificance, as he contemplates the falling snow.

Another use of comparison, common to Pound, Eliot and Joyce, is the use of quotations—songs, such as 'I dreamt that I dwelt in marble halls' in 'Clay'—and literary allusions, such as the quotation from Byron at the end of 'A Little Cloud' to illuminate Chandler's marriage. In 'Grace' the text chosen by the priest for his sermon is: 'For the children of this world are wiser in their generation than the children of light'. His interpretation of this, as 'a text for business men and professional men', casts an ironic light on this story of an attempt to redeem a drunkard. So does the parallel with Dante's *Divine Comedy* in the structure of this story. Kernan's alcoholic collapse in the first part corresponds to the *Inferno*; the resulting visit he receives from his concerned well-wishers corresponds to the *Purgatorio*; while the priest's sermon at the end offers a worldly *Paradiso*.

The use of the title-word 'Grace' instances another form of comparison, a comparison of different meanings of the same word, in this case of a spiritual meaning with a social one. Mr Kernan sets store by his silk hat and gaiters: 'By grace of these two articles of clothing, he said, a man could always pass muster'. Similarly, Mr Fogarty, we are told, 'bore himself with a certain grace, complimented little children and spoke with a neat enunciation'. The final use of the word, by the priest himself, shows that the redemption aimed at is no more than a return to the fold of bourgeois respectability. The repentant sinner, he declares, should say to himself: 'Well, I have looked into my accounts. I find this wrong and this wrong. But, with God's grace, I will rectify this and this. I will set right my accounts.'

By such comparisons, details which otherwise would have been only marginally significant are charged with meaning, because they point to a unifying theme—just as in Pound's example of the Chinese ideogram the signs for flamingo, cherry and the rest add up to mean 'red'. Another device is the use of repeated motifs in the action. The same action or relationship recurs, in different forms at various points in the plot. Thus Gabriel, in 'The Dead', is rebuffed by Lily at the beginning, by Miss Ivors in the middle, and at the end by his own wife. Another repeated motif is mourning. In addition to the examples already referred to, Gabriel, in his after-dinner speech, mourns the passing of old-fashioned hospitable virtues, and the guests discuss the great singers of a bygone era. Complementing this is the anticipation of death, expressed in the idea of 'going West', and the talk about monks who sleep in their coffins. Nor are these motifs confined to that particular story. They link it with previous stories, in which thoughts of the dead and dying repeatedly occur. Other motifs unifying the collection are the role of woman as gaoler, escape abroad or into the exotic, failure to seize a chance to break free, and the obligations of parenthood. Of particular interest, because of its use in Joyce's later work, is a Tweedledum-Tweedledee relationship between two male characters, each possessing qualities that the other lacks.

Another means of charging physical details with additional significance is the use of symbolism, again common to Eliot, Pound and Joyce. But before examining this feature, it is necessary to examine Joyce's view of the connection between plain truth and imagined truth.

Realism and Romanticism

Dubliners is a collection of stories about people who are too timid and conformist to see things as they really are. The stories are case histories, all pointing to Joyce's diagnosis of 'moral paralysis', arranged in accordance with Pound's ideogrammatic method. Pound himself claimed that this method was adapted to scientific study.

> [it] is very much the kind of thing a biologist does ... when he gets together a few hundred or thousand slides, and picks out what is necessary for his general statement. Something that fits the case, that applies in all cases.
>
> (*The ABC of Reading*, Routledge and Kegan Paul 1934)

This notion of putting slides under a microscope is directly comparable with the concept of the 'slice of life' which, according to Realist novelists, it was the function of the novel to display. The function of literature, according to this school, was medical. Zola had even compared the writer to a surgeon, and Joyce, at this period, came close at times to accepting that analogy. Vivisection is the process with which he makes Stephen Dedalus compare the art of the novelist, in *Stephen Hero*.

A further consequence of this view of literature was that many Realists saw their function as the exposure of injustice. In America, for example, Upton Sinclair exposed the brutal conditions of employment in the Chicago stockyards in *The Jungle* (1906) a novel that led directly to the reform of those conditions. But this was not intrinsic to the method. The truth could be seen as valuable for its own sake, and this was Joyce's view. Art, in his view, should be conducive neither to desire nor to loathing. Works which had such effects were either pornographic or journalistic. It was as journalism that he would have dismissed Upton Sinclair's novel. A work of art should promote 'stasis'—a state of mental satisfaction resulting from contemplation of the truth—in the reader, not 'kinesis', a state of unrest.

It is worth noting that he might well have proceeded differently. At the time he wrote *Dubliners* he had a stock of political ideas about the Irish question which he could have propagated in his stories. He called himself a Socialist, and took a lively interest in what Socialists were thinking and doing, especially during his stay in Rome. The Irish question, as he saw it, was not one of national oppression but of economic exploitation. He kept an eye on political developments at home, and sided with Griffith, whose programmes he found sympathetic. Some of the stories reflect this point of view. 'Grace', for example, satirises the teaching of the Church as the ideology of the bourgeoisie. But this propagandist element is rare. In the main, the stories reveal the unhealthy, imprisoned state of mind of the characters, without attributing blame for it. The only therapeutic aim they have is to provide such characters with a means of perceiving their personal condition. Protesting at Grant Richards's hesitation in publishing his work he told him: 'I sincerely believe that you will retard the cause of civilization in Ireland by preventing the people of Ireland from having one good look at themselves in my nicely polished looking glass.'

The age-old comparison of art with a mirror can imply different things. It may be a magic mirror, which reveals features of the object reflected in it which are invisible when you look directly at the object itself. Or it may be a plain mirror, whose only virtue is that it misses nothing out, and does not distort. It was in the latter way that the Realists sought to mirror life. Their ideal was that nothing should be censored and that every detail should be accurate.

The latter requirement produced a passion for 'documentation'. The writer who aimed at revealing the naked truth about some aspect of life was committed to research into details he did not already know. He must not invent such details. Joyce took great pains in this respect, and we find him writing to his brother for local

33

details that he had forgotten. His stories are full of such details, and in *Gas from a Burner*, attacking the Irish publisher who let him down, he makes him protest

> Shite and onions! Do you think I'll print
> The name of the Wellington Monument,
> Sydney Parade and Sandymount tram,
> Downes's cakeshop and Williams's jam?
>
> (Now published with *Poems Penyeach*)

The publisher's objections were not purely aesthetic. The recognisable local details Joyce crammed into his work produced a risk of libel actions.

There was also the risk of prosecution for obscenity, thanks to Joyce's refusal to censor anything. His inclusion of unsavoury details made him notorious. 'Mr Joyce has a cloacal obsession', H. G. Wells commented disapprovingly. 'He would bring back into the general picture of life aspects which modern drainage and modern decorum have taken out of ordinary intercourse and conversation.' (Review in *Nation* 1917). Joyce was quite willing to see himself as a sanitary engineer. In *The Holy Office*, he says of the Irish writers who were preoccupied with loveliness:

> That they may dream their dreamy dreams
> I carry off their filthy streams.
>
> (Now published with *Pomes Penyeach*)

Sanitary engineering, when all is said and done, makes for public health, and truth is truth. 'It is not my fault', he told Grant Richards, 'that the odour of ashpits and old weeds and offal hangs round my stories.'

It was in this role—that of the unflinching observer, remorselessly confronting the cowardly and hypocritical citizens with things they would rather not see—that Stanislaus loved to see his brother. But Joyce was aiming at more than that. His aim was to make the citizens see what these things meant. For this reason, his art could not be a plain mirror. For the Realist writer, Reality meant no more than those aspects of events which would be noticed by an average observer if he would only look for himself. The only order the Realist would allow was that of cause and effect. The only significance he could admit was environment, heredity and chance. For Joyce meaning lay far deeper. He followed the Realists absolutely in their refusal to alter the facts as they found them, but not in their insistence that facts could speak for themselves. For this reason his mirror had to be a magic one. Or, to use the comparison he himself affected, the artist, by his ministration, must transform the raw material of experience without altering its attributes, as, in the Sacrament of the Eucharist, the bread and wine were transubstantiated, without alteration of their attributes, by the ministration of the priest.

It is important to realise that this transformation of experience was not, as Joyce conceived it, a trick. On the contrary, art was only giving life its due when, by rendering it beautiful, it made it a source of satisfaction. In this his attitude was faithful to the spirit of Aquinas, from whom he had derived his doctrine. When Aquinas spoke of 'wholeness', 'harmony' and 'radiance' he was not analysing the properties of a work of art. He was analysing the properties of any God-created thing, and there was nothing that God had not created. Perceived as part of the divine creation, perceived, that is, in its proper place as God had disposed it in his scheme of things, everything was both beautiful and good. This did not mean that everything was perfect. The Fall had deprived creation of its original perfection. But as St Augustine observed, in a passage Joyce quoted both in the first version of *A Portrait*, and also later in *Ulysses*, imperfection is nothing to despair over. That was why the artist must not reject or tamper with the facts as he found them. 'So long as this place in nature is given us, it is right that art should do no violence to that gift,' the young Joyce declared. But this did not imply that the artist must merely list the facts as he found them. His function was to reveal their hidden significance by an artistic method 'which bends upon these present things and so works upon them and fashions them that the quick intelligence may go beyond them to their meaning, which is still unuttered'.

This intention of revealing the concealed beauty of common things is very similar to that which Coleridge, whom Joyce had also studied, ascribed to Wordsworth in the *Lyrical Ballads*:

awakening the mind's attention from the lethargy of custom, and directing it to the loveliness and wonder of the world before us; an inexhaustible treasure, but for which, in consequence of the film of familiarity and selfish solicitude we have eyes, yet see not, ears that hear not, and hearts that neither feel nor understand.

(*Biographia Literaria*, 1817)

Like the Realists, Joyce maintained that Romanticism had exercised a pernicious influence on literature by substituting fantasy for art, but he also believed this damage was due to a misunderstanding of Romanticism. This he makes clear in the early paper, from which the remarks about 'this place in nature' and the unuttered meaning have been taken ('James Clarence Mangan': published in *The Critical Writings*).

The romantic school is often and grievously misunderstood, not more by others than by its own, for that impatient temper which, as it could see no fit abode here for its ideals, chose to behold them under unsensible figures.

35

As this makes clear, his rejection of fantasy was not a rejection of imagination. At this stage of his development he accepted imagination as intrinsic to complete perception, and therefore to Art. Later, for reasons that will become apparent when his last works are examined, he was to disclaim imagination, declare that he himself had the mind of a grocer, and describe *Finnegans Wake* as a 'scissors-and-paste' work. But at the outset he exalted the power of imagination. This did not mean, however, that the Realist's concern with actuality should be abandoned. It was in his combination of these two qualities that Ibsen's distinction lay. 'Ibsen has united with his strong, ample, imaginative faculty a preoccupation with things present to him. Perhaps in time even the professional critics . . . will make this union a truism of professional criticism.'

In practice, the fusion of Realism with imagination proved a difficult task, and in his earliest attempts, his so-called 'epiphanies', he failed to achieve it. The word 'epiphany' means manifestation, and in the ecclesiastical calendar the Feast of the Epiphany commemorates the manifestation of the infant Christ to the Magi. Joyce's aesthetic concept of an 'epiphany' was an expression of his demand that a work of art should present things so that 'the quick intelligence may go beyond them to their meaning which is still unuttered'. The 'epiphany' was the revelation of hidden significance which occurs when, perceiving an object, 'We recognise that it is *that* thing which it is. Its soul, its whatness, leaps to us from the vestment of its appearance. The soul of the commonest object, the structure of which it is so adjusted, seems to us radiant. The object achieves its epiphany.' The religious source of this conception is evident in the notion that appearance is a vestment—a sacrament, or 'outward and visible sign of an inner and spiritual grace'. The influence of Thomas Aquinas is expressed in the definition of soul as inherent structure. For Aquinas, this characteristic pattern of relationships was concealed by human sinfulness, but occasionally revealed by God's grace. For the early Joyce it was something concealed by custom, to be revealed by the imagination of the artist—'the priest of the imagination'.

Joyce's early epiphanies themselves, however, fail to bring the imagination to bear upon 'these present things'. The definition of an epiphany, quoted above, is that given by Stephen Dedalus in *Stephen Hero*, who goes on to classify the material to be treated in this kind of writing into two distinct kinds. The first is 'vulgarity of speech and gesture'. Material of this sort was observed externally, in the behaviour of others, and recorded in brief glimpses of their behaviour. Some of these epiphanies were subsequently included in *A Portrait*. One is placed in the second section of the second chapter of the novel, in a scene where Stephen's aunt, looking at a picture in the evening paper, remarks, 'The beautiful Mabel Hunter!' and a little girl, gazing fascinated at it in her turn, repeats the exclamation and then murmurs: 'Isn't she an exquisite creature?' Taken by itself, it is an insignificant episode. It is only by including it in the larger structure of the novel that Joyce makes it light up with meaning, because the reader, having already witnessed the alert and speculative efforts made by young Stephen to connect words with experience, has something with which to compare this demonstration of tired cliché fastened to blinding stereotype. Read in isolation, as it was originally intended to be, this passage is a piece of uninspired realism.

The other kind of material was 'a memorable phase of the mind itself'. This material was observed inwardly by the artist. The resulting epiphanies were brief lyrics in prose, such as the passage later worked into the conclusion of *A Portrait* which begins, 'The spell of arms and voices: the white arms of roads, their promise of close embraces . . .' (Journal entry of 16 April). Here the arms and voices are certainly imagined, but they are not real. Once again the passage only becomes significant in the wider context of a novel, where it illustrates a psychology which has become real to the reader from earlier, recorded episodes.

This initial alternation of realism and romanticism did not amount to the union of a 'strong imaginative faculty' with 'a preoccupation with things present to him', for which Joyce had praised Ibsen. For this a fusion was required similar to the fusion that had been achieved in poetry by the Symbolists.

Symbolism

Poetry, according to Ezra Pound, was 'the most concentrated form of verbal expression'. By this he did not mean that language is used more concisely in poetry, but that it is more highly charged. The same expressions are used to convey different meanings simultaneously, as if a telephone wire was being used to convey several messages at the same time—messages which are different but are nevertheless associated with one another, so that the total effect is one of unity.

Thus in a poem, in addition to the explicit meaning of the words there is an additional meaning conveyed to what Eliot termed the reader's 'auditory imagination', by their rhythm and correspondence in sound, as in Pound's

> See, they return; ah, see the tentative
> Movements, and the slow feet
> The trouble in the pace and the uncertain
> Wavering.
>
> ('The Return')

Here the versification imposes breaks at the end of the first and third lines in just those places where, if they were written as running prose, the reader would move smoothly on. The resulting rhythmic effect is one of uncertainty and hesitation, corresponding with the explicit meaning of the words.

Although this extra meaning corresponds with the explicit meaning of the words which it accompanies, it is not derived from their explicit meanings, but from the movement produced by the way Pound has arranged them, from their rhythm. The meaning conveyed by a rhythm can be considered separately, and may even contradict the explicit meaning of the words which convey it, just as a tune may suit the words of a song, or jar with the words—as when a soldiers' song, like 'When the bleeding war is over', is sung to a hymn tune. It may therefore be considered as a musical effect.

Another additional source of meaning is the use of imagery. The use of imagery is a natural development of language. When we say that a sergeant-major 'barks out' an order, the meaning of the words is just as clear as if we had said that he 'shouted'. The correspondence between barking and shouting is obvious, even though in the literal sense of the word, only animals bark. But not all images are so obvious, and in the course of the nineteenth century a school of poetry had developed in France which deliberately cultivated obscurity in the use of imagery, so that, in the words of Baudelaire, the image had about it 'something a little vague, allowing scope for conjecture'. Pound and Eliot were influenced by this 'Symbolist' movement. A classic example of the use of symbols in English poetry is afforded by the opening lines of T. S. Eliot's 'The Love Song of J. Alfred Prufrock'.

> Let us go then, you and I,
> When the evening is spread out against the sky
> Like a patient etherised upon a table.

Here the image of the unconscious patient, with its implications of unnatural passivity and imminent surgery, cannot readily be tallied with the details of an evening sky. We cannot say exactly what features of the evening correspond with the features of the etherised patient. The image of the patient simply evokes a mood.

Although the correspondence between Eliot's image and its original remains obscure, however, the implication of the image is clear enough. We know what mood it evokes. We can translate the image into other words, and say it produces a sick, exhausted feeling of hopelessness. This precision is typical of Pound and Eliot. They viewed poetry as a means of conveying a clearer view of contemporary experience. The last thing they sought was vagueness. Yeats, on the other hand, also influenced by the Symbolists, cultivated vagueness as the essence of poetry, in his early work, as did also George Russell, and the other writers of the Irish Movement.

This 'Celtic Twilight' also veils the poems in Joyce's first published work, *Chamber Music*. The explicit meaning of the words is invariably subordinated to their music, and the images are faint. All that remains with the reader is his sense of the vaguely weary attitude of the lonely, loveless poet. Once or twice the weariness develops into faint mockery, or the loneliness becomes a source of pride, but there is no variety of tone or treatment.

The following poem (XXXV) may be considered as typical:

> All day I hear the noise of waters
>   Making moan
> Sad as the seabird is when going
>   Forth alone
> He hears the winds cry to the waters'
>   Monotone.
>
> The grey winds, the cold winds are blowing
>   Where I go.
> I hear the noise of many waters
>   Far below.
> All day, all night, I hear them flowing
>   To and fro.

The images of the sea-bird and the sound of waters are of considerable interest in the context of *A Portrait* and *Ulysses*, but in the context of the poem they make no impact. The sea appears to be heard from a remote distance. Instead of being told what kind of seabird is involved, we are told that it is sad. Indeed, as regards its imagery, the poem might have been designed to illustrate a warning from Pound!

> Don't use such an expression as 'dim lands *of peace*'. It dulls the image. It mixes an abstraction with the concrete. It comes from the writer's not realizing the natural object is always the *adequate* symbol.
>
> (*Literary Essays*, Faber 1954)

Comparison with the lines quoted above from Pound's 'The Return' also exemplifies the peculiar character of Joyce's rhythm, which is incantatory, not dramatic. The rise and fall of the alternate long and short lines carries all before it, overruling the syntax of the first stanza. (The poem is destroyed if one reads—'when going forth alone he hears the winds cry'). The monotony is emphasised by the rhyme, with nine of the twelve rhymes stressing the same dark vowel. The function of the rhythm is precisely the 'musical' one desired by Pater of submerging detail, 'modulating it to one dominant tone', or by Yeats, who declared:

> The purpose of rhythm, it has always seemed to me, is to prolong the moment of contemplation, the moment when we are both

asleep and awake, which is the one moment of creation, by hushing us with an alluring monotony, while it holds us waking by variety, to keep us in that state of perhaps real trance, in which the mind liberated from the pressure of the will is unfolded in symbols.

(*Essays and Introductions*, Macmillan)

So it was not in his poetry but in his prose writing that Joyce broke with the Irish Movement, and took his place as a modernist, along with Eliot and Pound. The stories in *Dubliners* employ musical effects and imagery no less deliberately then the poems of *Chamber Music*, but in the stories the effect is precisely calculated. As an example of musical effect, consider the opening paragraph of 'Two Gallants'. (Two sets of rhyming words have been identified, for convenience, by italics and capital letters.)

The grey *warm* evening of August had descended upon the city and a mild *warm* air, a memory of SUMMER, circulated in the streets. The streets, SHUTTERED for the repose of SUNDAY, *swarmed* with a gaily coloured crowd. Like illumined pearls the lamps shone from the SUMMITS of their tall poles upon the living texture below which, changing shape and hue unceasingly, sent up into the *warm* grey evening air an unchanging unceasing MURMUR.

The pattern revealed is even closer than the pointing adopted indicates, because the two sets—'warm' and 'summer'—besides being themselves closely linked, are joined by other similar sounding words, like 'memory' and 'illumined'. Repetitive forms are also used, 'grey warm' at the opening balancing 'warm grey' at the end, and, in the final sentence—'changing shape and hue unceasingly . . . an unchanging, unceasing murmur'. Highly contrived though it is, however, the 'music' of the passage does not distract the reader's attention. Conveying a sense of a continuous, circulating hum, it sets the initial atmosphere.

This is only one of many such passages, and the music is varied. Compare, for instance, the enervation of the above passage with the lively form of this sentence from 'A Little Cloud'.

Walking swiftly by at night be had seen cabs drawn up before the door and richly-dressed ladies, escorted by cavaliers, alight and enter quickly.

(78/69)

The placing of 'walking swiftly' at the beginning, and 'enter quickly' at the end, dramatises the fact that while the ladies were moving one way, Little Chandler was moving in the opposite direction, a fact which casts an ironic light on Little Chandler's later comparison of the ladies, in his thoughts, to 'alarmed Atalantas'. The arrangement reinforces the image, just as in the previously quoted paragraph from 'Two Gallants', out of the prevalent murmur arises the image of lamps shining like pearls upon a 'living texture'. The latter image, suggesting pearls upon a woman, introduces an association of women and wealth which is intrinsic to the subsequent story.

It was in the use of such imagery that Joyce achieved the fusion of imagination and realism for which he had praised Ibsen. The stories in *Dubliners* are so true to life that it was not until twenty years after they had been published that their symbolism began to be appreciated, because the symbols are recognisable objects of common experience. In this they conform perfectly with Pound's observation.

> I believe that the proper and perfect symbol is the natural object, that if a man use 'symbols' he must so use them that their symbolic function does not obtrude; so that a sense, and the poetic quality of the passage is not lost to those who do not understand the symbol as such, to whom, for instance, a hawk is a hawk.
>
> ('A Retrospect' in *Literary Essays*, Faber 1954)

Joyce's use of symbols in his stories is exactly what Pound required: images of everyday objects, occurring naturally in the action of the stories. The only fantastic images are reproductions of the characters' own fantasies, like the child's dream of the dead priest in 'The Sisters'. The author's imagination works entirely upon 'these present things' to endow them with extra significance, just as the imagination of Dickens, in *Bleak House*, converted the London fog into a symbol. What is new about Joyce's practice is the intensity and consistency of his use of this device.

The second point to note about the stories' symbolism is its explicitness. There is nothing vague about the correspondence between the image and its meaning. Its interpretation is clear, although various symbolic devices are employed.

One such device is the use of personal names, such as that of Gabriel, the central character of 'The Dead'. In Hebrew mythology the angel Gabriel is the prince of fire and the angel of death, as befits this character's attachment to warmth and his dull, compromising existence. Warmth itself, in the form of the cosy interior of the house as opposed to the bleak cold of the winter night outside, is another symbol—of huddled sociability and cosseted lust. As such it is imported into the story from common speech, where warmth conventionally suggests these qualities. Much of the symbolism in the story is of this kind, as for example the symbol of the goose. The wild goose is the conventional Irish symbol for the man who, refusing to surrender his freedom, flees abroad. Gabriel is a tame goose: his ventures abroad take the form of holiday cycling trips with friends. To refer again to common idiom, 'his goose is cooked', and he is called upon to carve it. Colour symbolism is also involved in the image of the cooked goose, which has lost its whiteness and become well browned, as the white snow outside is opposed to the cosy interior (not to mention the ubiquitous and bogus guest, Browne).

The significance of all these symbols is derived from a common code, already available in the reader's mind before he starts on the story. Other significant correspondences are created in the course of the narrative. Thus Gabriel tells a family anecdote about a horse so conditioned to working a mill that it failed to trot out proudly 'with the quality', walking round and round in a circle instead. Additional symbolism inheres in the detail that it was 'King Billy's statue'—symbol of the English yoke—that the horse walked round, and from Gabriel's insistence that the mill belonged to a glue-boiler (boiling down the bones of dead horses). As he tells this story, himself walking in a circle, he presents a parable of his own enslavement.

In addition to such analogies, there is a pervasive metaphoric pattern, which polarises contrasting moral attitudes—living death versus life in death. The inhabitants of the warm, brown, cosy world are still alive, but at the cost of spiritual death. The pure uncompromising world of snow beyond it cannot endure. Already, as the guests leave, the snow has begun to melt. Those, like Michael Furey, who belong to that world are dead, but Michael (the highest angel) will always live in the memory of Gabriel's wife. Nevertheless, this moral pattern is not unambiguous. As Falstaff pointed out, there is a lot to be said for staying alive physically, and the guests are not condemned in Joyce's presentation of them. They are presented with sympathy and affection.

All the images are clear. There is nothing mysterious about them. They are coded messages that can be deciphered and translated into non-figurative terms. They do not reveal a perception that cannot be put into other words. The image with which the story ends, however, is of a different order, an intimation in the manner of Symbolism proper, of a meaning otherwise incommunicable. This image is Gabriel's vision of the falling snow. The disagreement of critics as to its significance—whether the force it represents is beneficent, whether Gabriel's vision is a sign of returning health— is ample evidence that this image cannot be adequately interpreted. Here, at the end of the story, the snow no longer stands for one pole in a binary opposition of life and death but reconciles that opposition in a way that cannot be explained *but can be recognised.* Applied equally to the living and the dead alike, the phrase 'their last end' must refer to an end even beyond death. Simultaneously embellishing and obliterating, the snow represents a nameless process, engulfing living and dead alike. This indefinable and mysterious effect is not in the precise manner of Pound, but that of Symbolism proper, as described by Yeats.

All sounds, all colours, all forms, either because of their preordained energies or because of long association, evoke indefinable and yet precise emotions, or, as I prefer to think, call down among us certain disembodied powers whose footsteps over our hearts we call emotions; and when sound, and colour, and form are in a musical relation, a beautiful relation to one another, they become, as it were, one sound, one colour, one form, and evoke an emotion that is made out of their distinct evocations and yet is one emotion.

(*Essays and Introductions*, Macmillan)

The point of view

The vision of a mysterious process, presented at the end of 'The Dead', is Gabriel's vision, not the author's. It is not something there before him. It occurs in his mind, as he lies in bed with his wife sleeping beside him. Throughout the story we have seen his fluctuating attitude to the snow—circumspectly defensive, romantically attracted, ultimately resigned. This was another lesson the youthful Joyce had learnt from Ibsen, the preeminence of the dramatic method which, in Ibsen's case, he described as 'a principle of all patient and perfect art which bids him express his fable in terms of his characters'.

This observation shows that even before he began work on *Dubliners* Joyce had realised the importance of the question then engaging the attention of thoughtful novelists, and in particular of Henry James—the question of 'the point of view'. For a writer who aims at impersonality this is a question of crucial importance: where are the words that compose his writing supposed to be coming from if not from him personally? It concerned poets, like Eliot and Pound, no less than novelists. If the poet is not a man speaking to men, but a maker of poems, how is the reader to take the words in his poem? What could the source be considered to be, if not the poet himself?

At this stage in their development, both Eliot and Pound found a solution in putting words into the mouths of historical or fictitious characters, as in Eliot's *The Love Song of J. Alfred Prufrock*. The words in their poems were to be taken for what they were worth, without being felt to carry the personal endorsement of the poet himself. Presented as the speech of a dramatic character, the implicit direction to the reader which they carried was not 'Listen to me', but 'See what you make of this'. The words which these poets put into the mouths of their personae were not direct expressions of their personal attitudes.

A similar answer to the problem of where his words should appear to be coming from is open to the novelist. Instead of telling the story in his own words, he can tell it in the words of a character within the story. This is an old device. It is used, for example, in Defoe's

Robinson Crusoe (1719). In such early examples the aim is authenticity. The reader feels as if he were reading a memoir, not a fiction. Nevertheless, there was also an aesthetic gain in impersonality. Apparently the product of the very events it records, the text is formally self-contained.

At the same time, however, the relationship of the character to his adventures is altered. Instead of living through them he is reconsidering them. This perspective may be just what the novelist requires, if his object, as in the case of Proust, is to explore the reality of remembered experience. In the case of most novels, however, the result is a lack of immediacy which is a drawback. One solution found for this problem was to write the novel as a sequence of letters exchanged between the characters in the course of the incidents in the story. Immediacy resulted, because now the text of the novel appeared to have been generated in the heat of the events it related. Again, however, there was a drawback. The framework of incessant correspondence had a distracting effect, except in the exceptional cases of novels like Richardson's *Clarissa* (1747–8) where the letters themselves played a part in the story.

For the novelist in search of impersonality, the great attraction of the autobiographical or epistolary novel was that the personality of the author was excluded from the narrative by the use of a fictitious narrator. Without such a device, the very act of narrating his story seemed to compel him to declare his presence to his reader. No matter how impartially he told his story, he would still loom over it.

Suppose, for example, he is narrating a scene in which a man tells a woman he loves her, and produces the sentence: 'Jill was later to remember (poor) Jack's declaration with gratitude, but at that moment (the silly girl) was seized by a fit of laughter so irresistible that she was only just able to disguise it as a bout of coughing.' The author might well decide that he had shown his hand in the expressions placed in brackets, and cut them out. The resulting neutral version no longer expresses his sympathies. The complete authorial presence is no longer there. Nevertheless, a presence that has no part in the story is still felt. Who is it who knows what Jill is going to feel later, and can assure us that her pretence of coughing succeeds? This know-all presence, 'the omniscient narrator', was the contamination from which in the early twentieth century, some writers sought to free the novel by deliberately restricting the narrator's point of view.

By this stratagem, explained at length in Percy Lubbock's *The Craft of Fiction* (1921), the author denied himself not only the direct expression of his personal sympathies but also every advantage he enjoyed over his characters in seeing what was going on. At any given point in the novel, he would tell the story as if he could see no more than one single, selected character could see. Thus, the incident in our hypothetical example written from Jack's point of view might read: 'No sooner had he said these words than Jill was seized by a bout of coughing.' The sentence is not presented as if Jack had written it, but it is written from his point of view, with no indications of the limitations of that view.

Although the narrative does not tell him so, the reader may well realise that Jill was laughing, not coughing. The author expects him to see more in the narrative than is directly expressed in it. For this reason, like the autobiographical novel and the epistolary novel, the novel written from a point of view within the narrative is a form suitable to one kind of story and not to another. It was perfectly suited to Henry James's *The Ambassadors* (1903), where the centre of interest is the way in which a character changes his perception of a situation. The point of view of that character is precisely the field of the major action.

For the same reason the point of view within the narrative was perfectly suited to Joyce's purposes in *Dubliners*. His purpose is not quite the same as that of Henry James. He is not concerned with the operation of delicate minds, but rather with the operation of cowed and undeveloped ones. James's story is one of discovery: Joyce's stories are stories of failures to make discoveries. Thus in 'Eveline' the heroine is prevented from making a bid for freedom because she cannot conceive of living anywhere but at home. She has been condemned to life imprisonment by her own point of view. But no less than in *The Ambassadors*, a point of view is the centre of the story's interest.

The inherent irony of the method is intrinsic to such a story. The reader must realise what Eveline fails to see. In the same way, in 'Clay', the family party sees how Maria, herself blindfold, unwittingly picks the symbol of death in the game of saucers. But the irony is compassionate. Maria does not appear, to the privileged vision of her relatives, or to the superior vision of the reader, as a contemptible character. Her mental limitations seem pitiful, not reprehensible, and within those limits she is morally sympathetic. The same compassionate irony invests the one story which tells how a character does come to transcend the limited point of view from which he starts—'The Dead'. As a result of his wife's unexpected revelation, Gabriel takes a fresh look at himself, and finds himself contemptible.

> He saw himself as a ludicrous figure, acting as a penny-boy for his aunts, a nervous well-meaning sentimentalist, orating to vulgarians and idealizing his own clownish lusts, the pitiable fatuous fellow he had caught a glimpse of in the mirror.
>
> (251/216)

A new irony, however, invests this recognition. The reader had a similar view of Gabriel, as long as he did not have it himself, but now that Gabriel *has* taken this view of himself the reader's view of him is paradoxically enlarged. It is impossible to dismiss in such terms a character who can realise with humility:

> He had never felt like that himself towards any woman but he knew that such a feeling must be love.
>
> (255/220)

The ultimate direction of Joyce's irony in this story is the feeling Gabriel himself experiences towards his sleeping wife—'a strange, friendly pity'.

This friendly pity is the attitude which his dramatic method led Joyce to adopt to all his fellow citizens, in *Dubliners*, in the very act of exposing their defects. Nobody is pilloried, or condemned.

Style

'He held style, good or bad, to be the most intimate revelation of character', Stanislaus informs us. A dramatist, expressing his fable in terms of his characters, expresses it in the way those characters speak. In his stories Joyce makes the fullest use of this resource in the dialogue, which ranges from Gabriel's stilted after-dinner speech to the clichés of the political hirelings in 'Ivy Day in the Committee Room', where Mr Henchy, for example, observes of Edward VII: 'He's a man of the world, and he means well by us'.

The bulk of the writing, however, is not dialogue but narrative, describing the setting and relating the events, and it might seem that when he is writing narrative an author, even if he adopts the point of view of his characters, is obliged to put things in his own way, not in theirs. The sentence in which an English novelist describes a French-speaking character will be written in English, not French. The point of view in *The Ambassadors* may be that of the character, Strether, but the style of the narrative is the late style of Henry James. Similarly in 'Ivy Day in the Committee Room,' although the style of Mr Henchy's speech reveals his character, the style in which his entrance is described does not.

> Then a bustling little man with a snuffling nose and very cold ears pushed in the door. He walked over quickly to the fire, rubbing his hands as if he intended to produce a spark from them.
>
> (136/120)

On the other hand, this is not recognisably the style of James Joyce either. It is an anonymous style, derived from several novelists and Dickens in particular. In order not to come between his reader and his fable, the author has effaced himself. This faceless narrator, nevertheless, lives in a different world from Mr Henchy: Mr Henchy would not talk like that.

This anonymous style may have been what Joyce was referring

to when he told Grant Richards that his stories were couched in 'a style of scrupulous meanness'. He may, on the other hand, have been referring to another very different sort of meanness to be found in the style of a passage like the opening of 'Clay'.

> The matron had given her leave to go out as soon as the women's tea was over and Maria looked forward to her evening out. The kitchen was spick and span: the cook said you could see yourself in the big copper boilers. The fire was nice and bright and on one of the side-tables were four very big barmbracks. These barm-bracks seemed uncut; but if you went closer you would see that they had been cut into long thick even slices and were ready to be handed round at tea. Maria had cut them herself.
>
> (110/97)

This narrative passage, presenting us with Maria on the point of going out, obviously brings us much closer to her than we came to Mr Henchy in the first passage. The reason for this closeness is partly that the passage about Maria is narrated from her point of view, but this explanation is not enough to account for all the difference. Compare the opening of 'Eveline'. This too is narrated from a character's point of view, but it still keeps the reader at a distance from her, when it is compared with the opening of 'Clay'.

> She sat at the window watching the evening invade the avenue. Her head was leaned against the window curtains and in her nostrils was the odour of dusty cretonne. She was tired.
> Few people passed. The man out of the last house passed on his way home; she heard his footsteps clacking along the concrete pavement and afterwards crunching on the cinder path before the new red houses.
>
> (37/34)

In this passage the narrator sees no more than the character sees. The reader is conscious of nothing of which Eveline is not also conscious, and the context-bound use of the definite article in the phrase 'the man out of the last house' is comprehensible only in relation to her particular circumstances, which it implies. Never-theless, the presence of the narrator is still felt in that he talks above his character's head. In employing the metaphor of the invading evening, the literary word 'odour', and the precise distinction of clacking and crunching, he is using linguistic skills, and therefore offering perceptions, beyond her competence.

This is not the case in the passage from 'Clay'. The situation is not only presented from Maria's point of view. Her point of view is expressed in her own language, as if it had been written by someone who belonged to her circle. The narrator is using the same language as the cook who remarked that 'you could see yourself in the big copper boilers', when he commends the 'spick and span' appearance of the kitchen, and the 'nice and bright' fire. The narrator is clearly no less impressed by the expertise with which the barmbracks have been sliced than Maria is proud of it. We can imagine Maria nodding complacently at the information: 'Maria had cut them herself'.

The narrator in 'Clay' therefore is not faceless but sympathetic. Although not actually a character in the story, the narrator tells the story as if he belonged to the social world in which it takes place. Clearly, in this respect, the narrator is not Joyce, the author, but an imaginative projection created to be part and parcel of the story. The author has completely disappeared, no longer visible even in the narrative style. To use Stephen Dedalus's phrase, in *A Portrait*, the author is 'refined out of existence'. As *Dubliners* progressed, Joyce came more and more to rely on a sympathetic narrator in telling his stories, employing this device with the utmost flexibility in 'The Dead', where not one but several narrators are at work.

Before the entry of Gabriel, the narrator belongs to the social world of 'the Misses Morkan', and employs its language. 'Lily, the caretaker's daughter, was literally run off her feet.... It was well for her she had not to attend to the ladies also.... It was always a great affair, the Misses Morkan's annual dance....' With the entry of Gabriel, a more educated narrator takes over. 'Gabriel smiled at the three syllables she had given his surname and glanced at her. She was a slim, growing girl, pale in complexion and with hay-coloured hair.' The second of these two sentences reveals something of his facile Romanticism. He is not a simple character, and more than one narrator is required to express his shifts of mood. Sometimes, because Gabriel is not sensitive enough to register his own perceptions, the narrator too stumbles into banality, as in the scene where Gabriel admires the spectacle of his wife, transfixed on the stairs by Mr D'Arcy's singing of the fateful song. 'There was a grace and mystery in her attitude as if she were a symbol of something.' But at the end of the story, when he is seized, swooning, by the power of the falling snow, the prose develops the incantatory rhythm recommended by Yeats for the prolongation of a contemplative moment. 'His soul swooned slowly as he heard the snow falling faintly through the universe and faintly falling, like the descent of their last end, upon all the living and the dead.'

With this dramatic use of style, Joyce broke the limits of the point of view as employed by Henry James. The reason he gave for this development, in an essay on Ibsen's *Catalina*, transcends aesthetic considerations. 'As the breaking up of tradition, which is the work of the modern era, discountenances the absolute and as no writer can escape the spirit of his time, the writer of dramas must remember now more than ever a principle of all patient and perfect art which bids him express his fable in terms of his characters.' Truth was relative. There could therefore be no such quality as omniscience. That, according to the youthful Joyce, was why an omniscient narrator had no part in a modern work. He would be falsely representing the ideology of his group as if it possessed absolute value. For this reason, in *Dubliners*, he produced a text which does not appear to come from himself, but from his characters. The style is not a parody. It is not a caricature, set up for ridicule. Its object is sympathetic understanding. Instead of mocking the style appropriate to his characters, he forges it meticulously and faithfully.

Style is a symptom of sensibility. In *Dubliners* Joyce develops a style symptomatic of the conditions he portrays. This development of narrative therefore adds a new dimension to the practice of realistic fiction. The realists themselves had paid scant attention to the problem of style. Balzac defined his role as to act as secretary to the society in which he lived. His task, as he saw it, was simply to keep minutes of the proceedings of those about him. Later realists were less naive. They understood well enough that the standpoint of the secretary would colour his minutes. 'A work of art', said Zola, 'is a corner of creation seen through a temperament.' This apparently inevitable fact did not, however, appear to them as a limitation. In his work, the novelist was addressing his fellow citizens on the subject of modern life. It was his duty to tell them the truth as he saw it, to present them with 'a slice of life'. Joyce went further. He offered his readers a slice of language. His stories read like documents for sociological study, bearing witness to the conditions which produced them in such turns of phrase as: 'Lily, the caretaker's daughter, was literally run off her feet.'

They read like that, however, only to the studious reader who is prepared to focus his attention in the appropriate way. It is in this provision for a new kind of reader that Joyce's profound originality is to be found. For previous writers, as also for most subsequent ones, style is a means of sharing their deepest perceptions with the reader. For Joyce, style is a means of presenting the reader with a problem: why is the text written in this particular way? Such a style can only operate as an obstacle to the reader who wishes to share Joyce's vision, as he is able to share, for example, that of D.H. Lawrence. But for the reader who, as he reads the text, would rather share in the writer's labours, he offers a peculiar pleasure. This he lucidly expounded as early as his *Fortnightly Review* article on Ibsen's *When We Dead Awaken*, where, describing the treatment of Professor Rubek, he wrote:

By degrees the whole scroll of his life is unrolled before us, and we have the pleasure of not hearing it read out to us, but of reading it for ourselves, piecing the various parts, and going closer to see wherever the writing on the parchment is fainter or less legible.

It was to cater for such a reader—the reader who pores over a text—that Joyce loaded his sentences with meaning, to the point of burying it, so that finally, in *Finnegans Wake*, reading becomes an exercise in excavation.

Original sin

The impersonality of Joyce's prose style is thus not secured by the omission of any expression which reveals emotion, prejudice, or a personal point of view. On the contrary, he writes in several styles which express all those things. What makes these styles impersonal is that the feelings they express are never his. They are standpoints he has understood, and whose limitations he has seen.

At this point in their development, T. S. Eliot and Ezra Pound also employed a variety of limited styles with a similar detachment. The dramatic use of style is strikingly illustrated by T. S. Eliot's *The Love Song of J. Alfred Prufrock*. For instance, the protagonist reflects:

> I grow old . . . I grow old . . .
> I shall wear the bottoms of my trousers rolled.
>
> Shall I part my hair behind? Do I dare to eat a peach?
> I shall wear white flannel trousers, and walk upon the beach.

The whimsical, self-deprecating irony is a symptom of the speaker's self-pity, combined with his intelligence, matching the characteristic speech that Joyce puts into the mouths of his characters in *Dubliners*. It is not T. S. Eliot speaking, although no doubt he has a personal investment in Alfred Prufrock, just as Joyce had in Gabriel Conroy. And, like Joyce, Eliot does not confine his dramatic use of style to the speech of his characters. In *The Waste Land*, for example, he employs a variety of poetic voices, just as Joyce employs different narrators in 'The Dead'.

There was, however, one respect in which Joyce differed from Eliot, Pound, and other writers associated with them in 1914, such as T. E. Hulme and Wyndham Lewis. This was his tolerance of weakness and vulgarity. He had as sharp an eye as they for human failings, but not to chastise them, only to understand. He was not interested in worthies. From his youth he maintained that art must represent what was 'constant' in human experience. In his view an extraordinary event was material for a journalist, not an artist. 'Man bites dog', has been said to be the quintessential news story. As Joyce saw it, an artist should be concerned with the commonplace occurrence 'dog bites man', or, to take an example from *Dubliners*, 'man strikes child'. For this reason, he had no use for heroes.

This feature of his work is enough to mark it off from that of Pound.

Eliot, on the other hand, also found much material in the gutter. The real distinction of Joyce only appears when we compare his treatment of the same material—a sordid sexual affair, for example. In *The Waste Land* Eliot describes the man in such an incident:

> He, the young man carbuncular, arrives,
> A small house agent's clerk, with one bold stare,
> One of the low on whom assurance sits
> As a silk hat on a Bradford millionaire.

The attitude expressed is clearly a combination of moral and social contempt. In Joyce's story, 'The Boarding House', Mr Doran has been involved in a similar incident. He too is a clerk, and 'one of the low'. There is, however, no contempt in Joyce's presentation of him. To some extent this is because Eliot regarded modern civilisation as depraved: for him the function of art was to recover the perspectives of a lost civilisation. The carbuncular young man is a product of the horror of modern life. Joyce, on the other hand, did not regard modern man as peculiarly horrible. He regarded human nature as constant, unchanging, although its folly might take different forms in different ages and places. If (in all his work before *Finnegans Wake*) his attention was concentrated on the modern world, this was simply because the modern world was what was present to him, not because it offended him.

But Eliot's loathing for modern man was not merely topical. It was part of a deeper disgust with humanity in general, at least at this early stage in his development. Like many of his contemporaries, he was opposed to the attitudes of positivists and humanists, who maintained that history was a record of progress, that man was capable of continuous improvement, and that it was rational to struggle for perfect life on earth. Perhaps it was because Eliot had absorbed these optimistic assumptions in childhood that he reacted so violently against them when his experience gave them the lie. To him, as to many others, the doctrine of orginal sin appeared in the light of an important discovery, investing religion with a new authority. As T. E. Hulme confessed:

> I have none of the feelings of *nostalgia*, the reverence for tradition, the desire to recapture the sentiment of Fra Angelico, which seems to animate most modern defenders of religion. All that seems to me to be bosh. What is important, is what nobody seems to realize— the dogmas like that of Original Sin, which are the closest expression of the categories of the religious attitude. That man is in no sense perfect, but a wretched creature, who can yet apprehend perfection. (*Speculations*, Kegan Paul, 1924)

An unrelenting awareness of this gap between glimpsed perfection and actual wretchedness, the notion of 'some infinitely suffering thing', informs all Eliot's early poetry, preparing the ground for a later religious art.

Joyce's development lay in the opposite direction—the direction of comedy. As a pupil of the Jesuits he had been taught, as a child, to take original sin for granted. He had also learnt that sin could be forgiven, and when his Christian faith had disappeared he continued to view human failing in a forgiving light. There was nothing rational—nothing justifiable—about this forgiving spirit. Forgiveness did not result from a demonstration that, in a given case, a lapse was to be condoned as the product of particular circumstances. On the contrary, forgiveness was the result of a resigned and charitable sense that no human performance can maintain the highest standards for long, however favourable the circumstances.

Moreover, the more dignified the figure a man cuts, the more certain is it that he is about to tread on a banana skin. Falls are repeated and inevitable, yet always come as a surprise. Human life is therefore intrinsically comic—or rather, offers a continuously comic spectacle to a spectator with a sense of humour, a possession Joyce explicitly prized as a way of deriving satisfaction from the recognition of defeat.

This comic impulse is not very evident in his early work, but in his *Paris Notebook* he had already argued: 'tragedy is the imperfect manner and comedy the perfect manner in art'. His basis for this perference was that comedy excited joy in the audience directly, whereas the direct products of tragedy were pity and terror. Nevertheless, although the 'friendly pity' with which he presents the ignominious characters of *Dubliners* is already far removed from Eliot's disgust, the stories are not comic, and such elements of comedy as they contain are rather satirical than humorous. A sense of humour involves more than 'friendly pity' for moral ignominy, although 'friendly' comes close to it, with its suggestion of fellow feeling.

Notoriously a sense of humour implies a readiness to laugh at one's own weaknesses, or, in other words, to recognise oneself among the ignominious. This self-knowledge is something Joyce gained from the self-inflicted indignities that marked his early years as a family bread-winner and husband. The resulting sense of humour first makes itself felt in the character of Freddy Malins in 'The Dead'. Instead of requiring the firm handling that has been arranged for his arrival, this deplorable and embarrassing drunkard proves, in the event, to be the life of the party.

Part Two
Critical Survey

3 A Portrait of the Artist as a Young Man

Biography and fiction

'O, Stephen will apologize', his mother assures the neighbours at the opening of the novel. We must beware of reading *A Portrait of the Artist* as Joyce's own apology—an apology not in the sense Mrs Dedalus intended, but in that used by his early stylistic mentor, Newman in his *Apologia Pro Vita Sua* as an act of self-justification. In the first place, Stephen Dedalus is not to be confused with James Joyce. 'Stuck-up Stephen' was Stanislaus' nickname for the fictitious character, and Stephen certainly differs markedly from the character portrayed in *My Brother's Keeper*. We cannot imagine Stephen being known as 'Sunny Jim', or, in his student days, collapsing into a passing empty perambulator, and asking the nursemaid who was pushing it how far she was going. And when we match the incidents incorporated in the fiction with their originals in real life, we find they have been re-shaped to accommodate a participant far less sanguine, vigorous and zestful than the young James Joyce. The visit to Cork with his father can be taken as a case in point. In the novel it occasions contemptuous, weary disgust in Stephen. The corresponding event in real life, however, according to Stanislaus, provoked his brother's amusement.

This re-shaping of Joyce's autobiography into fiction is especially clear when the Stephen of the *Portrait* is compared with the more faithful picture presented in *Stephen Hero*. Family relations, and in particular the close relationship with Stanislaus, figure largely in the earlier novel. In the final version Maurice (the name of Stanislaus's fictitious counterpart) has all but disappeared, and there is no incident to match the death of a younger brother which provides a pathetic episode in *Stephen Hero*. The later hero is far less conscious of 'what the heart is and what it feels' than the earlier one. The statement that a mother's love is one of the few sure things in a disappointing world, which was a favourite observation of the young James Joyce, is put into the mouth of Cranly in the final version, by way of reproof to Stephen.

The aesthetic theories enunciated are similarly modified. The idea of the epiphany, for example, fully explained in *Stephen Hero*, is omitted from the *Portrait*. So is the devotion to Ibsen, which features largely in *Stephen Hero* as 'the most enduring influence of his life'. In the *Portrait*, Ibsen is mentioned only once. We are told that whenever Stephen walked past a stone-cutting works, the spirit of Ibsen would

'Once upon a time and a very good time it was . . .' Joyce as a child with his mother, father and maternal grandfather.

blow through him, 'a spirit of wayward boyish beauty'. The phrase is taken straight from *Stephen Hero*, but with a significant alteration. In the earlier novel the phrase is not 'boyish beauty' but 'boylike bravery'. The emphasis given to the aesthetic theories in the *Portrait* stresses their detachment, whereas in *Stephen Hero* they serve a revolutionary attitude, in tune with what the hero terms 'the modern spirit', which he defines as 'vivisective'. At that stage of his development, according to Stanislaus, his brother's literary aim was to develop 'grim realizations that dethrone tyrannical secrets in the heart and awaken in it a sense of liberation'. The truth of this observation is proved by the stories Joyce actually went on to write, in *Dubliners*—stories quite beyond the range of the young man presented in the *Portrait*.

No less striking is the difference between the two novels in the treatment of the central character. The tone of *Stephen Hero* is that of the biography of a great man written by one of his disciples. Speech is observantly and realistically reported when the speakers are minor characters, but Stephen himself makes authoritative pronouncements, and when the narrator makes comments they have the humourless solemn style of an obituary. We are told, for example, that:

> It was not part of his life to undertake an extensive alteration of society but he felt the need to express himself such an urgent need, such a real need, that he was determined no conventions of a society, however plausibly mingling pity with its tyranny, should be allowed to stand in his way . . .

Corridor at Clongowes Wood College

In the *Portrait* on the other hand, when the narrative turns to explanatory comment, the tenor of the observations is far more critical and objective, as for example:

> In vague sacrificial or sacramental acts alone his will seemed drawn to go forth to encounter reality: and it was partly the absence of an appointed rite which had always constrained him to inaction whether he had allowed silence to cover his anger or pride or had suffered only an embrace he longed to give.
>
> (162/159)

In general, however, the narrative in the *Portrait* is conducted ironically from the point of view of Stephen, exposing the limitations of his responses, the blindness produced by his pride. Seeing himself always in a heroic role, Stephen in the *Portrait* is by way of figuring as a mock-heroic, comic figure, comparable with Don Quixote or Parson Adams. In the interest of realism, this feature of the novel is never emphasised to the point of absurdity. Nevertheless it is present from the moment when, as a boy demanding justice at Clongowes, he sees himself as a legendary Roman hero, and the ridicule is plain enough, as when his saintly exercises following his confession are related in the style of hagiography.

> To mortify his smell was more difficult as he found in himself no instinctive repugnance to bad odours, whether they were the odours of the outdoor world such as those of dung and tar or the odours of his own person among which he had made many curious comparisons and experiments.
>
> (154/151)

It is a measure of his growing maturity that, at the end of the book, Stephen himself comes to appreciate this comic aspect of his behaviour, as when he remarks that, making 'a sudden gesture of a revolutionary nature' in the course of his last meeting with Emma, he 'must have looked like a fellow throwing a handful of peas into the air'.

Significantly, although Stephen's exposition of his aesthetic doctrine follows Joyce's *Paris Notebook* closely, it omits the declaration that comedy is the highest form of art, and concentrates on tragedy. He lacks humility, and thus a sense of humour, which, as Joyce explained to his friend Arthur Power, is an acknowledgement of one's 'inferiority before life'. 'No Frenchman will admit his inferiority before life. His vanity prevents it. But an Englishman is better balanced, and he will admit his powerlessness before fate by means of his humour', Joyce told him.

It was because Joyce had come to realise his own inferiority that he dropped the earlier, heroic version of his life and substituted the *Portrait*. When he first began to convert the material of his past into a work of art he felt himself to be a master of life, who had already fought and won those battles behind the forehead in which Ibsen had been victorious before him. In the event, this battle proved to be the task of writing the novel itself. Or rather, there were two battles. The first, on winning which he justly prided himself, was the battle to free himself from the mental shackles imposed on him by family, church and nation, in order to become a free spirit. His very first autobiographical work, *A Portrait of the Artist*, was a short rhapsodic effusion in celebration of that victory. *Stephen Hero* was a full account of the rebellion which achieved it. Its arrogance was a sign of the writer's ignorance of the cost at which the victory was achieved, which was isolation. Recognition of that cost was the second battle, in which victory was not an intellectual but a moral feat, the acknowledgement that he was not a superior being, but a man as other men were. In artistic terms, it meant seeing himself not as a rebel angel but just another Dubliner.

Significantly it was after writing 'The Dead' that he scrapped *Stephen Hero*. In this story he came to terms with a personal problem which had revealed to him his own weakness—the shock resulting from his wife's revelation that, before he met her, a young man had 'died for love of her' as Michael Furey had died for Gretta in the story. In the story Gabriel surmounts his humiliation because he comes to see himself with humility. For Joyce the story itself was his way of doing the same thing. His treatment of the material, however, is not to produce a faithful portrait of himself. Gabriel Conroy is not James Joyce, but a character governed by that aspect of Joyce's character which was most relevant to the situation, namely his complacency. In the same way, in the *Portrait*, Stephen Dedalus is not identical with his creator, but a character governed by that aspect of his character most relevant to the story of his rebellion, namely his egoism. That is why his more amiable, sympathetic characteristics are excluded. It is not *the* portrait, but *a* portrait, one of several possible renderings of the original material. In *Stephen Hero*, the subject's egoism is frequently referred to, but not criticised. In *A Portrait* it is never mentioned, but ironically presented in an extended and developed application of the method Joyce had discovered in the course of writing *Dubliners*.

Structure

A Portrait of the Artist as a Young Man is a study in egoism, and Stephen's egoism manifests itself in different forms throughout the action. Egoism itself, however, is not a motive. What motivates Stephen throughout the novel is an unsatisfied desire to harmonise his experience, which finds its eventual answer in the wholeness, harmony and radiance of art. Before this conclusion has been reached, however, a series of provisional solutions are adopted only to be outgrown. At the beginning of each chapter Stephen is presented as the subject of a distressing tension, which develops to a crisis leading to a resolution. At the beginning of the following chapter, however, this resolution is seen to have produced a new tension, and the process is continued in a new form.

This wave-like, pulsating movement is characteristic of every scene, and is formulated clearly from the beginning, as when the infant Stephen notes the way in which a wetted bed is first warm, then cold, or, as a schoolboy at supper he alternately shuts out and lets in the noise of the refectory by applying his hands to his ears. In this first chapter the conflict lies between his desire to find peace in conformity and his awareness of anomalies in the teaching and conduct of those in authority. At home his elders are in violent opposition over politics: both sides cannot be right. At school his teachers do not always practise what they preach. This tension comes to a head when he is unjustly punished, but when he demands justice things are put right, and his trust in the perfection of orthodoxy seems to be justified.

At the opening of the second chapter, however, he has left Clongowes and is the victim of a new tension, this time between his romantic aspirations and the unsatisfactory environment in which he finds himself as a result of the decline in the family fortunes. He has to harmonise a vivid inner world with a sordid outer one. A detailed analysis of the sequence of scenes in this chapter will serve to illustrate the pattern of presentation which governs the structure of all the chapters. The tension which is its theme is presented by an alternation of realistic and romantic scenes.

The chapter opens with a realistic account of his excursions with Uncle Charles, followed by a romantic account of his daydream about Mercedes, succeeded by a realistic account of the changes that came with autumn, when the cows came in from their lush pasture to the filthy farmyard. The section closes with a return to his daydream and the theme of the chapter is clearly formulated. 'He wanted to meet in the real world the unsubstantial image which his soul so constantly beheld.'

This alternation is continued in the succeeding sections. In the second, a realistic account of the family removal to Dublin is followed by the romantic fiasco with Emma on the tram, and ends with the realistic scene in which his schooling is discussed at table. In the third (shifting in time with the use of flashbacks) the behind-the-scenes preparation for the Whitsuntide festivities (realistic), is followed in succession by a romantic flashback related to Emma, a realistic account of schoolboy persecution, a subjective description of the stage performance, and finally a realistic recovery of realism amidst horse piss and rotted straw.

Alternation between inner excitement over his 'cold and cruel and loveless lust' and his objective observation of his father's moral disintegration during the visit to Cork in the next section is too continuous to be plotted. A hint of resolution appears when he is shocked to find, in the word 'foetus' carved on a desk, 'a trace of what he had deemed till then a brutish and individual malady of his own mind'. This hint is repeated in his reaction, in the final section, to obscene graffiti in a urinal, which points to the 'dark peace' which he finds at last in the arms of a prostitute. Even in this final section the alternation continues. The highly coloured account of his wanderings in the red-light district is preceded by a realistic account of his attempt to make his home respectable with the help of his scholarship money.

The same movement continues through the rest of the book. In the third chapter the measured, rhetorical warning of the sermons alternates with his fevered sense of guilt, to be resolved in his confession and sense of redemption. In the fourth chapter his sense of personal perfection is at odds with his sense of mortal weakness, to be resolved in the vision of the wading girl, in which he recognises the existence of 'mortal beauty' and embraces life, with all its imperfections. In the final chapter his detachment and suspicion are at war with his awareness of the demands of personal feeling, a tension which is resolved by going into 'exile'.

REPETITIONS AND ECHOES It is not only by this wave-like motion that the incidents are unified. In every chapter similar scenes occur—there is, for example, a passage where Stephen has a vision of his situation in the cosmos; a scene where he recalls a past incident; a scene where he is alone in a room, usually in bed; a scene where he imagines an event which he has not actually witnessed; a scene where he is catechised or accused; a scene where he rejects or refuses to accept something; a family meal-time; a scene of Stephen among his peers; a scene of squalor; a scene with a girl; an encounter with a woman by the wayside. All these similarities invite comparisons. To take obvious examples, the family meals are increasingly squalid; Stephen's handling of accusations becomes increasingly cool and adept.

This systematic repetition, however, is only one aspect of the continuous mounting of comparisons. Sometimes these comparisons are explicit, as when Davin's account of his meeting with a peasant woman at the doorway of her cottage reminds Stephen of the peasant women he had seen at their doorways on his way to school, or his writing of a villanelle after cutting Emma on the steps of the library reminds him of his childhood attempt to write a love poem after refusing to kiss her on the steps of the tram. Sometimes they are obvious, like the matching of the kiss of the prostitute at the end of chapter 2, with the administering of the sacraments at the end of chapter 3, or the recital of the seven deadly sins at the beginning of chapter 3 with the listing of Stephen's seven-fold religious observances at the beginning of chapter 4. Sometimes they are buried deep in detail, but nevertheless significant, like his father's trick of whistling to call him, or passing his plate for his son to eat the remnants of his food. These pairings are sometimes far distant, like the humiliation Stephen feels in the second chapter when, putting his fingers to his collar he is aware of its frayed condition, which invites comparison with putting his fingers in the same position, in the final chapter, to kill a louse. Nevertheless, they are there to be pondered for their significance. We can see what a long way Stephen has come when we compare his answer to the schoolfellows who bother him at Clongowes with questions about his father, with the answer which he gives to Cranly's similar question at the end of the book. We can nevertheless also see that he is the same person when we compare his attitude to burdened Brother Michael, raking the infirmary fire in the first chapter, with his attitude to the no less burdened dean of studies, lighting a fire in the physics theatre in the final chapter.

Incident is not linked to incident in a causal chain. The scenes, and even more the chapters, are separated by gaps in the manner Pound termed 'ideogrammatic'. They illuminate each other in a harmonious, 'radiant' wholeness. They add up. When he first described the book he intended to make out of his past experience, the youthful Joyce told Stanislaus that it was to be 'a stream of presents'. At each succeeding moment we are only allowed to perceive the here and now. The pattern, however, becomes clearer as time passes. In a sense one reads the book for the first time only when one comes to read it again, and the future joins with the past to illuminate the present.

Above all, what gives the novel its cohesion is the character of Stephen. The method of the point of view is adhered to with the utmost fidelity. The reader only sees what Stephen sees, and what he cannot see clearly and objectively remains nebulous to the end. This is particularly true of the nebulous figure of Emma, in marked contrast to *Stephen Hero*, where she is a strongly marked character in her own right.

Stephen himself is both fluid and consistent. Like the book itself he simultaneously develops and remains the same—weary, proud, speculative, sensitive, narcissistic, timid yet bold, resentful, preoccupied by language, lonely, afraid of love. These unifying traits, however, manifest themselves in the flow of minutely registered experiences, so that a careless reading, ignoring the possibility of irony, might treat the novel as a piece of self-justification. The treatment to which he is subjected, however, remains throughout the book what it is at the beginning, when we see him in his infancy—

understandingly ironic, and kindly comic.

It is worth considering this opening section in detail. Containing as it does the whole work in miniature, it exemplifies the structure of implication that sustains the entire work. To begin with, it states the theme. The encounter with the moocow symbolises Stephen's million 'encounters with reality', to which he refers at the end. The cow is not a recurrent symbol in the book, but the phrase 'encounter with reality' is frequently employed and the cow's significance is clear enough if we ignore its conventional uses and see it simply as the supplier of natural nourishment (which alternately attracts and repels Stephen in chapter 2). The story of all these encounters is then summed up in the ensuing action. At first Stephen conforms. Authority has two faces—one, his father's scrutinising hairy one, which is alarming, the other his comforting mother's. He dances to authority's tune, and is applauded and rewarded for obedience. The girl next door attracts him, and he weaves a fantasy about her. Then comes his offence. Authority threatens him and demands a confession. But Stephen refuses, and goes into voluntary exile under the table, to compose a poem.

The character of Stephen is also demonstrated. The tone of the passage is introverted and reflective but all the senses are active. He is cunning in his compliance, but, when the crisis comes, he proves self-willed. He sees himself as a fictitious character, and confuses reality with fantasy. Words preoccupy him, and can lead him astray (the 'green rose'). But, in the end, he uses the words which others have to offer, when he converts the language of Dante into a song.

The passage also exemplifies the structure of the entire novel. The incidents are not causally linked, but juxtaposed ideogrammatically. The wave movement governs the sequence, and is formulated in Stephen's registration of the successive heat and cold of the wetted bed. Other structural features, which we shall proceed to examine next, are also present. Symbols which are to be used throughout the book are introduced—heat and cold, colours, birds—and the narrative is conducted in a style in which the author's presence is not felt because the language is the language of the child he writes about.

Symbolism

In the last chapter the final section of narrative opens with Stephen, standing on the steps of the library, watching the circling swallows.

And for ages men had gazed upward as he was gazing at birds in flight. The colonnade above him made him think vaguely of an ancient temple and the ashplant on which he leaned wearily of the curved stick of an augur. A sense of fear of the unknown moved in the heart of his weariness, a fear of symbols and portents, of the hawklike man whose name he bore soaring out of his captivity on osierwoven wings, of Thoth, the god of writers, writing with a reed upon a tablet and bearing on his narrow ibis head the cusped moon.

(229/224)

Here, for the first time, we find Stephen in the situation in which Joyce has placed the reader from the outset: he feels himself confronted with a symbol. The symbol was no less potent for Joyce himself than for his fictitious counterpart, who, by proceeding to connect it with lines from Yeats's *The Countess Cathleen*, supplies us with a context for the poem from *Chamber Music* already discussed on page 39. Stephen recalls the lines in which the dying countess compares herself with a swallow, taking a last look at its nest before it flies away to 'wander the loud waters'.

He thus interprets the swallows as a symbol of departure or of loneliness—departure because of the birds' migratory habits; loneliness because of the hostility of the nationalistic mob to Yeats, the solitary artist. Without this new association, however, the symbol is already sufficiently explicit. It can be read as part of a pattern already woven. Indeed, such a reading includes implications which Stephen himself is not aware of. The reader finds it significant enough that Stephen should identify himself with birds. In the earlier chapters they were symbols of accusation and punishment. That they no longer seem to threaten him is the result of his vision of 'the angel of mortal beauty', in the shape of a wading girl who was herself formed like a bird. Associated with that vision was that of the hawk-like man—the great artificer himself—in flight. Art and escape (by association with Daedalus) are thus fused, together with a sense of rebellion, for Thoth is not the god of the Jesuits. The sense of priesthood Stephen experiences under the colonnade is exotic. Indeed it must be exotic, for the hawk-like man has its counter-image—that of the 'bat-like soul'—imprisoned at home, who must call on strangers for rescue from the blind darkness in which she awakes. As for reading loneliness into the details of the scene, the cusped moon marks the reappearance of a repeated symbol first identified in the second chapter, where, acknowledging his sense of isolated superiority, Stephen repeats to himself a fragment from Shelley:

> Art thou pale for weariness
> Of climbing heaven and gazing on the earth,
> Wandering companionless . . . ?

PUBLIC SYMBOLS This passage also serves to illustrate the symbolic method of the novel. This method has two sources. The first source is determined by the culture shared by Stephen and the reader, and is public, as for example the allusion of his surname, the association of the colonnade, the emblem of the ashplant, the analogy with augury. The second source, although also shared by Stephen and the reader, is private. It is the peculiar associations with his earlier personal experiences which the scene awakens. These two categories inevitably overlap. Nevertheless, the distinction serves as a basis for considering the overall symbolic structure of the book.

The most obvious kind of culturally determined symbolism is the use of historical and mythological analogies, such as that invited by the hero's name. As Stephen he invites a comparison, simultaneously valid and exaggerated, with the first martyr. The significance of his surname, which is particularly dear to him, is no less ambiguous. Is he Daedalus, the successful artificer, or only the vainglorious and ineffectual son, who fell to his doom in the water? As one who fell, incidentally, he himself accepts the comparison with Lucifer which Cranly suggests to him when he declares his *non serviam*, while the threat of torment by divinely commissioned birds links him with Prometheus (who also bore light).

None of these comparisons is structural. In *Ulysses* the comparison of Mr Bloom with his Homeric prototype remains continuously operative. The analogy is intrinsic to the action. The comparison between Stephen and Icarus, Prometheus, and the rest is, on the other hand, merely incidental. Something more like a sustained allusion might seem to be offered in the last chapter, where Stephen compares himself with Christ, in defending his relationship with his mother, and in his identification of Cranly with John the Baptist. These, however, prove only incidental references. A sustained analogy would require the development of the story along lines parallel with the New Testament. In particular, the climax of the story must be an event corresponding, in some way, with the Crucifixion, which it is not.

There is another difference between the cultural references in *A Portrait* and those in *Ulysses*. Not only are they less sustained and less numerous. They are also simpler. Only in one place is there a reference of that esoteric kind which was to provoke admiration or annoyance in readers of Joyce's later work. It occurs in the diary entry for March 21, morning, where, after justifying an analogy between Cranly and John the Baptist, Stephen observes, 'Puzzled for the moment by saint John at the Latin gate'. The reference here is to a church in Rome which, although originally dedicated to Christ, was later re-dedicated to St John the Baptist and St John the Evangelist. The church thus instances the supplanting of a saviour by his inferior, as Stephen suspects he is being supplanted in Emma's esteem by his friend. But perhaps this detail should be regarded as a piece of psychological realism rather than of symbolism, anticipating the way in which ideas emerge in the mind of Mr Bloom in *Ulysses* in a manner which he himself cannot account for, although the reader, as he comes to know him, can. This is not the only place in *A Portrait* where the unconscious mind is seen at work. In the first chapter, for example, Stephen cannot understand the older boys when they speak of the crime of 'smugging', but his thoughts fly immediately to the occasion where Eileen had put her hands in his pockets, and observed that pockets were funny things to have.

The most intrinsic and structural comparison is that with Dante. Not until the end do Stephen's own thoughts consciously turn to him although in his Mercedes fantasy he plays the role of Dantès (hero of *The Count of Monte Cristo*), and the name 'Dante' does appear in the novel, attached to Mrs Riordan. The action itself however offers a close parallel, which is sufficiently apparent to the reader. Stephen's life is bound up with that of a city, he has an ecstatic vision of a pure young girl, sees a rose in heaven, and finally goes into exile. As Stephen's own eventual reference makes clear, however, the comparison is a source of irony—'opened the spiritual-heroic refrigerating apparatus, invented and patented in all countries by Dante Alighieri'. A similar irony invests the other heroic comparisons, even when he is not himself aware of it.

Typical of the conventional, public symbols which illuminate the action is that of the rose, which he celebrates at the very start of the book, and which is intertwined with his life at many of its subsequent crises. At school, where his badge is a white rose, he broods on the beauty and colours of roses. His romantic reveries about Mercedes centre on a rose-clad cottage. After his repentance, he offers up to the Virgin his 'heart of white rose'. His artistic vocation is signalled to him by the appearance of a rose shape in the sunset sky. His composition of a villanelle in his bedroom is accompanied by a sense of 'rose and ardent' light, as well as 'staring at the great overblown flowers on the tattered wallpaper'. At the end of the book we are reminded that he has not yet met 'sweet Rosie O'Grady'.

COLOUR SYMBOLS The significance of roses in the novel varies with their colours—another source of conventional symbolism. White represents purity; red represents excitement; green represents creativity; yellow represents corruption; grey represents nullity. These definitions do not, of course, imply that the colours are unambiguous. Purity, for example, may be positive, with an attractive whiteness, like that of 'tower of ivory', or the recollection of Emma dancing at a party—'her white dress a little lifted, a white spray nodding in her hair'. On the other hand, it can be repulsively anaemic, like the food at Clongowes.

> He sat looking at the two prints of butter on his plate but could not eat the damp bread. The tablecloth was damp and limp. But he drank off the hot weak tea which the clumsy scullion, girt with a white apron, poured into his cup. He wondered whether the

scullion's apron was damp too or whether all white things were cold and damp.

(12/12)

(This passage illustrates another use of conventional symbols—partial communion—a gesture which also features in *Dubliners* and *Ulysses*.) It is a measure of Stephen's self-betrayal, when he repents, that he can prize this feeble purity, once again presented as a menu.

He sat by the fire in the kitchen, not daring to speak for happiness. Till that moment he had not known how beautiful and peaceful life could be. The green square of paper pinned round the lamp cast down a tender shade. On the dresser was a plate of sausages and white pudding and on the shelf there were eggs. They would be for the breakfast in the morning after the communion in the college chapel. White pudding and eggs and sausages and cups of tea. How simple and beautiful was life after all! And life lay all before him.

(149/146)

Similar ambiguities attend the other colours. For example, a misty greyness invests Dublin with beauty, when Stephen sees it in the distance, as he walks by the sea. More generally, however, the colour grey conveys an ashen lifelessness. The prefect of studies has a 'white-grey' face and 'white-grey' hair to match his 'no-coloured' eyes. Greyness, associated with rain, is continuously present in the

Customs House Quay, Dublin

last chapter, as the manifestation of a force in Ireland which 'seemed to war with the course of Stephen's thought'. Thus, in the scene of incestuous intercourse which Stephen imagines (after encountering the degenerate offspring of an incestuous union), the background features a grey lake, grey rainy light, and a woman dressed in grey.

What governs the positive or negative implications of colours in the novel is the context in which they occur, and in particular Stephen's state of mind. This is especially evident in the case of redness, with its associated excitement. Defined by Dante's hair-brushes as the colour of orthodox Davitt as against heretic Parnell, it has threatening implications of righteous indignation, starting with the blazing faces at the Christmas dinner, and ending with the warning signal that alerts Stephen, in chapter 4, against entering the priesthood.

> His name in that new life leaped into characters before his eyes and to it there followed a mental sensation of an undefined face or colour of a face. The colour faded and became strong like a changing glow of pallid brick red. Was it the raw reddish glow he had so often seen on wintry mornings on the shaven gills of the priests? The face was eyeless and sour-favoured and devout, shot with pink tinges of suffocated anger.

(164/161)

Interior of the National Library of Ireland

Stephen himself is much given to flushing and blushing. When this is for shame, it is connected with indignation. But red also stands for positive ardour. His encounter with the wading girl sets his cheeks 'aflame', and culminates in the vision of a sunset 'breaking in full crimson and unfolding and fading to palest rose'.

Green, the colour of the 'little green place' and of Parnell is no less ambiguous, for although it plainly promises change its freshness is questionable. There is something mouldy about it. It is the colour of the turf-coloured bogwater in the loathed swimming bath at Clongowes, of the scum that mantles the filthy farmyard pool, of the weeds infesting the derelict field in which Stephen sees circling demons. As such it is connected with the colour of excrement— yellow, which tints the vocabulary of dung-eating Lynch, the colour of the gas-lit haunts of prostitutes, and of 'horse piss and rotted straw'. This significance is conventional enough especially at the turn of the nineteenth century. (W. S. Gilbert would have recognised in Stephen a kindred spirit of 'greenery-yallery' Bunthorne.) But decadence itself is an ambiguous concept. Decadent periods have often been fruitful ones, and it is by embracing corruption that Stephen develops. The significance of the symbolism shifts in tune with his development, even when it is conventional.

SUBJECTIVE SYMBOLS In addition to the conventional symbolism, however, there is also the symbolism which derives a peculiar significance from Stephen's own personal experience. Thus, for example, hands have special associations for him. In the scene of incest, already referred to, the lover's face is not seen, but his hand is Davin's hand. That it should be Davin is in itself significant, because for Stephen Davin is, above all else, the man who refused sexual intercourse with a stranger, just as he refuses all contact with foreigners. In this imagined scene, therefore, we have a comment on Irish patriotic xenophobia—as incestuous, and productive of monstrosity. But the emphasis on the hand is also significant. 'Is he as innocent as his speech?' is the question Davin poses. The emphasis on his hand in the imagined scene links him with priests, and, as such, with untrustworthiness. Ever after the traumatic pandybatting, Stephen is on his guard against the apparent friendliness of priests. On that occasion the prefect of studies took the boy's hand in his own smooth, cool, well-kept hand, as if to give it a friendly shake, but in fact to prepare it for the infliction of pain. Thereafter, when he is in the company of priests, Stephen is aware of their hands —symbols both of friendliness and punishment. And very often those hands frame themselves into further, instructive symbols. Thus, at the retreat: 'The preacher began to speak in a quiet friendly tone. His face was kind and he joined gently the fingers of each hand, forming a frail cage by the union of their tips.' Similarly, warily waiting for the director of Belvedere College to come to the point, Stephen watches 'the slow deft movements of the priestly fingers' as they form the cord of the blind into a noose. (Consideration of this scene exemplifies the impossibility of distinguishing Joyce's symbolism from realistic description: the director has his back to the light; the lines of his skull are visible; the blind is a crossblind.)

A similar symbolism results from the experience of being pushed into the square ditch at Clongowes, which colours his reaction to the water in the swimming-bath, the farmyard-pool, the dirty water of Dublin docks, sea water and greasy food. Contamination is an obsessive fear of Stephen's, which has very deep roots. Longing for peace, he longs for immunity—symbolised by candles, ivory, ecclesiastical vessels and vestments, and above all the moon. Feelings are experienced as painful inflictions from outside, external seizures, contaminations to be got rid of. Even his refusal to communicate, as he explains to Cranly, is due to fear of admitting within himself the operations of an external power. His confession, whereby he gets rid of impurities, is described in terms of an enema. His sex appears to him as an external thing, parasitically attached to him, threatening his self-possession. Indeed, any kind of affection presents itself to him as an infection. His horror of contamination is a manifestation of his fear of intimacy.

Purity, thus conceived, means imperviousness. Symbolised by 'the barren shell of the moon', it implies sterilisation and isolation. It is essentially cold. Despite his egoism, these are not qualities which attract Stephen, and he suffers from weariness as a result. Moreover, he is subject to impulses of a very different nature. For example, although afraid of contamination he shows no enthusiasm for coldness or for cleanliness when he thinks of the Jesuits as 'men who washed their bodies briskly with cold water', or consigns Emma to the love of 'some clean athlete who washed himself every morning to the waist'. At Clongowes he preferred the smell of the peasants— 'air and rain and turf and corduroy'—to the cold smell of the chapel. His attitude to corruption is ambiguous. He does not like the feel of it, but the smell of it does not offend him. 'That is horse piss and rotted straw', he tells himself in Lotts Lane, in the second chapter. 'It is a good odour to breathe.' A similar odour—'the faint sour stink of rotted cabbages . . . from the kitchen gardens'—comes to his aid when he is considering joining the priesthood.

His rejection of the priesthood, followed by his vision of mortal beauty, marks the end of his fear of corruption, his acceptance of imperfection and the inevitability of falling. The symbolism which has developed in the earlier sections of the book here receives its most intense use, particularly the symbol of the sea as a contaminating force, not only seen as such from the quayside, but used as a metaphor of contamination in the second chapter, and again, in the fourth, where the danger of falling once again into sin presents itself to Stephen in the image of a tide threatening his feet as it advances to the place where he is standing on a dry shore. This serves almost as an interpretation of the final section of the chapter, where despite 'a faint click at his heart' caused by his phobia, Stephen stays on the shore, and at last bares his feet and wades into the sea. (This aspect of the sea symbolism is reinforced by another aspect. Stephen's revery of Daedalus's flight, interrupted by the shouts of his school-fellows splashing in the water, recalls the fate of Icarus, who also ended up in the waves.) His reward is a vision that incorporates, symbolically, the full range of his experience.

A girl stood before him in midstream, alone and still, gazing out to sea. She seemed like one whom magic had changed into the likeness of a strange and beautiful seabird. Her long slender bare legs were delicate as a crane's and pure save where an emerald trail of seaweed had fashioned itself as a sign upon the flesh. Her thighs, fuller and softhued as ivory, were bared almost to the hips, where the white fringes of her drawers were like feathering of soft white down. Her slateblue skirts were kilted boldly about her waist and dovetailed behind her. Her bosom was as a bird's soft and slight, slight and soft as the breast of some darkplumaged dove. But her long fair hair was girlish: and girlish, and touched with the wonder of mortal beauty, her face.

$$(175/171)$$

The image of the bird as an authoritative agent—an angel, in fact—is here, although now the angel has come 'from the fair courts of life'. The white purity of ivory is there, in significant conjunction with green weed, which implies corruption. The repeated image of the dove introduces the element of greyness. Only the red is missing, to be presented in the next paragraph when a 'faint flame trembled on her cheek'.

Most remarkable is the way in which the imagined bird and the seen girl remain, although united, perceptibly distinct, as if to serve as a monument to the process of metamorphosis by which, in the rest of the book, realistic detail is transformed into symbol. The more often the novel is read, the deeper the significance that attaches to each recorded feature. Thus, turning back to the beginning, after the opening infancy passage already discussed, we find:

The wide playgrounds were swarming with boys. All were shouting and the prefects urged them on with strong cries. The evening air was pale and chilly and after every charge and thud of the footballers the greasy leather orb flew like a heavy bird through the grey light.

$$(8/8)$$

Table 1   A Portrait of the Artist as a Young Man

	FACTOR	COLOUR	QUALITY	FORM	POSITIVE ASPECT	NEGATIVE ASPECT
(a)	Stimulation	Red	Hot	Surface	Ardour e.g. fire sunset	Disturbance e.g. anger smarting
(b)	Immunity	White	Cold	Surface	Purity e.g. tower of ivory white rose	Alienation e.g. shell Clongowes ghost
(c)	Fecundity	Green	Thick	Fluid	Fertility e.g. manure kitchen garden	Corruption e.g. slime grease
(d)	Passivity	Colourless	Thin	Fluid	Rapture e.g. dewy wetness fountain	Nullity e.g. clammy things rain

The allegorical import of the opening sentences is clear enough. (Half the novel is concerned with Stephen's struggle to ignore 'the prefects' and evade 'the game'.) The third sentence, however, only reveals its import when all the rest of the book has been absorbed. The pale chill, the grey light, the greasy ball, take their places together in a complex pattern. And the metamorphosis of the greasy ball into a bird is, in Stephen's language, the act of 'a priest of the eternal imagination, transmuting the daily bread of experience into the radiant body of everlasting life'.

Language

Written in the speech of an infant, the opening passage prepares the reader for the irony which characterises the writing of the novel as a whole. Joyce employs the device he developed in *Dubliners* of couching his narrative in a style which the fictitious subject would himself have chosen to represent him, the style of a sympathetic narrator. As in the course of the novel the fictitious subject, Stephen, changes considerably, there is a need for many narrators employing a multiplicity of styles. Stephen's development can, in fact, be plotted by selecting specimens of prose from successive sections of the narrative.

Thus, at Clongowes:

It made him very tired to think that way. It made him feel his head very big. (16/16)

At Belvedere:

A shaft of momentary anger flew through Stephen's mind at these indelicate allusions in the hearing of a stranger. For him there was nothing amusing in a girl's interest and regard. (79/77)

At University College:

It was the windless hour of dawn when madness wakes and strange plants open to the light and the moth flies forth silently. (221/228)

The quotations do not of course imply that the narrative falls into three stages, with three corresponding styles. On the contrary, in each chapter the variations of Stephen's attitudes and moods call for several different styles. Never before had a novel been written in such a variety of different styles, and this fact is an indication of Joyce's originality. A more instructive clue to the nature of his genius, however, is the way in which style is thrust into the reader's face, as an object not for his admiration but for his critical inspection. Transparency was the last thing Joyce aimed for in style. He deliberately employed style as an obtrusive factor, claiming the reader's critical attention as an essential component of the understanding which the writing was intended to convey. Thus, in the passages quoted, the obtrusive features—the artlessness of the first, the stilted self-consciousness of the second, and the cosmetic aestheticism of the third—are there to be noticed. They are gestures expressing Stephen's state of mind, and they serve to focus attention on the limitations of that state of mind.

This variety is itself enough to provoke comparisons, but Joyce also provides material for more immediate contrast. One such ground for comparison is provided by the dialogue. Although the novel is written from Stephen's point of view, this does not prevent other characters from speaking for themselves. Indeed it is characteristic of Stephen to pay close attention to the way in which people speak. Side by side with passages written in styles sympathetic to Stephen we therefore find passages couched in alien styles. The most massive of these is the series of sermons in the third chapter. Other extended examples are Mr Casey's anecdote at the Christmas dinner, Simon Dedalus on many occasions but most notably his anecdote about his father, and Davin's anecdote about the village woman. All of these have their characteristic styles, which contrast with Stephen's. No less characteristic, and equally effective as background, are brief utterances such as bring to life the prefect of studies: 'lazy, idle little loafer'—the dean of studies: 'when may we expect to have something from you on the aesthetic question?'—or Cranly's 'let us eke go'. To these samples may be added the memorabilia that surround Stephen, like Napoleon's reply when asked what was the happiest day of his life: 'Gentlemen, the happiest day of my life was the day in which I made my first holy communion.'

When it occurs in discussions with Stephen, this alien speech inevitably produces a contrast with his own utterances. But it also serves for purposes of contrast when it interrupts passages of sympathetic narrative. Thus Stephen's fanciful response to a hellfire sermon

> He passed up the staircase and into the corridor along the walls of which the overcoats and waterproofs hung like gibbeted malefactors, headless and dripping and shapeless. (128/125)

is juxtaposed with the more normal reactions of his classmates

> – I suppose he rubbed it into you well.
> – You bet he did. He put us all into a blue funk.
>
> (128/125)

Similar effects are also, for example, produced in the fourth chapter, when Stephen's reveries, as he walks beside the sea, are twice interrupted by the hearty (and fortuitously relevant) shouts of other schoolmates.

SUBJECTIVE AND OBJECTIVE NARRATIVE. On this occasion, however, Joyce also offers for contrast with the sympathetic narrative style another, anonymous narrative style. The sympathetic narrative style, conveying Stephen's exaltation, is conveyed in writing like this.

> So timeless seemed the grey warm air, so fluid and impersonal his own mood, that all ages were as one to him. A moment before the ghost of the ancient kingdom of the Danes had looked forth through the vesture of the hazewrapped city. Now, at the name of the fabulous artificer, he seemed to hear the noise of dim waves and to see a winged form flying above the waves and slowly climbing the air. What did it mean? Was it a quaint device opening a page of some medieval book of prophecies and symbols, a hawk-like man flying sunward above the sea, a prophecy of the end he had been born to serve and had been following through the mists of childhood and boyhood, a symbol of the artist forging anew in his workshop out of the sluggish matter of the earth a new soaring impalpable imperishable being?
>
> (173/169)

His perceptions are visionary and vague, marked by words like 'ghost', 'haze-wrapped', 'dim' and 'mists', and by the frequency of abstract terms like 'form', 'prophecies', 'symbol' and 'being'. The synthetic quality of the experience is also accentuated by the inclusion of words remote from common speech—'vesture', 'fabulous artificer', 'quaint device'. But, above all, the sentences lack thrust. They dwell rather than do. This effect is accentuated in the first sentence by inversion ('So timeless seemed . . .'), and in the last, long sentence by use of the interrogative form to conceal assertion. In both these sentences, also, an appositional structure delays progression. 'So timeless . . . so fluid . . .', and 'Was it a quaint device . . . a hawk-like man . . . a prophecy . . . a symbol?'

The tendency of certain sentences to *dwell* rather than *do* is a recurrent feature of the prose throughout the novel. It registers a persistent feature of Stephen's mind—his contemplativeness. Once a perception has ignited his mind, it is deliberately held there until it fades away. This process is what Stephen, in his conversation with Lynch, calls 'the enchantment of the heart'. 'The mind in that mysterious instant Shelley likened to a fading coal.' Stylistically it is registered by a sequence of phrases in apposition—'like drops of water in a fountain falling softly in the brimming bowl'. The last sentence of the quotation, 'Was it a quaint device. . . . ?', will serve as an example of this construction. It is long, but lacks the periodic effect of climax. It merely undulates and lingers. This construction has little use for the main verb, and can even dispense with it, as in this from the later journal: 'Faintly, under the heavy night, through the silence of the city which has turned from dreams to dreamless sleep as a weary lover whom no caresses move, the sound of hoofs upon the road.'

The style in which the objective setting for Stephen's revery is described provides a complete contrast to that kind of writing.

> He looked northward towards Howth. The sea had fallen below the line of seawrack on the shallow side of the breakwater and already the tide was running out fast along the foreshore. Already one long oval bank of sand lay warm and dry amid the wavelets. Here and there warm isles of sand gleamed above the shallow tide, and about the isles and around the long bank and amid the shallow currents of the beach were lightclad gayclad figures, wading and delving.
>
> (174/170)

Instead of dwelling on an impression by indefinitely extending it, the sentences in this passage deliver their message in a business-like way, and stop as soon as they have done so. Besides being thus direct, they are lively, and their life depends upon finite forms of the verb. The vocabulary, also by way of contrast, is concrete and familiar.

Another typical example of dialogue, reinforced by a brisk narrative style, to act as a foil to a style expressive of Stephen's own sensibility, is provided by the Christmas dinner scene. Stephen's perceptions are essentially bewildered and naive. 'It was not nice about the spit in the woman's eye.' The contrast provided by vigorous adult dialogue requires no illustration, and comprises the bulk of the writing. It is interesting, however, to note the third stylistic component, the description of physical details, in sentences like

> Mr Casey struggled up from his chair and bent across the table towards her, scraping the air from before his eyes with one hand as though he were tearing aside a cobweb.
>
> (40/39)

This simile clearly did not originate in Stephen's mind. Nor could Stephen have perceived, at the end of the scene, that the face he raised to see his father's tears was 'terror-stricken'. The narrator, therefore, is not restricting himself to the character's point of view, let alone his language.

Although the novel is unusually dramatic, in that much of the story is told in characteristic dialogue and ironically restricted narrative prose, in places where the reader might expect reliable guidance Joyce does not scruple to assert his authority as author. The kind of narrative prose just quoted is one example of this process. So also is the inclusion in each chapter of at least one conclusive statement sign-posting the current direction of Stephen's development with a perspicacity which Stephen himself does not command.

For example, we are told in the second chapter:

> The causes of his embitterment were many, remote and near. He was angry with himself for being young and the prey of restless foolish impulses, angry also with the change of fortune which was reshaping the world about him into a vision of squalor and insincerity. Yet his anger lent nothing to the vision.
>
> (69/67)

What we have here is not an analysis of the boy's situation as he sees it himself, but authorial guidance to assist our reading of the three epiphanies which immediately ensue.

Yet another means of authorial control, used consistently throughout the book, is the reiteration of key words. Sometimes such repetition, contributing to the rhythm of a paragraph, is an expression of Stephen's prolongation of the contemplative moment, as in the description of the wading girl—'But her long fair hair was girlish: and girlish, and touched with the wonder of mortal beauty, her face.' It is, however, also used in passages of objective background description, as in the passage quoted earlier in this section, describing the beach: the inviting repetition of 'already' and 'warm', and the insistent repetition of 'shallow'. The same device is extended to entire chapters: thus the words 'nice' and 'nasty' continuously recur in the first chapter, marking the poles of conformity and disobedience which plot Stephen's childhood during the Clongowes period. By an even more extended use of this device, key words like 'pride' and 'weariness' recur from chapter to chapter. More subtly, chapters are linked by repeatedly connecting a particular word and a particular sort of situation. Thus, in the quoted sentence describing Mr Casey's confrontation with Dante, he 'bent' across the table, just as in the anecdote he is about to tell, he 'bent down' to spit in the eye of a woman who confronted him in the road, and Stephen 'bent towards' the flower girl who stopped him in the street, and 'bent down' also to ask an old woman in the street the way to a chapel where he could make his confession.

TRUTH AND STYLE. Such a highly conscious deployment of style may be either the result of a scrupulous aptitude, or a self-indulgent virtuosity. The tension between these alternatives enlivens the entire book. In part this tension manifests itself in the reader: there are so many places where he may have a sense that, despite its appropriateness, a word, a phrase, a sentence or even a whole passage solicits his admiration as a treasure in its own right—like the treasures in Stephen's word hoard. The other way in which this tension manifests itself is the way in which Stephen himself experiences it. The story of the novel is the story of his encounters with reality, and all these encounters are verbal.

Truth, after all, is a question of using the word that fits the case, and Stephen is sometimes indifferent to the fit, an indifference that is the complement to his self-preoccupation:

> – A day of dappled seaborne clouds.
>
> The phrase and the day and the scene harmonized in a chord. Words. Was it their colours? He allowed them to glow and fade, hue after hue: sunrise gold, the russet and green of apple orchards, azure of waves, the grey-fringed fleece of clouds. No, it was not their colours: it was the poise and balance of the period itself. Did he then love the rhythmic rise and fall of words better than their associations of legend and colour? Or was it that, being as weak of sight as he was shy of mind, he drew less pleasure from the reflection of the glowing sensible world through the prism of a language manycoloured and richly storied than from the contemplation of an inner world of individual emotions mirrored perfectly in a lucid supple periodic prose?   (170/166)

This separation of language and reality starts early, with his infantile misquotation that produces 'the green rose'. This misquotation finds its matching counterpart in the final chapter, where another misquotation indicates a falsification of feeling, because it refuses to fit. This occurs when Stephen is waiting for Cranly who is talking to other students under the colonnade of the library. Emma has just passed by, and Stephen romantically attributes the vacancy and silence of the evening to her passing. Seeking once again to match the hour and scene with a phrase from his word hoard he produces: 'Darkness falls from the air.' We have already been informed that his mind 'often turned for its pleasure to the dainty songs of the Elizabethans'. He takes the sentence that has now entered his mind to be a quotation from a song by Nashe. But the words do not yield the expected pleasure. There is something wrong with their sweetness, which is 'only . . . a disinterred sweetness like the figseeds Cranly rooted out of his gleaming teeth'. Presented with an image of lustful eyes, opening at dawn, shimmering with desire, he misses the daintiness he expected and reflects that in any case the Elizabethan period was not a dainty one. ' . . . what was their shimmer but the shimmer of the scum that mantled the cesspool of the court of a slobbering Stuart.' He protests at the unpleasing images the words have conjured up. 'That was not the way to think of her.'

Eventually, however, despite himself, he has to acknowledge the excitement of the thought of her body smell and her underclothing. The image which he cannot dismiss from his mind may be a false one, but the attendant feelings are undoubtedly his, just as the louse in his collar is his. Joyce's basic methods are clearly demonstrated in this fascinating episode. Images from actual experience—the filthy pool in the farmyard when he was a boy, the dawn awakening that produced his lustful villanelle, Cranly's eating habits, the louse in his collar—all came together to convey a message he has only to decipher. And language joins in the process, contributing its share to the final revelation, because, try as he may, he cannot constrain the words he has quoted to produce images of darkness. The images they produce—gleaming teeth, shimmering eyes, a shining shower of lice—are images of brightness. He had mis-quoted his line in the first place. What Nashe had written was: 'Brightness falls from the air.' His original misquotation was an expression of his attempt to falsify the true nature of his feelings—to render them as dainty and romantic when in fact they were crude and lustful.

THE NET OF LANGUAGE. Behind this process can be discerned a view of the relationship between reality and language. As we have already seen from his proclamation of the modernity of the dramatic method, he did not believe in the existence of an objective reality, which was common to all (see p. 48). Reality varied according to the experience of each individual who encountered it. The truth of any account of reality, therefore, could be tasted by its ring—whether it rang true for the individual in question. The irony which characterises the account of Stephen's experience in the novel derives from the fact that he seeks to force his experience into moulds which he has selected for it in advance.

Stephen himself does not arrive at this view of reality and its embodiment in words, even at the end of the book. (Something like it is enunciated by Stephen in *Ulysses*, in the discussion in the National Library.) From the very beginning however, he believes in the correspondence of language and the nature of things. He expects words, upon inspection, their use being known, to reveal truths about the world. As the Christian brothers pass him on the bridge, in chapter 4, he reflects

– Brother Hickey.
  Brother Quaid.
  Brother MacArdle.
  Brother Keogh. –
  Their piety would be like their names, like their faces, like their clothes . . .

(170/166)

(One reflects that, like his creator, Stephen learned a lot from his father. 'Christian brothers be damned!' Simon Dedalus explodes at the idea of his son being taught by such humble folk. 'Is it with Paddy Stink and Micky Mud?') Language and world are inseparable. It is the 'language' he has heard used at the Christmas row which, Dante warns, the boy will remember all his life, and the threat with which

Father Dolan intimidates his hearers in his sermon is that it may be their lot 'to hear that language' (which, incidentally, is the language in which Cranly addresses the figseeds he spits out of his mouth).

It is appropriately from the Church that Stephen learns his reverence for the word. His life at Clongowes is characterised by an unrelenting, anxious effort to acquire words and understand them— even when they are forbidden. (Even at the height of the Christmas dinner row, he pauses to wonder: 'But what was the name the woman had called Kitty O'Shea that Mr Casey would not repeat?') His first sense of serious anomaly comes not from injustice or divided authority, but from his realisation that both answers to the question whether he kisses his mother are unacceptable. His sense of order calls for an arrangement like that of the intriguing wash basin with the two taps marked 'hot' and 'cold', which produce water at temperatures to match their names—a model both of the ordered universe into which his Jesuit teachers are inserting him, and also of the aesthetic universe which Stephen is constructing for himself in the final chapter, where he continuously connects the personalities of his friends with their styles of speech.

It is the appropriateness of a style which reveals reality, just as it is the appropriateness of a word which reveals truth. This obvious point needs to be made because linguistic forms are not inevitably appropriate. They have a life of their own, as Stephen discovers on the very first page, with his 'green rose'. Later instances of the same autonomy multiply as he becomes increasingly enthralled by words. The sentences in the school spelling book take on the unintended form of verse. Given a rhythm, even that of a train, words will fall into place to produce a pattern regardless of sense, into which he can retreat from the world. Although he is critically aware of this tendency, it still operates in the final chapter. As he walks through the streets 'among heaps of dead language', words in his head 'set to band and disband themselves in wayward rhythms', producing 'whining ivy' to match the 'green rose' of his infancy.

By the word 'rhythm', as his *Paris Notebook* makes clear, Joyce meant *all* the relations between the words which compose a sentence, paragraph, or other unit of literature. Stephen's discussion with Lynch makes it plain that he means the same thing. It is therefore safe to assume that when the word 'rhythm' is used in *A Portrait* it means the pattern of language in all its aspects. Stephen's own efforts at composition show how difficult it is for a writer to construct an appropriate rhythm. Not only when he is sitting passively in a railway train, but also when he is actively trying to express his personal feelings, he finds himself gripped by wayward forces. The first time he attempts to write a poem, it disintegrates into a versification of the names of his classmates. The second time (the poem for Emma after the débâcle on the tram) the form of a conventional love lyric seizes control of his pen, obliterating all traces of the incident the poem was intended to celebrate. A similar disturbance—failure to take an initiative with Emma—motivates his next attempt to write a poem, but no sooner has he found his first words than rhymes suggest further words, and he feels 'the rhythmic movement of a villanelle pass through them'. The result is a poem which rings false.

The romantic explanation of these failures would be that Stephen is prevented by literary forms from finding the right words. Joyce's explanation is more radical. It is because Stephen is emotional that he is gripped by mechanical forces. He is working in the lyric mode, which, as he has already explained to Lynch, is that of a man 'more conscious of emotion than of himself as feeling emotion'. The resulting form is automatic, 'a rhythmical cry such as ages ago cheered on the man who pulled at the oar or dragged stones up a slope'. To achieve the form which objectified his meaning, the dramatic form, he needed to become conscious of *himself* as feeling emotion, rather than directly of the emotion itself. In other words, he had to detach himself from himself and become the object of his own impersonal vision.

By itself the villanelle is valueless, even ludicrous: ('languorous look and lavish limb' is a phrase which would have nestled very comfortably in the memory of Mr Bloom, alongside the phrase from *Sweets of Sin* which so enchanted him—'opulent curves'). Joyce in his adolescence did write it, but he excluded it from *Chamber Music*. Why was it worth inclusion in *A Portrait*? Because in the novel it is treated ironically. It becomes dramatic by juxtaposition with other contrasting pieces of writing, such as those which accompany the account of its composition. For example: 'Bah! he had done well to leave the room in disdain. He had done well not to salute her on the steps of the library!' In this context, the absurdities of the villanelle became comic—as comic as other expressions of Stephen's erotic perplexities, like the command he earlier imagined the pair of them receiving from the Virgin: 'Take hands, Stephen and Emma. It is a beautiful evening now in heaven.' This pathetic injunction, quite possibly the product of a reverential imagination when it first appeared, becomes part of an ironic and dramatic work when it joins the concourse of utterances which comprises the text of Joyce's *Portrait*.

No doubt it was natural for Joyce to disassociate himself from the language of his earlier utterances, and so put them to dramatic use. At the time he was writing the novel in which he appeared as another person, he was also expressing himself directly in letters, in his own person. The difference between these utterances, however, is not merely that those included in the novel belonged to an earlier period of his life. The meaning of a letter depends upon external factors, in particular the personal relationship of writer and reader. The meaning of a work of art does not. It was, as Joyce saw it, the distinction of a work of art to be impersonal. That was why it had to be dramatic. The words in it must not be the author's own words: like the words 'Apologize, Pull out his eyes' in Stephen's first artefact, they must be borrowed, or at least seem to have been.

In short, the novel is a forgery. It has been questioned whether Joyce intended the word 'forge' to carry that additional implication, in Stephen's finally stated ambition—'to forge in the smithy of my soul the uncreated conscience of my race'—although he certainly makes a jocular reference back to it, in that sense, in *Finnegans Wake*. In any case, as soon as the reading offers itself, it is seen to be relevant. As for the painter *trompe l'œil* is the directest form of realism, so is forgery for the writer.

More significant, however, is the comparison of the soul with a smithy. There is nothing natural in this image. Things do not grow in smithies. They are hammered into shape there, by the application of skill and industry to refractory material. There is no organic connection between the smith and the metal he works: there is no organic connection between the writer and the words he assembles, as Joyce sees it.

In the final chapter, this alienation from language becomes an explicit theme. His discussion of the word 'tundish' with the Dean of Studies is a sharp reminder to Stephen that English is not *his* language. He is not at home in it. 'My soul frets in the shadow of his language.' This realisation does not, however, lead him to join Davin in the Gaelic League. He is not looking for a language to be at home in, for to be at home in a language would mean being at home in a prison. Language is one of the three nets of which he speaks to Davin.

> When the soul of a man is born in this country there are nets flung at it to hold it back from flight. You talk to me of nationality, language, religion. I shall try to fly by those nets.
>
> ... 1203

If a man is to fly by a net, it is just as well that his soul should fret under it. And, when it came to the word 'tundish', as Stephen discovers, the Irishman to whom the language was alien proved his mastery of it to be greater than that of the Englishman upon whose lips it felt at home.

Irony

The theory of art held by Joyce when he wrote *A Portrait of the Artist as a Young Man* can be summarised in three requirements. First, a work of art must be a treatment of actual experience: the artist must therefore be satisfied with the material life has to offer him. Secondly, a work of art must be truthful: the artist must therefore enjoy independence of mind, to be able to reject the false pictures of reality which society seeks to impose. Finally, a work of art must be impersonal: the artist must therefore know himself, so that he can see through himself.

These requirements were not all clearly recognised by Joyce, when he wrote his first autobiographical study, in 1904. It was only as a result of his experience of writing in the next ten years that he came to realise the full cost of impersonality. The need to be satisfied with the material life had to offer was, however, clear to him from the beginning, and the main action of the original *Portrait* is the hero's acceptance of this necessity. At the outset the hero is a 'fantastic idealist' who, after leaving the Church, devotes himself to an other-worldly mysticism by means of which, through esoteric studies, he hopes to achieve spiritual emancipation. 'A thousand eternities were to be reaffirmed, divine knowledge was to be re-established.' In due course, however, he discovers that his associates in this enterprise are hopelessly compromised. 'Wherever the social monster permitted they would hazard the extremes of heterodoxy.' Accordingly he abandons other-worldliness, and turns his attention to the world as he finds it. 'Sceptically, cynically, mystically, he had sought for an absolute satisfaction and now little by little he began to be conscious of the beauty of mortal conditions.' It is in this context that he quotes the saying of Saint Augustine, that 'those things be good which yet are corrupted'. This realisation, interestingly, is associated with wanderings on the sea shore. It corresponds, of course, with the realisation which comes to Stephen at the end of the fourth chapter, when he sees the wading girl.

INDEPENDENCE. The later *Stephen Hero* concentrates the reader's attention on the second requirement, emphasising Stephen's moral courage, his independence of shibboleths, and his acceptance of the resulting isolation. In *A Portrait of the Artist as a Young Man*, Stephen's freedom of thought is manifest from the start. 'By thinking of things you could understand them.' When he seeks conformity in the first chapter, or forgiveness in the third, he cannot check his thought processes, even though they lead him to question authority. (Thus, on his way to confession, he cannot prevent himself from questioning why his body should have been equipped, by a beneficent creator, with a bestial member which leads it into sin.) By the time it comes, at the end of the last chapter, his declaration of *non serviam* is the outcome of a long struggle which his nature rendered inevitable. In all three works, Joyce thus endowed his fictitious counterpart with the first two requirements of an artist, as he saw them.

As regards the third requirement—self-knowledge—the case is very different. In the first two attempts, not only does Stephen lack this essential quality, but Joyce lacks it as well. It is not just that in neither the first *Portrait* nor in *Stephen Hero* does Stephen see himself as others might see him: such a deficiency in the hero could be a source of comedy or irony. That it fails to act in this way is due to the fact that the blindness of the character is shared by the author. It is not just that Stephen cannot see himself as others see him: Joyce cannot see Stephen as the reader sees him, either. In the case of both these works it is pointless to ask whether the narrative is told from the point of view of the character or of the author. The two points of view are identical.

The following passage from *Stephen Hero* is typical in this respect.

> As he walked slowly through the maze of poor streets he stared proudly in return for the glances of stupid wonder that he received and watched from under his eyes the great cow-like trunks of police constables swing slowly round after him as he passed them.
> (151)

It is notable how active Stephen's eyes are in this sentence. He stares and watches, and the reader is unequivocally invited to share his observations. What Stephen saw was what was there to be seen. The relations of reader and character is quite different in a comparable sentence from *A Portrait*.

> But, when this brief pride of silence upheld him no longer, he was glad to find himself still in the midst of common lives, passing on his way amid the squalor and noise and sloth of the city fearlessly and with a light heart. (180/176)

The dismissal of the city in the brief list of abstractions—squalor, noise, sloth—is Stephen's gesture, not the author's. There is no suggestion that anybody but Stephen saw it in that way, nor that the reader would have shared his view. And in the same way, the picture of Stephen himself is Stephen's private picture. There is no suggestion that anybody else perceived this figure, passing on its way 'fearlessly and with a light heart', and indeed we are offered evidence to the contrary, in the flower-girl, for example, not to mention 'a girl who had laughed gaily to see him stumble when the iron grating in the footpath near Cork Hill had caught the broken sole of his shoe'. Most important of all, the reader cannot accept this picture because of the style of the painting: the passage is not written in a style in which we expect truth to be told. This fearless and light-hearted character belongs to fiction. He is a figment of Stephen's imagination. We do not believe we should have seen him ourselves, if we had been there.

SELF-KNOWLEDGE   On the other hand, as the novel nears its close, Stephen does show signs of a sense of humour. In his account of his last meeting with Emma he explicitly takes an external look at himself:

Talked rapidly of myself and my plans. In the midst of it unluckily I made a sudden gesture of a revolutionary nature. I must have looked like a fellow throwing a handful of peas into the air.

(256/252)

The laconic good humour of this is characteristic of the poise Stephen is developing throughout the chapter. In scene after scene we find him smiling. He makes jokes frequently. There is even an element of appreciation in his relations with his friends and family. The final touch of self-mockery, however, is something new. His good humour in the earlier passages has always been a feature of his mockery of other people, the badge, in fact, of his indifference. It is the jollity of the Miller of Dee in the ballad, the burden of whose song forever used to be: 'I care for nobody, no not I, if no one cares for me.' He feels independent in a very literal sense of the word, namely that he is emotionally dependent upon nobody, or, at least, upon nobody but Emma. The main development in the last chapter is his achievement of a detachment with regard to her similar to that which he already enjoys with regard to his family, for example, at the beginning of the chapter.

- Good morning, everybody, said Stephen, smiling and kissing the tips of his fingers in adieu.

In the course of the chapter he kisses his finger-tips in adieu to everybody, although it is only on the penultimate page that he succeeds in doing so to Emma.

This new lightness of touch marks an advance—in terms of silence, exile and cunning—on any of his more youthful performances. The advance, however, has been taken along a path on which he first set foot in the second chapter. After suffering a beating which reduced him to tears for his refusal to admit his heresy in preferring Byron to Tennyson, he learnt that honour could be satisfied on both sides by a mock confession. There is, he comes to realise, no reason to declare his feelings. Hence the jocular *confiteor*, when Heron calls on him to admit his feelings for Emma. The result is a spurious kind of impersonality. His refusal to sail under false colours expresses itself as a refusal to sail under any colours at all. Associated with this refusal is a distrust of his own feelings. Whenever an emotion seizes him, he plunges away in an attempt to shake it off in solitude. As early as the second chapter, he has learnt how to separate himself from an emotion and slough it off—'as a fruit is divested of its soft peel'. He has a compulsion to reject his own desires. Even his fantasies about Mercedes culminate in a scene of repudiation:

an image of himself, grown older and sadder, standing in a moonlit garden with Mercedes who had so many years before slighted his love, and with a sadly proud gesture of refusal, saying:

  – Madam, I never eat muscatel grapes.

(65/63)

Small wonder that when his opportunity comes on the tram journey home from the children's party, and he sees Emma 'urge her vanities, her fine dress and sash and long black stockings', his reaction is to remain 'listlessly in his place, seemingly a tranquil watcher of the scene before him'. This compulsion to reject what offers itself stands him in good stead. He has it to thank for his escape from the priesthood, and the ease with which he avoids the solicitations of various public movements in the final chapter. These advantages, however, are purchased at high cost. He has to dismiss his own feelings into the bargain.

Dismissal, of course, does not result in his feelings going away. They remain, but he ignores them. The continually repeated proof of his failure to recognise his own motives is his repeated failure to act intentionally in a crisis. At each crucial moment, from the moment when he turns into the corridor that leads to the rector's study of Clongowes, he finds that he has made the fatal decision without knowing how he has done so. This listlessness does not amount to the impersonality of the dramatic artist, the man who, to quote Stephen himself is more 'conscious of himself as feeling the emotion' than he is of 'the instant of emotion'. They are the qualities of a man who is certainly self-conscious, but not of himself as feeling any emotion at all. Small wonder that 'all the descriptions of fiery love and hatred which he had met in books had seemed to him therefore unreal'. Small wonder, too, that he should regard everybody in sight as a threat to his invulnerability, from whom he must therfore ensure his complete detachment.

The ease with which, in the last chapter, Stephen shrugs off the claims of family and friends is therefore a sign of the efficacy of a defence mechanism. His helplessness in the grip of the conflicting emotion Emma, all unwittingly, provokes in him is a sign of that mechanism's defects. When the mechanism succeeds, it yields him a clear, if unsympathetic insight into the minds of others, as when Mrs Dedalus washes her son's ears before he leaves for college.

  – Well, it's a poor case, she said, when a university student is so dirty that his mother has to wash him.
  – But it gives you pleasure, said Stephen calmly.

(178/174)

When the mechanism fails, he is simply blind. The figure of Emma which torments him is a projection of his own emotion, at one minute impossibly lecherous, at the next minute impossibly chaste. At last the mechanism works and he frees himself by total rejection. 'Well then, let her go and be damned to her! She could love some

85

clean athlete', etc. Once free Stephen's way is to test his understanding and detachment by some act of coldness. 'Of whom are you speaking?' he enquires, when Cranly asks whether he is ready to forfeit the companionship of someone who would be more to him than the noblest and truest friend a man ever had. 'About whom?' he similarly enquires, when Emma, during their last meeting, asks whether he has been writing poems.

On this occasion, however, his thrust makes him feel 'sorry and mean', and he is aware of a novel feeling, sympathy. He finds that he 'likes' her. This feeling of friendliness is akin to the 'friendly pity' that illuminated Gabriel's vision of the commonality of the living and the dead, at the end of 'The Dead', or the spirit which governs the sympathetic irony with which Stephen himself is handled by Joyce, in this novel. At last, as we have noted, Stephen seems almost to meet the third requirement of the artist—self-understanding. Realising that he 'likes' her, he begins to see his previous fantasies for what they were. 'Then, in that case, all the rest, all that I thought I thought and all that I felt I felt, all the rest before now, in fact. . . . O, give it up, old chap! Sleep it off!'

None of this, however, amounts to an acknowledgment of the inevitability of his human dependence, the need one person has of another. As his mother tells him, he still has to learn 'in his own life and away from home and friends what the heart is and what it feels'. Or as Cranly reminds him, he has not yet met Rosie O'Grady. Even at the end of the book, as Joyce pointed out to Frank Budgen, the artist is still a young man. He has a long way to go, before he can see himself as clearly as the artist who created him could see him. That clarity of vision was the clarity with which Joyce could see himself, the clarity he attributed to Ibsen's dramatic imagination. 'Calm' and 'ironical' were the terms he used to describe Ibsen's mind, and they can be attributed as well to his own. To describe his mind thus is not, however, to claim that Joyce was a superior being. The artist is not cured of his weaknesses just because he can see himself, however ironically and calmly, as a dramatic character. The effort involved was contemplative, not ethical, directed not to the future but to the past, recognising the characteristic feeling *after* it had been felt, and the typical deed *after* it had been done. The victory lay in the abandoning of self-justification. 'I haven't let this young man off very lightly, have I?' Joyce observed to Frank Budgen. He was speaking of his treatment of Stephen in *Ulysses*, but the remark is no less true of *A Portrait of the Artist as a Young Man*.

Joyce as a student (right), with George Clancy ('Davin') and John Byrne ('Cranly')

In *A Portrait* Joyce had constructed a character to dramatise one limited aspect of his personality as a young man. The youthful Stephen was to be employed again in *Ulysses*. Between these two major works, however, came two other pieces in which he presented versions of himself at a more mature stage of development. Joyce never attempted to have the first and slighter of these two pieces published, and its title *Giacomo Joyce* was not supplied until it appeared in 1968. It is written in the first person, and the narrator—who is named Jim and has a wife named Nora—can hardly be distinguished from the author, Joyce himself. It is composed of fifty brief epiphanies all related to the writer's infatuation with a rich young Jewess, to whom he teaches English in Trieste. (A girl who was one of Joyce's actual students at Trieste can be identified with this character.)

Probably written at a time when work on *A Portrait* was nearing completion, this piece is interesting for its development of the method used, at the end of the novel, in the journal entries, but the tone, especially the tension, of the writing is very different. Gone is the laconic ease, alternating with lyrical exultation, which marks the manner of Stephen as he prepares for flight. These passages— with their brooding prolongation of the furtive disturbance produced by chance encounters—serve more as explorations of those aspects of his sensibility which Joyce was later to dramatise more fully in the character of Bloom. By the same token, however, they serve as a link between Bloom and Stephen. The latter's obsession with Emma, while it lasts in the final chapter of *A Portrait*, is a similar case of 'sex in the head'. In the later instance, however, the character does not eventually emerge into sanity as Stephen did. The last section of *Giacomo Joyce* is a brief, sardonic envoi. 'Love me, love my umbrella.'

The implication of fetishism in this sally is not accidental. Joyce makes no attempt to conceal or embellish the distortions that result from a passion too timid to seek active expression. But, like Freud with whose work he had already become acquainted, he found in such material the key to general principles. Considered as a process whereby objects in themselves insignificant become invested with a compelling power, fetishism provides a clue to symbolism. The nature of this kind of power is indeed the centre of interest of the narrative, such as it is. There is no action to speak of, but the tension which activates the brief scenes and reflections arises from the question—how far is the girl aware of her power over the teacher? Are her apparent cruelty, disdain, indifference and occasional encouragement mere figments of his imagination? Does she really know nothing of his feelings, or is she, as he would prefer to believe, deliberately entangling him in her toils? This problem of the connection of the inner with the outer world is a recurrent theme with Joyce. It is clearly formulated for Stephen in *A Portrait*—'he wanted to meet in the real world the unsubstantial image which his soul so constantly beheld'—and, in *Ulysses*, for Shakespeare: 'He found in the world without as actual what was in his world within as possible.' It is this same gap which, as a student, Joyce had praised Ibsen for bridging.

The connection of *Exiles* with Joyce's own life history is less direct. It is more a dramatisation of his preoccupations. No doubt he was fascinated by thoughts of being betrayed, and entertained such thoughts with tell-tale readiness. In practice, however, when it came to the question of his wife's fidelity, his attitude was very direct. When a friend in Trieste began to show too lively an interest in her company, Joyce did not hesitate to have it out with him and reduce him to tears. In the similar situation dealt with in Joyce's only play, the conduct of his counterpart figure, Richard Rowan, is very different.

An older character than Stephen, he is a might-have-been version of his creator, Joyce as he might have been if he had returned to Dublin after his first literary success. He is also endowed with characteristics which Joyce would perhaps have liked to possess but lacked —characteristics which would certainly have made him less sympathetic. This self-improvement even extends to the detail that although, like Joyce, Richard Rowan was a heavy drinker in his youth, he pointedly abstains from alcohol now he has put his past behind him. In this as in other points Joyce failed to live up to him. It is clear enough that Richard Rowan is an even more difficult person to live with than Joyce was.

The centre of interest in the play is the nature of freedom. Just as Joyce and Nora lived together without marrying and had a son, so do Richard and Bertha in the drama. Bertha, an attractive and lively woman who is Richard's intellectual inferior and cannot understand him, considers them to be as good as married. In other words, they are tied to each other, in her view. Perhaps it was Joyce's reluctance to accept that this was certainly true in his own case which led him, in his only play, to ignore the principle of drama which he had previously enunciated—that the fable must be presented in terms of the characters. In this case the fable is presented in terms of its moral, that free men and women do not protect themselves from their freedom by hiding behind obligations and rights. The audience is always aware of a force behind the action which will manifest itself as soon as Richard shows his hand, and, in this respect, Bertha and Richard's friend Robert feel much as the audience does. Everything hinges on one man who clearly, as the author's appointed representative, knows what it is all about. Even the clandestine meeting of Robert and Bertha can only take place when they know that he knows it is happening, and intends it to benefit them as a lesson in free choice.

Although Joyce's notes makes it clear that he does not intend Richard to appear as a superior being, a superior being is none the less what everybody on stage (including himself) sees him to be, and the audience is not discouraged from sharing in that vision. As Richard's attitude becomes clearer, the audience finds it harder to do this, but the play offers no basis for a corresponding irony. The action is presented not in terms of all the characters but of one alone.

This advantage which Richard enjoys over everybody else resembles that of Prospero over the rest of the *dramatis personae* of *The Tempest*, and indeed one way of reading—if not watching—*Exiles* is to treat it as an allegory of the dramatist's art. As such it is interesting and informative about Joyce. Beatrice Justice, the woman who was so close to Richard in his youth, would feature in such a reading as his early muse—the inspiration of Joyce's first stories, with their heroic aim of liberating people by dethroning the tyrannical secret that enslaved them. (In this connection it is relevant that her cousin Robert is a journalist.) Bertha, Richard's maturer choice, represents the inspiration of Joyce's middle period—his devotion to unrefined 'mortal conditions'. It is of the essence of this devotion—as of Richard's relationship with Bertha—that it offers no scope for authority. Both Bertha and Robert expect Richard to claim rights and exercise them: they even wish it. His refusal to do so corresponds with Joyce's refusal to exercise the privilege of authorship to modify, restrict or correct reality. His work is guided by a faith he cannot justify, that when the critical test is made reality will be found to belong to the artist, not to the journalist.

An allegory succeeds, however, only if its argument (however interesting) works also on the level of plot. It must make sense literally as well as figuratively, and this cannot be claimed for *Exiles*. There is something sinisterly prejudiced about the situation which Joyce simply failed to see. Nevertheless, the play features new developments, interesting for the consideration of his later works, both *Ulysses* and *Finnegans Wake*. (There are close parallels between elements of the closing dialogue and the last page of *Finnegans Wake*.) The most noticeable of these developments is the pairing of male characters. This has already been noted, in its embryonic form, in *Dubliners*—the coupling of Gallaher and Little Chandler, for example, or Michael Furey with Gabriel Conroy. The structure of *A Portrait* could not accommodate such a division: its ambivalence is expressed in the alternatives of Stephen's attitudes. In *Exiles*, however, the systematic opposition of Richard and Robert prefigures that of Stephen and Buck Mulligan, Bloom and Blazes Boylan—as also of Stephen and Bloom themselves—in *Ulysses*, not to mention the proliferating mythological and historical antagonisms that stem from the rivalry of Shem and Shaun in *Finnegans Wake*. Within each character additional antitheses are in operation. Bertha, Robert and Richard himself are all three torn by conflicting impulses. One aspect of this ambivalence, the subject of keen comment by Joyce in his notes, is Richard's masochism, a feature to be further developed in *Ulysses*.

Most basic of all the polarities exhibited in the play is that of sex. In the character of Bertha Joyce presents, for the first time, his sense of the deep division between the understandings and expectations of men and women—the incompatibility of giving and taking, and the paradoxical way in which each sex has a way of taking and giving that complements the other's. Fundamentally, although more durable, the woman is also seen as more dependent because she cannot exist in isolation while the man can. 'Richard', Joyce observes in his notes, 'must not appear as a champion of woman's rights', and goes on to explain that it is his own rights Richard is fighting for, when he forces freedom on his wife. Unlike a man, a woman cannot face the void of freedom: she needs a man to do it for her. For her part, on the other hand, woman makes a profound affirmation of life. Bertha, the notes remark 'is the earth, dark, formless, mother, made beautiful by the moonlight, darkly conscious of her instincts'. As such she is the harbinger of Molly Bloom and Anna Livia Plurabelle.

N don the gloves

— Talking about violent exercise, says Alf, were you at that Keogh-Bennett match?

— No, says Joe.

— I heard So and So made a cool hundred quid over it, says Alf.

— Who? Blazes? says Joe.

And says Bloom:

— What I meant about tennis, for example, is the agility and training of the eye.

— Ay, Blazes, says Alf. He let out that Myler was on the beer to run up the odds and he swatting all the time.

— We know him, says the citizen. The traitor's son. We know what put English gold in his pocket.

— True for you, says Joe.

And Bloom cuts in again about lawn tennis and the circulation of the blood, asking Alf ·

— Now don't you think, Bergan?

— Myler dusted the floor with him, says Alf. Heenan and Sayers was only a bloody fool to it. See the little kipper not up to his navel and the big fellow swiping. God, he gave him one last puck in the wind. Queensberry rules and all, made him puke what he never ate.

It was a historic and a hefty battle when Myler and Percy were scheduled to box for the purse of fifty sovereigns. Handicapped as he was by lack of poundage Dublin's pet lamb made up for it by superlative skill in ringcraft. The final bout of fireworks was a gruelling for both champions. The welterweight sergeantmajor had tapped some lively claret in the previous mixup during which Keogh had been receivergeneral of rights and lefts, the artilleryman putting in some neat work on the pet's nose, and Myler came on looking groggy. The soldier got to business leading off with a powerful left jab to which Myler retaliated by shooting out a stiff one flush to the point of Bennett's jaw. The redcoat ducked but the Dubliner lifted him with a left hook, the punch being a fine one. The men came to handigrips. Myler quickly became busy and got his man under, the bout ending with the bulkier man on the ropes, Myler punishing him. The Englishman, whose right eye was nearly closed, took his corner where he was liberally drenched with water and when the bell went came on gamey and brimful of pluck, confident of knocking out the fistic Eblanite in jigtime. It was a fight to a finish and the best man for it. The two fought like tigers and excitement ran fever high. The referee twice

∧ Handed

S. gave him the father and mother of a beating.

⊢ the Irish gladiator

4 Ulysses

A portrait of the artist as Shakespeare

Reading *Ulysses* is like finding your way through a forest. There are several paths that will see you through, but they cannot all be taken at the same time, and in the end they bring you out at different places. You can, if you like, set off without a guide but if you do so you are likely to waste a lot of time, when so many foresters have been there before you. On the other hand it must be acknowledged that even the most skilled foresters are not in agreement about the best route. All that is certain about the forest is that it would not exist without the trees. The life of *Ulysses* is all in its details.

Joyce himself offers less real help than in the case of the far less complex *Portrait*. Conceived originally as a short story for *Dubliners*, and started as a kind of sequel to *A Portrait*, *Ulysses* soon developed into something gigantically different from both, and with two masterpieces to his credit, Joyce no longer had time for the literary theorising which might have explained the corresponding development of his intentions. Instead of a statement of his general approach, all he vouchsafed were casual observations about specific aspects of the book. These revelations are partial, provocative, and often self-contradictory. In this, it might be said, they resemble the revelations vouchsafed by the divine creator to whom, once again, Stephen Dedalus in this novel likens the artist.

One obvious approach to *Ulysses* is to read it as a rendering of autobiographical material. Stephen Dedalus is a major character in it. The entire action takes place in Dublin on a single day—16 June 1904. It was on this day, in history, that Joyce first went out walking with Nora Barnacle, whom he had met casually in the street some days previously. According to his subsequent acknowledgment, it was therefore the day on which he took his first steps towards manhood. This incident, however, has no direct counterpart in the novel. There is no character in the novel who stands to Stephen in the relationship that Nora stood, in history, to Joyce. Stephen, however, is not Joyce's only representative in the novel: there is also Bloom, a personality very different from Stephen but none the less very like Joyce, especially Joyce after ten years of family life. And there is a character who stands to him in a relationship Nora maintained with Joyce later—his wife Molly Bloom. What happens in the novel is not that Stephen meets a girl but that he meets a man, a man who embodies those aspects of himself which Joyce had excluded in creating that earlier portrait of himself as a young man. Looked at from the biographical point of view, the story of *Ulysses*—the story of how Stephen and Bloom meet on that day—is allegorical. It is an allegory for a process that began on that day, although of course it was not completed on it—a process of maturation.

Naturally, as they are two aspects—albeit conflicting—of their creator's personality, Stephen and Bloom have much in common. Each dressed in black, each without the key of his dwelling, they are not at home in the city in which they spend their day. At the best their presence is tolerated by their associates and at times it is even rejected. Both are repelled by violence. Their minds are alike in being speculative and alive to the implications of words. They are both sensitive to music. Moreover, in the course of the day, before they actually meet their paths have crossed more than once, and several times, in response to similar stimuli, they have shared the same thoughts. What unites them is their common consciousness of alienation—not merely their uneasy social positions but their homelessness in that deeper sense that makes them both pilgrims. Thus, in the penultimate chapter, we are informed:

> He [Stephen] affirmed his significance as a conscious rational animal proceeding syllogistically from the known to the unknown and a conscious rational reagent between a micro- and a macrocosm ineluctably constructed upon the incertitude of the void.
> Was this affirmation apprehended by Bloom?
> Not verbally. Substantially.
> What comforted his misapprehension?
> That as a competent keyless citizen he had proceeded energetically from the unknown to the known through the incertitude of the void.

> (817/618)

Nevertheless, as this comparison also shows, the two characters are also markedly different. Stephen represents very much the same aspects of Joyce's personality as he did in *A Portrait* in the final chapter. In the interval since his exultant departure into exile his pride has taken a knock. He has returned with no success to show, hardened and embittered by his humiliating poverty, prouder, more lonely and more suspicious than ever, and even more preposterous. The sense of humour that flickered on the last pages of *A Portrait* has largely given way to self-pity and self-mockery. When, in the opening chapter, Mulligan calls him 'an impossible person', the reader is inclined to agree. But the reader is also inclined to agree when Stephen regards Mulligan as his intellectual and moral inferior. His mind is more perceptive, clearer and swifter than in *A Portrait*, and he struggles egotistically yet none the less courageously to retain his integrity. The occasion of his return from Paris was his mother's fatal illness, but he refused to grant her dying wish that he should pray at her bedside. In consequence, despite his personal declaration of independence he is suffering under the conscience which parents and teachers planted in him before he was strong enough to resist. He has not yet won the battle behind his forehead to free, as he himself phrases it, the mind from the mind. In short, Stephen represents those qualities in Joyce which, while they emboldened him to see the truth for himself, threatened to cut him off from mankind.

Bloom, on the other hand, incorporates all those tendencies of Joyce which made him a dependent husband and an anxious father. He has never reconciled himself to the death in infancy of his only son Rudy—a trauma which has put an end to normal sexual relations with his willing wife Molly. Molly, nevertheless, occupies a large part of his attention, speculation and memories. Her sexuality fascinates him, and his attitude to her infidelity, although he is distressed by it, is ambiguous. There are masochistic elements in the fantasies to which his own furtive sexual gratification is now chiefly confined. Although not confessional, in these features Joyce was exploring his own nature with extraordinary honesty—in some instances recapitulating details of incidents, as in the repetition of features of his flirtation with Marthe Fleischmann in Bloom's clandestine correspondence with Martha Clifford. Bloom also shares Joyce's preoccupation with facts. He is endlessly curious, not only about Molly but about everybody he meets and everything he sees. Even in the way in which he has one eye cocked, in an amateur way, for business opportunities he resembles Joyce, one of whose returns to Dublin was connected with an attempt to start a cinema there, and who was entrusted, when he went to Eastern Europe, with a vague agency for Irish tweeds. In his job as an advertisement canvasser, Bloom is even involved in an indirect kind of authorship— to which Joyce himself did not scruple to stoop from time to time.

The great quality possessed by Bloom which Stephen lacks and needs is his resilient realism. He has learnt to accept the way of the world without being crushed by it. Although he has learnt the limits of the possible, he still hopes and cares. When *Ulysses* first appeared, even those readers who praised the book failed to see this heroic quality in Bloom, whom they could only regard as a satirical figure exemplifying the collapse of European culture. Joyce on the other hand intended, as he told Budgen, that as the novel progressed Bloom should come to overshadow all the other characters morally, to be revealed at last, despite his weakness, as the type of the good man.

In this, however, he was extending the fictitious character beyond the limits of autobiography—even figurative autobiography. Considered as a counterpart to Stephen, what aspects of Joyce's mind does he present? This question is put, almost in so many words, in the catechistic 'Ithaca' chapter, and the answer supplied is that he stands for Science, while Stephen stands for Art. This answer has the explicit, and hence unsatisfying, baldness of all the categorical statements offered in the chapter. The antithesis art/science is too vague and too stereotyped to define the difference. Nevertheless it does indicate a fundamental difference between two alternatives that Joyce was concerned to reconcile—an interest in significance and an interest in brute fact. Treading in the footsteps of the mystic Boehme, Stephen reads all things as signatures: Bloom looks at everything in the light of common sense and popular science. This disjunction had engaged Joyce since he was a student. In his article on Ibsen's early play *Catalina*, he had contrasted two worthless kinds of modern writer—on the one hand the latter-day Dante 'who chooses to wander amid his own shapeless hells and heavens', on the other hand the fact-monger 'for whom Balzac is a great intellect'. Each lacks what the other is confined to. The meeting of Stephen and Bloom in the novel represents Joyce's fusion of symbolism and realism in the novel, and his acknowledgement, biographically, of two conflicting aspects of his own personality. *Ulysses* thus constitutes a landmark of Joyce's understanding of himself, an understanding so complete that—comparing his art to a machine for processing experience—everthing that he encountered became grist for his mill.

In the course of the novel this claim—'everything was grist to his mill'—is made for Shakespeare, and it is therefore not surprising that when the reflection of Stephen's face is mysteriously fused with Bloom's face in a mirror the resulting features are those of Shakespeare too. Shakespeare has replaced Ibsen as the type of the artist—in his art no less 'ironical and calm', but in his personal life as vulnerable as Bloom, and, like Bloom, a cuckold. This theory is propounded by Stephen in the 'Scylla and Charybdis' chapter, so named because of the opposing extremes between which the modern writer, and like him the modern man, must steer—the opposing extremes between which Joyce claims to have steered his novel.

But taken as directions for reading *Ulysses*, Stephen's theory about Shakespeare tells us more than that about the novel which contains it. It advises us to read the novel as a dramatisation of the author's unresolved tensions. Stephen insists that Shakespeare's personal problems are reflected in his plays, even down to the detail of the characters' names. The plays, in his view, constitute a mastery of those problems achieved by an objective vision of them. Although these same problems remained insoluble in the world Shakespeare inhabited, they were solved in the world he created. His dramatic world was a complete re-creation of the world in which he suffered, harmonised by art. By implications Joyce makes a similar claim for himself and his novel.

It is in this context that Stephen's preoccupation with the relationship of the members of the Trinity is to be understood. The Father-

Son relationship in particular is a model of the relationship of the author with his fictitious representative—of Joyce, for example, with Stephen. By entering their own creations in the persons of their sons, God the Father, Shakespeare the dramatist, and Joyce himself, father themselves forth—become their own fathers, as Stephen phrases it. To achieve this recreation of oneself calls for complete self-knowledge. More than that, it calls for complete knowledge of the world one inhabits, for the two things are the same. As Stephen observes:

> Maeterlinck says: *If Socrates leave his house today he will find the sage seated on his doorstep. If Judas go forth tonight it is to Judas his steps will tend.* Every life is many days, day after day. We walk through ourselves, meeting robbers, ghosts, giants, old men, young men, wives, widows, brothers-in-love. But always meeting ourselves. The playwright who wrote the folio of this world and wrote it badly (He gave us light first and the sun two days later), the lord of things as they are whom the most Roman of catholics call *dio boia*, hangman god, is doubtless all in all in all of us ...
>
> (273/213)

This, then, is one way to read *Ulysses*, as the presentation of a world we walk, meeting and finding all manner of people and things, but always, in doing so, meeting and finding Joyce because it is his recreation of the world he himself walked through on a particular day—recreated completely, inclusive of all those aspects which he had not been able to acknowledge on the day in question because he did not know himself yet. It is impossible to read Stephen's observation on the relationship of the Son with his consubstantial father without recognising, behind the figure of God the Father, and the shade of Shakespeare, the presence of Joyce himself. 'So in the future, the sister of the past,' Stephen prophesies in the Library, 'I may see myself as I sit here now but by reflection from that which then I shall be.'

Not that as Shakespeare's analogue Joyce is claiming wisdom for himself, as he reflects upon his past. The writer can see clearly, but his vision does not make him wise. In the case of Shakespeare, Stephen makes clear, drama was not a cure for his sores but only a way of licking them. He remains 'untaught by the wisdom he has written or by the laws he has revealed'.

What is interesting is that Joyce should have seen himself not as Ibsen or as Dante but as Shakespeare. Perhaps he professed enthusiasm for Ibsen and Dante more readily because he was less jealous of them. Shakespeare, he told Budgen, was the writer whose works he would choose to take to a desert island if his choice was

Painting of 7 Eccles Street, by Flora Mitchell

confined to one author. The reason he gave for this preference was Shakespeare's richness. Richness—a complex density—was the quality he sought increasingly in each successive work of his own. So was the myriad-mindedness Coleridge praised, praise which Joyce took care to work into the discussion in the Library. This Protean quality is essential to the impersonality for which, in *A Portrait*, Stephen commends the dramatist. He 'refines himself out of existence' not so much to disappear as to become many. To introduce another quotation which features in the Library discussion, while 'others abide our question' Shakespeare is free. Even historically, he cannot be pinned down, and various identities are offered as the talk proceeds—he may have been a Catholic, a Jew, Lord Bacon, the Duke of Rutland, an ambitious provincial. As Lyster remarks in this discussion, everyone can find his own Shakespeare. It is tempting to believe that Joyce may have had that sense of seeing Shakespeare in a mirror when he read the portrait given by Frank Harris in his *The Man Shakespeare*, a book which contributed generously to Stephen's disquisition.

> He had to be true to his higher nature or to the conventional view of his duty; he was true to himself and fled to London and the world is the richer for his decision. . . . The Shakespeares of this world are not apt to take up menial employs, and this one had already shown that he preferred idle musings and parasitic dependence to uncongenial labour. . . . There is a certain weakness, however, shown in the whole story of his marriage; a weakness of character, as well as a weakness of *morale*, which it is impossible to ignore; and there were other weaknesses in Shakespeare, especially a weakness of body. . . . He found no wonderful phrase for any of the manly virtues; he was a neuropath and a lover, and not a fighter, even in youth. . . . All the evidence we have is in favour of Shakespeare's extravagance, and against his thrift. . . . With all his sensuality he only knew one woman . . . and only one man, himself, profoundly apprehended in every accident and moment of growth.

The Homeric outline

Even the uninstructed reader must be aware that Stephen Dedalus is, to some extent, a representative of Joyce. It is, however, very possible to read *Ulysses* with no sense of any further reference—to be ignorant, for example, of any connection between Joyce and Bloom, and to regard Stephen's discourse on Shakespeare and Hamlet as merely an interesting feature of his day. By and large it is possible to read the book in its entirety as a story about two characters and the way in which the disconnected events of a random day finally brought them together. Despite the inclusion of eccentric and boring passages which seem perverse when it is read as simple narrative, the novel does work at that level. And indeed it has to work at that level if it is to work at any other. If it does not claim the reader's attention for the sake of the behaviour of the two main characters, it cannot claim his attention as analogy, or symbol, or sample, or in any other way. The novel fails unless we believe in Stephen and Bloom, and are so concerned by them that we are prepared to work through the penultimate chapter avidly, despite its dry-as-dust presentation, because, although by now we know them both inside out, we cannot imagine what is going to happen—and then, having seen the meeting and having recognised why it had to be like that, to read it again.

For many, although by no means all, of his readers Joyce does succeed in creating just such an interest. And yet the comparison with finding one's way through a forest is still valid. There is so much that gets in the way of the straight narrative. Even the details which give the setting its solidity accumulate into thickets that block the way. In such a situation it is natural to look for a route map, and the title offers one. The path runs parallel with the action of the Odyssey, if not in detail at least in its main essentials.

In this respect the Homeric parallels in the novel serve a more important purpose than the other allusions with which it abounds. For example when he proclaims the doctrine of love in Barney Kiernan's, Bloom is compared with the prophet Elijah. There is, however, no sustained parallel between his actions and those of the prophet elsewhere in the book. (Bloom feeds the gulls: they do not feed him.) Other comparisons with such miscellaneous figures as Don Giovanni, Jesus, Moses, Pyrrhus, and many others, are similarly momentary. They are only incidental allusions.

More sustained, because although not continuous it is repeated, is the analogy with *Hamlet*. Thoughts of Hamlet recur to Stephen throughout the day. Like Hamlet he is dressed in black and beset by false friends. His situation does not, however, offer a structural correspondence. The ghost that haunts him is that of his mother, and if the ghost points an accusing finger it is levelled at Stephen himself. The ghost is not to be trusted in this version of the story. Hamlet's task is not to avenge her (upon himself), but to forget her. It is, indeed, a re-enactment of that struggle behind the forehead for waging which so fearlessly the young Joyce had commended Ibsen. The comparison, in short, breaks down in detail. It works only as a general metaphor for Stephen's inner state. The revenge theme has been removed. Hamlet's task in respect of his father is simply to be re-united with him, not to punish his murderer. This is the theological interpretation of the play, outlined by Haines in the first chapter; 'The Father and the Son idea. The Son striving to be atoned with the Father.' To be able to atone, Stephen must first discover who his father is, which leads us back to the theological analogies discussed in the previous section. The true author of Stephen's being is clearly not Simon Dedalus. No more is he the hangman god—feeding on remorse—who made such a botched job of creation. He is Shakespeare/Joyce, which means that to be atoned with him Stephen must be united with Bloom. The analogy with Hamlet therefore does not offer a map of the novel, but is subordinated to it, being offered only as and where it fits.

Comparison with Homer's *Odyssey*, however, does offer a map. Each chapter has a matching episode in Homer's epic, and was originally named accordingly in the serialised version. (For this reason, the Homeric titles are usually retained for ease of reference: they will be found displayed in Table 2.) Moreover, the suppression of the revenge theme in favour of the paternity theme effects less distortion in the *Odyssey* than in the case of *Hamlet*. Ulysses's safe homecoming was effected with the help of his son, and homecoming was his main object: revenge was a contingency. So when Bloom at last returns home (ousting his wife's suitor—in his absence, admittedly, but still doing so in his own way), he too has the assistance of a son—Stephen. The action of *Ulysses* as it regards Bloom—and this is the central action of the novel—can thus sustain an overall comparison with that of the *Odyssey*. There is one major difference. Viewed literally, Bloom's return to his house in Eccles Street is a less hazardous enterprise than the voyage of Ulysses. This is not to make the superficial point that he is in less physical danger, but the more fundamental one that his return is, barring unlikely accident, a foregone conclusion. What is less certain, however, is that he will return in the form of an adequate husband, father and householder. It is that moral achievement which, in the novel, corresponds with Ulysses's final success in the epic. The homecoming of the hero is an allegory of Bloom's moral survival of moral perils. In this allegorical reading of the *Odyssey* Joyce was following Charles Lamb, whose version of the story had given him his first experience of it. It was, Joyce told a friend, the 'mysticism' of the legend which first attracted him to it. The character and conflicts in it, as Lamb had explained to his readers, could be regarded as 'external forces or internal temptations which influence human life'. Thus the episode in the *Odyssey* with which any given chapter of *Ulysses* is associated can be interpreted as an allegory of the moral action in that chapter.

The difficulty of matching episodes literally is illustrated clearly enough by the first chapter. In Homer we find Telemachus, surrounded by enemies even under his paternal roof, where his mother's suitors are living off the fat of the land, and threatening him. Disguised as Mentor, Athena advises him to settle things by getting some definite news about his missing father. He sets out to do so. It needs only to point out that Stephen knows very well where to find his father, while his mother is dead, to show that there is no literal parallel. Even if we substitute the absent Bloom for Simon Dedalus the parallel remains inoperative at the literal level. Allegorically, however, the parallel is clear enough. The threat which faces Telemachus is the loss of his inheritance. Stephen similarly sees the danger that he will not realise his potential as long as he allows himself to be patronised by a treacherous entertainer (Mulligan) and a condescending alien (Haines). Leaving the tower to these two he obviously does not know that he is setting out to find Bloom, but his theories of paternity, as explained in the previous section, make it clear enough that search for his birthright as an artist means search for his true father—in other words, the mature understanding necessary to create himself.

This application of the Homeric original fits the case but may seem arbitrary. Certainly it is not obvious. That it was the application Joyce made is, however, more than probable. When *Ulysses* was being serialised Joyce provided a friend, Carlo Linati, with a plan of the entire novel, showing how each chapter conformed in detail with a scheme of correspondences and also indicating in a word or phrase the general meaning of each chapter. Table 2 (page 109) sets out that part of this information which is of help in determining the general tenor of the narrative. The meaning of the first chapter—dispossessed son in struggle—picks out precisely that aspect of Tele-machus's situation which, metaphorically, equates the threatened prince with the ineffectual artist. The symbols—Hamlet, Ireland, Stephen—suggest an identification of the danger. All three are oppressed, and need to know their friends from their enemies.

That Homer's *Odyssey* affords this allegorical illumination of the novel is best demonstrated by proceeding chapter by chapter, pausing only to observe that the sequence of episodes in the novel does not correspond exactly with the order of the Homeric original. The beginnings and the conclusions do match, but as for the rest, Homer offers archetypal situations, rather than an archetypal process.

The next two books of the *Odyssey* tell how Telemachus visited two of his father's old comrades, from whom he gained encouraging news. Stephen is not in search of information, but he is in need of qualities of mind. Some of these qualities are represented in the next two chapters of *Ulysses*. Matching Telemachus's visit to wise old Nestor, Joyce gives us Stephen's conversation with an opinionated and sententious old schoolmaster. The irony of the correspondence is obvious enough. 'Wisdom of antiquity' is Joyce's tag for this chapter: clearly, Mr Deasy is not a worthy representative. And yet he does make some observations to Stephen which are apt enough. 'Common sense' is one of the 'symbols' Joyce listed. This certainty is a sufficiently ancient form of wisdom, and if Mr Deasy is not in fact Bloom's old comrade, at least they do possess this quality in common, while Stephen certainly needs it.

The other old comrade of his father visited by Telemachus is Menelaus. He has no counterpart physically present with Stephen on the sea-shore in the third chapter, although he can be regarded as Bloom's comrade in cuckoldry. What Joyce seizes upon for re-enactment in this chapter is the account Homer's Menelaus gives to Telemachus of how he gained news about the whereabouts of Ulysses from Proteus. The latter had mythical characteristics of the deepest significance for a reader of *Ulysses*. He was a sea-god, and had the gift of prophecy. Unfortunately, however, it was not easy to consult him, because as soon as he was addressed he changed shape, not once but over and over again. Only the man who was brave and strong enough to hold him fast while he went through a series of frightening or elusive transformations would eventually be rewarded with a truthful answer to a question. Menelaus had performed this feat. In *Ulysses* the struggle with Proteus is undertaken by Telemachus, not by Menelaus. In other words, it is Stephen who, in his meditation by the endlessly changing sea, attempts to grasp the reality which lies behind shifting appearances. He is victorious, at least in the sense that he is not defeated. Despite his awareness of mutability and 'ineluctable modality', he retains his sense of being confronted by an object. Bloom's sense of unavoidable reality is, of course, his dominant trait and the source of his sanity. (There is no need to refer here to the supporting entries in Table 2 which the reader is invited to refer to in the case of this, as of the remaining chapters as they are discussed.)

With the fourth chapter we come to the central, main body of the narrative, whose hero is Bloom, and which corresponds with Homer's account of the perils of Ulysses. In Homer we find the hero on the island of Ogygia, where he has delayed his return home for seven idle years in the pleasing company of the nymph Calypso. The correspondence between this situation and Bloom's position, when we first encounter him, is highly figurative. Physically there is no correspondence at all, because we find Bloom already at home, preparing his wife's breakfast. Morally, however, he is a long distance away from the moment (to which his thoughts return in the course of the day) when Molly lay on the hill in his arms and said: 'yes I will Yes'. Both as husband and as father he is far from home. Just as in Homer the hero has been long absent from Ithaca, so Bloom has not had normal sexual intercourse with his now unfaithful wife since the death of their infant son, Rudy, eleven years before the opening of the novel. As for Calypso, the nymph who detains him, she is represented by the picture over the bed, symbolising the substitution of fantasy gratification for flesh and blood. The return home which Bloom has to achieve is a return to full domestic responsibility. One of the symbols to which Joyce relates this chapter is 'Israel in bondage', a motif which recurs intermittently in the novel and relates Bloom's plight to that of his people (just as Stephen's is comparable with that of Ireland). As the advertisement Bloom reads in this chapter proclaims, the waste land in the desert must be reclaimed as the Promised Land. The desert must bloom again.

Bloom's return home in this metaphorical sense is a journey beset with moral perils, just as physical perils beset the homeward voyage of Ulysses. In the subsequent chapters Joyce presents a series of such perils, matched. In 'Lotuseaters' the peril comparable with the enervating lotus is the relief of giving up the quest for real satisfactions and making do with substitutes. The symbols listed in Table 2 suffice to illustrate this. In the following chapter, attending a funeral, Bloom faces an even greater moral peril—'the descent into Nothingness' as Joyce designates it in the notes. He imagines his own death—'Mistake must be: someone else. Try the house opposite.' His imagination, however, is too lively to be put down. It notes the use of cemeteries as sanctuaries by birds, and devises an improvement of memorials by the use of gramophone records. Although the Irishman's home may (as Bloom reflects) be his coffin, his own is in a warmer place. He survives the descent to the Underworld, just as Ulysses did.

'Mockery of Victory' was the tag Joyce assigned to the 'Aeolus' chapter. Its relevance to the corresponding Homeric episode is clear enough. Ulysses, with the help of Aeolus's gift of the winds, came within sight of home, only to be blown off course when his crew let all the winds loose at once by opening the bag that contained them. Returning to his erstwhile benefactor, the unlucky hero was refused further help. Bloom suffers a similar reversal in the course of this chapter, leaving the editorial office hopefully, and returning with an unexpected problem only to be dismissed. The moral analogy, however, is provided by Moses upon Mount Pisgah, seeing the Promised Land but not entering it. The possible application of this to Bloom's case is obvious. The location of the scene in a newspaper office makes its application more general. What is illustrated in this chapter, by a host of offered instances, is the gap between inspiration and achievement, and the delusive bridge between them offered by words.

The Lestrygonians were cannibals encountered by Ulysses on his way home. The next chapter contains instances of eating and images of digestion, but again there is also a moral analogy with the original incident. In this chapter the physical devouring of man by man is matched with the way men prey upon one another's afflictions—as, for example, the lunacy of Breen or, for the matter of that, Bloom's cuckoldry. This chapter continues a process which has been developing from the first chapter of the 'Odyssey' section of the novel— the section that deals with Bloom's adventures. His perils became less and less peculiar to him personally, more and more common to mankind in general. For this reason he can be regarded as an everyman figure.

In the next chapter—the discussion in the Library—Bloom barely makes an appearance, and then not in the role of Ulysses. This role is temporarily taken over by personages to whom Stephen refers in his discourse, most notably Shakespeare. As we have seen, Stephen's central point is the writer's ability to convert the raw material of his experience into art. This capacity depends upon his success in steering a course between a crass submission to brute fact on the one hand, on the other an untruthful idealism. Shakespeare achieved this feat by the fusion of his inner world with his perception of the outer world. He thus, triumphantly if metaphorically, repeated Ulysses' negotiation of Scylla and Charybdis.

Bloom's role is similarly small in the tenth chapter—Wandering Rocks. In the *Odyssey* this danger was not actually encountered by Ulysses: he was only told about it. In Joyce's novel we find him involved in it no more and no less than a collection of other Dubliners. The citizens themselves are the dangerous rocks, clashing and colliding at random, subject to no harmonising direction from Church or State, despite their formal deference to Father Conmee and the Viceroy. Bloom's modest virtues stand out markedly against such a background. The generosity of his contribution to the fund for Paddy Dignam's widow is noted, and Lenehan's remark that Bloom is 'a cultured allroundman' indicates the direction of the reader's sympathy. As the novel progressed, Joyce told Budgen, Bloom would increase in moral stature until he dwarfed the other characters.

At this stage of the novel, however, Bloom still has a long way to go. In the next chapter—Sirens—a new test reveals another of his weaknesses, his sentimentality. Sentimentality is hardly a failing of which Homer's Ulysses can be accused, and the way in which Joyce interprets his treatment of the sirens as a manifestation of it is a good example of his metaphorical method. Sentimentality is indulgence in an emotion for the sole purpose of feeling that emotion. The moral defect of such indulgence is spelt out in the remark from Meredith which Stephen has already communicated to Mulligan by telegram: 'The sentimentalist is he who would enjoy without incurring the immense debtorship for a thing done.' One way of procuring this sterile enjoyment is offered by sentimental songs, such as are sung at the 'Ormond' in this chapter. Ulysses' trick of having himself bound to the mast of his ship, so that he was prevented from responding outwardly to the sirens' song, while still moved by it inwardly, is a diagrammatic representation of sentimentality, so regarded. Listening to the words

– Co-ome, thou lost one!
Co-ome thou dear one!

Bloom, through self-pity, converts his forlorn state into a source of satisfaction. There is nothing he can do about it, except savour it. Nevertheless, he does not allow himself to be deceived. The sirens move his curiosity, as well as his feelings. In this too he resembles Ulysses.

The 'Cyclops' chapter ends with Bloom narrowly escaping assault in Barney Kiernan's bar from which he emerges followed by a biscuit tin, but even Ulysses's corresponding triumph over Polyphemus amounted to no more than a clean get-away. In the course of the episode Bloom, like Ulysses, has demonstrated his superiority. It has become clear that his unusual humility is something more than mere passivity. He has made a stand for humane values against the monstrous forces Joyce lists as symbols for this chapter—Nation, State, Religion, Dynasty, Idealism, Exaggeration, Fanaticism and Collectivity. Like Stephen, he is an opponent of the hangman god. 'Force, hatred, history, all that', he roundly denounces as 'the very opposite of that that is really life'. What is really life is individual, as Joyce's summary of the chapter's meaning makes clear. It is the ego which is threatened by the giant.

The sense of the next chapter is 'projected illusion,' the trick of seeing what one wants to see instead of what is there. The parallel here between Joyce's scene and the episode of Nausicaa in Homer is ironic. When Nausicaa recognised a royal hero in the naked castaway she found on the shore, and desired him for her husband, she was penetrating appearances to perceive the truth. When Gerty recognises, in the stranger on the shore, a hero from a cheap novelette she is projecting an illusion. When Bloom matches her exhibitionism with masturbation he is doing the same. When she moves away he sees that she is crippled. His realistic yet compassionate response to this discovery is proof of the moral resilience that underlies his immediate subservience to fantasies. More than this, he has a solemn sense of the value of marriage and birth, which distinguishes him, in the next chapter, from all the other men at the gathering in the maternity hospital. So in Homer, Ulysses did not join in the slaughter of the sacred oxen. In consequence, he alone escaped divine retribution. So, at the end of the chapter when the party breaks up in confusion, Bloom is the only man who remains sensible and sober.

The 'Oxen of the Sun' chapter has thrown Stephen into the company of Bloom, although, if a strict parallel with the *Odyssey* were to be maintained, this should not happen for two more chapters. In the next 'Circe' chapter the Homeric parallel is ignored even more markedly, for Stephen plays a central role in it whereas Telemachus never set foot on Circe's magic island. Circe, by her magic, changed men into beasts. Joyce's version of this situation is Bella Cohen's brothel. The bestiality which overcomes her clients is not lust, but the loss of manhood induced by psychological fixations. Thus something in Bloom wants him to be treated like a woman, and ridden like an animal. The transforming magic is the power of the unconscious mind. This is the greatest of the perils Bloom encounters and survives. Although he has entered the place only to look after Stephen, he is severely tested, but he retains his humanity.

The last three chapters of the book match the climax of the epic, although the victory they relate is more subdued. Homer tells how father and son are united in a swineherd's hut, and return to the palace together. With some help from Telemachus, Ulysses slays the leading suitors and puts the rest to flight. At first sceptical, Penelope finally recognises her husband, long-lost but now at last returned. It is a conclusive ending, fitting in an epic. Joyce, on the other hand, is dealing with a world in which conclusive endings should not be looked for.

In Stephen's case the search for the father means the approach to maturity. This could not be realistically represented by a sudden enthusiasm for the company of Bloom. Stephen does accompany Bloom home, and accept refreshment from him. He also spends a considerable time in amicable conversation with him. Nevertheless when he leaves it is clear enough that he is unlikely to renew the acquaintance. In no sense can he be said to have found a father. What can, however, be said is that their relationship has been quite unlike any other in which we have seen Stephen engaged. Bloom's manifest solicitude has evoked a corresponding friendliness in Stephen. His behaviour shows none of the suspicion, contempt and display which have characterised it in the earlier scenes. He has not suddenly become mature, but he has at least taken a step towards maturity.

Bloom too has taken a step. He has not entered the Promised Land, but he has received more than a Pisgah sight of it. He has emerged from the various forms of moral bondage that beset him through the day, and now, flattered and excited by the presence of an intellectual guest, he can think his way out of the pain of Molly's betrayal, which has so far dogged him at every turn. He forgives it as relatively harmless, and, in the circumstances for which he is himself partly responsible, both natural and inevitable. Thus he goes peacefully to bed, sufficiently assured of his role to tell her, as he does so, to get his breakfast in the morning. He has slain the suitors in the battlefield behind the forehead.

As for Penelope's recognition of her husband, it is all the more convincing for being the product of undirected thought. Mentally reviewing the men in her life, Molly finds her thoughts gravitating to Bloom, and the incident he too has been recalling of his proposal of marriage. In spite of everything, she decides to give him another chance. She will even get him his breakfast. So Bloom may not have entered the Promised Land, but his domestic affairs are not un-promising.

The epic with which Joyce matched his novel, as the preceding account makes plain, is not a legend but a legend interpreted as a moral fable. Joyce read the *Odyssey* as a kind of *Pilgrim's Progress.* By matching his novel with a work of that kind, he provided his readers with another way of reading it, not as a portrait of the artist but as an unidealised portrait of a model man.

Table 2   Thematic correspondences in *Ulysses* (based on the Linati plan)

	TITLE	PLACE	TIME	MEANING	SYMBOL
	I *Telemachia*				
1	Telemachus	Tower	8–9	Dispossessed son in struggle	Hamlet, Ireland, Stephen
2	Nestor	School	9–10	Wisdom of antiquity	Ulster, woman, common sense
3	Proteus	Strand	10–11	Primal matter	Word, signature, moon, evolution, metamorphosis
	II *Odyssey*				
4	Calypso	House	8–9	Departing traveller	Vagina, exile, family, nymph, Israel in bondage
5	Lotuseaters	Bath	9–10	Seduction of faith	Host, penis in bath, foam, flower, drugs, castration, oats
6	Hades	Graveyard	11–12	Descent into nothingness	Cemetery, Sacred Heart, the past, the unknown man, the unconscious, heart trouble, relics, heartbreak
7	Aeolus	Newspaper	12–1	Mockery of victory	Machines, wind, hunger, stag beetle, failed destinies, press, mutability
8	Lestrygonians	Lunch	1–2	Dejection	Bloody sacrifice, foods, shame
9	Scylla and Charybdis	Library	2–3	Two-edged dilemma	Hamlet, Shakespeare, Christ, Socrates, London and Stratford, scholasticism and mysticism, Plato and Aristotle, youth and maturity
10	Wandering Rocks	Streets	3–4	Hostile surroundings	Christ and Caesar, errors, homonyms, synchronisations, resemblances
11	Sirens	Concert Room	4–5	Sweet deception	Promises, feminism, sounds, embellishments
12	Cyclops	Tavern	5–6	Egocidal terror	Nation, state, religion, dynasty, idealism, exaggeration, fanaticism, collectivity
13	Nausicaa	Rocks	8–9	Projected illusion	Onanism, female, hypocrisy

| 14 | Oxen of the Sun | Hospital | 10–11 | The eternal herds | Fecundation, frauds, parthenogenesis |
| 15 | Circe | Brothel | 11–12 | Man-hating monster | Zoology, personification, pantheism, magic, poison, antidote, reel |

III *Nostos* (Homecoming)

16	Eumaeus	Shelter	12–1	Ambush at home	(Sailors)
17	Ithaca	House	1–2	Hope in arms	(Comets)
18	Penelope	Bed	∞	The past sleeps	(Earth)

Note: The symbols placed in brackets are taken from the Gilbert plan, because these items are omitted from the Linati plan (see p. 114).

Coincidental detail

Until each section of *Ulysses* finally went to press, Joyce was busily drawing on an inexhaustible stock of details to make additions to the text. In Stephen and Bloom he had two characters he knew as well as he knew himself. He had so much knowledge about them that some of it had to be excluded—for instance, as his notes reveal, the idea that Bloom's response to Gerty MacDowell is in part due to his attraction to his daughter Milly, as a rejuvenated version of Molly. Similarly he had a detailed knowledge of the setting—the city in which he had grown up, as it was on a day he had particular call to remember. Memory however was not enough for him. He sometimes had occasion for research. Thus Bloom, who is represented as living at 7 Eccles Street, could not be described climbing into the premises over the area railings until Joyce's aunt had confirmed that a man of Bloom's age and size, in his condition, could actually have performed such a feat at the address in question. Another tool of topographical research was *Thom's Official Directory*, thanks to which Father Conmee cannot walk along the North Strand Road without passing Gallagher's the grocer's and Grogan's the tobacconist's, established at numbers 4 and 16 respectively. (The extent of this kind of documentation, when it is added up at the end of the book, can be inferred from the fact that in *A topographical guide to James Joyce's 'Ulysses'* by Clive Hart and Leo Knuth, nineteen addresses separate Gallagher from Grogan in the alphabetical list.) And the American shipping disaster, news of which is announced on a placard as Father Conmee passes Grogan's, did actually occur on that day.

Even the invented details often read like straight documentation. For instance, a threemasted schooner, the *Rosevean*, with a cargo of bricks from Bridgwater docks in the course of the day. She is sighted off port in the third chapter by Stephen. In the tenth chapter a handbill announcing a revivalist meeting, thrown over O'Connell bridge by Bloom in the eighth chapter, floats past her in the dock. In the sixteenth chapter Bloom and Stephen meet a member of her crew who has come ashore. The total effect of such an accumulation of apparently insignificant details can be suffocating, and many readers have found it so. No doubt an accumulation of details adds solidity to a story, and may contribute to an understanding of the characters' environment. Beyond a certain point, however, it acts as an impediment to the reader who expects a novel to be understandable in a way similar—different only because every detail is relevant —to the way in which he makes sense of his own everyday experience. Applying that common sense expectation to *Ulysses*, it appears at first that what we have is something far more like everyday experience than a novel, because so many of its details add nothing to our understanding of what is going on, and merely hold up the progress of the story.

Even common sense, however, can come to perceive beneath a mass of apparently unconnected details a pattern which explains their presence. This is clearly what happens in *Ulysses* in those passages where the stream of consciousness of a character is presented as interior monologue. The interior monologue appears to be entirely unstructured, the product of chance encounters and chance associations, but as he follows it the reader finds a pattern developing beneath the surface details, delineating the preoccupations of the character whose mind he has been reading. There is, however, a limit to the need for details to establish such psychological recognition. Beyond a certain point, they add nothing to the reader's understanding.

Other patterns, however, become possible if the writer can count on something more in his reader than mere common sense. If the reader was confined by common sense, he would pay no attention to the sound of words, but concentrate on their meaning. Given a reader who is prepared to pay special attention to sounds, a writer can give words an additional meaning which the common-sense reader misses. These additional patterns, of course, depend on what the writer selects for the reader's special attention. Joyce does use the physical properties of words. But what distinguishes *Ulysses* is the incorporation of patterns of a kind quite fresh, when he wrote, in fiction. This new kind of pattern is composed of narrative detail.

Take, for example, the invented detail of the *Rosevean*, to which reference has already been made. She first appears when, urinating on the shore, Stephen senses a presence behind him and turns to see what is there, namely: 'Moving through the air high spars of a threemaster, her sails brailed up on the crosstrees, homing, upstream, silently moving, a silent ship.' The 'homing' ship is, of course, an omen of Ulysses's return, but that kind of symbolic reinforcement was nothing new. The peculiarly Joycean device is manifest in another word, the 'crosstrees'. Budgen, who had sailed on schooners, informed Joyce that this was not the word he wanted. It should be 'yards'. Thanking him for the correction, which he declared to be of the kind of criticism he found most useful, Joyce nevertheless insisted that 'crosstrees' had to stay, as it was repeated elsewhere in the book. This repetition occurs in the Library discussion, where, listing the scenes in which God cast himself, as Son, in his own creation, Stephen includes 'starved on crosstree'. Joyce's ideal reader does not, however, have to wait for six chapters to make this connection. The word 'crosstrees' in combination with the number three, is enough to remind him immediately of Calvary.

Pound had a suggestive word for Joyce's interest in correspondences while ignoring the incompatibility of the objects compared as here, the immense discrepancy between the ship and the Crucifixion. He called it Joyce's 'medievalism', and the term is exactly applied. Like Fluellen in Shakespeare's *Henry V*, Joyce found 'figures in all things'—and 'figures' here can be taken to mean not only typical forms but even numbers. The three crosstrees is only one example of many numerical correspondences. For instance, in the last chapter, besides being herself Molly represents the earth. The chapter is therefore divided into four quarters—each beginning with the word 'yes'—thus matching the four cardinal points of the compass and also, as Joyce explained to Budgen, the four cardinal points of the female anatomy. In the same way there are nine passages of parody, historically arranged, in the chapter in the maternity hospital, to match the nine months of pregnancy. Or figures can be used more emblematically: Molly's birthday, 8 September, is the Nativity of the Blessed Virgin. In the sixteenth chapter of a novel set in the sixteenth of June, we meet a sailor with the figure sixteen tattooed on his chest, and, in the next chapter, we learn that Bloom is sixteen years older than Stephen. It is true that this information is then made the starting-point for a series of manifestly pointless calculations which mock this kind of thing, but in this novel mockery does not imply rejection. (Bloom's proclamation of love as against punishment, in 'Cyclops', receives exactly the same treatment.) Bloom later suspects astrology as being 'fallacious analogy', but Bloom is only half of Joyce. The Stephen in him is writing for the reader Dante knew, who could not be told of a rainbow without remembering that its colours numbered seven, and that each separate colour also had its meaning.

Colours were included in the structural factors Joyce listed in the schemes he supplied to show how the different chapters were all components of a tight system. Examination reveals that the systems in question were not as tight as they appeared, and their importance can be exaggerated. Nevertheless, like the details they are supposed to organise, they should not be ignored. As will be seen in Table 3, each chapter of the novel is supposed to display a particular colour, to exemplify a particular art, and to be dominated by a particular organ of the body.

There are two ways of considering such a scheme. It might be taken as a set of constraints which governed the actual writing of the novel so that when writing the Calypso chapter, for example, Joyce gave Bloom kidneys for breakfast because he had already decided that the kidney was the appropriate organ for this chapter. On the other hand, it can just as reasonably be conceived that Joyce gave Bloom kidneys for breakfast because they suited his character—his ability to digest impurity and turn it into living water—and then realised, after finishing the chapter, that the kidney could be

Table 3   Minor structural factors in *Ulysses*

	CHAPTER	COLOUR	ART	ORGAN
1	Telemachus	Gold, white	Theology	—
2	Nestor	Brown (chestnut)	History	—
3	Proteus	Green (blue)	Philology	—
4	Calypso	Orange	Economics	Kidney
5	Lotuseaters	(Brown)	Botany, chemistry	Genitals
6	Hades	White, black	Religion	Heart
7	Aeolus	Red	Rhetoric	Lungs
8	Lestrygonians	(Blood)	Architecture	Esophagus
9	Scylla and Charybdis	—	Literature	Brain
10	Wandering Rocks	(Rainbow)	Mechanics	Blood
11	Sirens	(Coral)	Music	Ear
12	Cyclops	(Green)	Politics	Muscle
13	Nausicaa	Grey, blue (grey)	Painting	Eye, nose
14	Oxen of the Sun	White	Medicine	Womb
15	Circe	(Violet)	Magic	Locomotor apparatus
16	Eumaeus	—	Navigation	Nerves
17	Ithaca	—	Science	Skeleton
18	Penelope	—	—	Flesh

Note: Items in brackets indicate discrepancies between the Linati plan and the Gilbert plan.

regarded as its appropriate organ. In fact it is known that both processes were involved. Some chapters, especially those which were written later, were planned with a full set of constraints from the start. Other chapters, the first to be written, were completed in first draft before Joyce had conceived of his categorical scheme. The assignment to such chapters of a colour or an organ therefore amounted, in the first place, to nothing more than a retrospective criticial comment. By the time the chapters in question had been re-written for the appearance of the novel in book form, however, these assignments had been taken as instructions, and appropriate details had been subsequently worked into the final text. This is probably one reason why between 1920 and 1922 Joyce changed his mind about some of the details. In 1920 he provided Carlo Linati with a plan which has already supplied us with material for an examination of the major Homeric correspondence. In 1922 he supplied Valéry Larbaud with a plan which, although similar, was by no means identical. This second plan was subsequently made public in Stuart Gilbert's *James Joyce's 'Ulysses'*.

The details given in Table 3 are those supplied by Gilbert. As an example of discrepancies, however, the colours named in the Linati scheme are also shown (in brackets), wherever they differ from those named by Gilbert, or where Gilbert shows no colour at all. That these discrepancies exist is not, of course, a sign of careless-ness but of deep consideration. It is also a sign that some factors played no significant part in the genesis of the novel. Often, indeed, they amount to little more than external comment. Gold and white, for example, are not assigned to the first chapter because special attention should be paid to their appearance in the narrative (as gold fillings in Mulligan's teeth), but because of their sacerdotal associations, which relate them to the Mass, mocked by Mulligan. Blue, similarly, has a conventional association with the Virgin Mary. Accordingly it is assigned to the 'Nausicaa' chapter, in the Gilbert scheme. This appropriation, however, is an afterthought. The Linati scheme only assigns grey to that chapter, and gives blue to 'Proteus' (perhaps as the traditional colour of the sea, instead of 'snotgreen'). Clearly enough, the Gilbert scheme is preferable in the sense that it is more explicable, but none of these details can be seen as a structural factor. They operate more as marginal notes. Similar qualifications must be made with regard to some other entries. Thus no organs are assigned to the opening three chapters. Joyce explained this as a sign that Stephen was not yet full-grown. This absence of organs cannot, however, be connected with any difference the reader feels between the opening chapters and 'Scylla and Charybdis', where Stephen reappears but an organ is neverthe-less awarded—the brain. It would seem that this organ is no less present in 'Proteus'. Arts, too, vary in their relevance. Architecture is not intrinsic to the action of 'Lestrygonians', for example, in the way that Rhetoric is to that of 'Aeolus'.

One can only reflect that Joyce was not upon oath when he filled in some of his columns. Each entry is no doubt justifiable, but they are justifiable in very different ways, some of them trivial. Others, however, are revealing, and can be seen to have operated as guides in the process of writing. Botany, for example, can be seen to operate as a controlling factor in the structure of 'Lotuseaters'. It was not included in the list of Arts in the Linati scheme, which only showed Chemistry (although 'flower' was given as one of the symbols). Its addition registers an additional direction given to the chapter, when the version published in the serialised version was rewritten for the book. References to flowers were worked carefully into the original passages to add, with their suggestions of perfume and vegetation, to the original narcotic atmosphere of drugged passivity. The opiate lotus constitutes the link between flower and drug—no less than the name of Bloom himself as he saunters on his way to the oriental-style public baths. The perfumed atmosphere is one of an Eastern paradise, complete with the eunuchs to whose ignoble ease he devotes some thought as he proceeds. And when, at the end of the chapter, he anticipates his bath, he is all but transformed, like Narcissus, into a flower himself.

> Enjoy a bath now: clean trough of water, cool enamel, the gentle tepid stream. *This is my body.*
> He foresaw his pale body reclined in it at full, naked, *in a womb of warmth*, oiled by scented melting soap, softly laved. He saw his trunk and limbs riprippled over and sustained, buoyed lightly upward, lemonyellow: *his navel, bud of flesh:* and saw the dark tangled curls of his bush floating, floating hair of the stream around *the limp father of thousands*, a languid floating flower.
> (107/88) (my italics)

The words in italics are those added in the final version. The 'languid floating flower', the key image, was there in the original, but the navel as bud has been inserted to support its effect, together with a suggestion of yoga contemplation of the self. Other additions also serve the same scheme. The Eucharist, suggested by 'This is my body', is a listed symbol—the *opium* of the people, according to Bloom's assessment of it earlier in the chapter. The thought itself also suggests the element of self-absorption, the *narcissism*, which is added to by the reference to self-enclosed, passive womb-life. ('Narcissism' is the 'technic' assigned to this chapter in the list given in Table 5.)

This is only one of many examples where the schemes draw our attention to consistent factors in the structure of a chapter, factors which serve to emphasise its meaning. In 'Sirens', to take another example, the art is Music, and reference is made to over a hundred and fifty musical works; 'Lestrygonians' is full of images of eating. These structural factors operate in a different way from the association of the colour blue with 'Nausicaa', which is a precise application of knowledge, external to the text. By contrast an element like the flower imagery in 'Lotuseaters' is part and parcel of the text which may, without the reader's consciously registering its presence, work upon his mind suggestively to modulate his reading in a relevant way.

Nowhere is the variety of kinds of reference more evident than in the Homeric parallels. As we have already seen, they provide a fundamental moral structure. They also operate, however, at the level of narrative detail in a multitude of ways which vary from the illuminating to the trivial. In the *Odyssey*, for example, Ulysses is protected from Circe's magic because he carries on his person the root moly. What eventually enables Bloom to recover his sense of reality in the brothel is a combination of factors, listed by the realist Joyce as 'indifference due to masturbation, pessimism congenital, a sense of the ridiculous, sudden fastidiousness in some detail, experience'. To satisfy the medievalist Joyce, however, Bloom also had to have a root about his person—namely the potato which, obedient to his dead mother's behest, he carries in his pocket as a prophylactic against rheumatism. In the same way the fact that Polyphemus was one-eyed in the *Odyssey* is matched, very significantly, by making his counterpart in *Ulysses*, the Citizen, into a violently prejudiced chauvinist with a one-track mind. Other correspondences, however, are trivial although they contribute an element of mock-heroic comedy. Where Ulysses was armed with a fire-hardened stake, Bloom has a cigar. Polyphemus flung a rock at the departing hero: the Citizen throws a biscuit tin after Bloom.

In addition to pairing Bloom and Stephen with Ulysses and Telemachus, Joyce also found Homeric counterparts for many of his minor characters. These pairings (taken from the Gilbert scheme) are given in Table 4 (page 117). The significance of these minor correspondences varies considerably. Some serve as useful signposts. The coupling of Gerty MacDowell with Nausicaa is obvious. The authorial identification of the milkwoman in 'Telemachus' with Mentor, however, invests Stephen's departure from the Martello tower with a motive more precise than is immediately apparent in the narrative. In the same way in 'Nestor', the matching of the feeble schoolboy Sargent with Pisistratus—who, in the *Odyssey*, became Telemachus's companion for a time—directs the reader's attention to an important relationship—Stephen's relationship with the boy who had kept timidly out of the scrum at Clongowes in *A Portrait*.

Table 4   Detailed Homeric correspondences in *Ulysses*

	TITLE	HOMERIC FEATURES	JOYCE'S FEATURES
1	Telemachus	Telemachus	Stephen
		Antinous	Buck Mulligan
		Mentor	Milkwoman
2	Nestor	Nestor	Deasy
		Pisistratus	Sargent
		Helen	Mrs O'Shea
3	Proteus	Proteus	Primal matter
		Menelaus	Kevin Egan
		Magapenthes	The cocklepickers
4	Calypso	Calypso	The nymph
		The Recall	Dlugacz
		Ithaca	Zion
5	Lotuseaters	Lotuseaters	Cabhorses, communicants, soldiers, eunuchs, bather, watchers of cricket
6	Hades	The Four Rivers	Dodder, Grand and Royal Canals, Liffey
		Sisyphus	Cunningham
		Cerberus	Father Coffey
		Hades	Caretaker
		Hercules	Daniel O'Connell
		Elpenor	Dignam
		Agamemnon	Parnell
		Ajax	Menton
7	Aeolus	Aeolus	Crawford
		Incest	Journalism
		Floating Island	Press
8	Lestrygonians	Antiphates	Hunger
		The Decoy	Food
		Lestrygonians	Teeth
9	Scylla and Charybdis	The Rock	Aristotle, dogma, Stratford
		The Whirlpool	Plato, mysticism, London
		Ulysses	Socrates, Jesus, Shakespeare

10	Wandering Rocks	Bosphorus European Bank Asiatic Bank Symplegades	Liffey Viceroy Conmee Groups of citizens
11	Sirens	Sirens Isle	Barmaids Bar
12	Cyclops	Noman Stake Challenge	I Cigar Apotheosis
13	Nausicaa	Phaeacia Nausicaa	Star of the sea Gerty
14	Oxen of the Sun	Trinacria Lampetie, Phaethusa Helios Oxen Crime	Hospital Nurses Horne Fertility Fraud
15	Circe	Circe	Bella
16	Eumaeus	Eumaeus Ulysses Pseudangelos Melanthius	Skin the goat Sailor Corley
17	Ithaca	Eurymachus Suitors Bow	Boylan Scruples Reason
18	Penelope	Penelope Web	Earth Movement

Other correspondences of character offer ironic comments. Molly is not faithful in the way Penelope was. Mr Deasy is not wise in the way Nestor was. Nevertheless, these correspondences do have their appropriateness. In the same way, although nobody in Dublin regards Bloom as a leader there are signs in Homer that Ulysses also was something of an outsider among the other heroes: in conversation Joyce commended him for his attempt to dodge military service, no less than for the business-like way he got on with the war once he was involved in it. Far from ironic, however, is the identification of Ulysses's bow in 'Ithaca', with Bloom's reason, and of the suitors he slew with his scruples. From Joyce's point of view, Bloom's was the more heroic deed. The analogy, however, is certainly 'medieval'.

Yet other correspondences add little or nothing to the narrative, although their ingenuity may please the reader. Two examples from 'Hades' are typical of this supererogatory process. The problem of Sisyphus, eternally rolling a boulder up a hill which promptly rolled down again, is matched with the domestic problem of Martin

Cunningham who has an alcoholic wife. The shade of Ajax in the underworld snubbed Ulysses, on account of an old grudge. For the same reason John Henry Menton snubs Bloom in Glasnevin Cemetery. Although they contribute nothing to our appreciation of the characters concerned, these correspondences cannot be said to be forced. The linking in 'Proteus' of Menelaus with the absent Kevin Egan, on the other hand, would seem to have been made simply for the sake of nominating somebody for the vacancy, while the identification of the nameless narrator of 'Cyclops' with the alias used by Ulysses, 'Noman' is simply the author's joke.

The most significant aspect of Joyce's use of these similitudes, however, is that he did not allow it to get out of hand. Clearly he had a taste for conundrums, but he controlled it. He discovered many more resemblances than he actually made use of. Asked, for example, why a barmaid was like a siren, he once replied that just as the sirens were alluring only down to the waist, so a barmaid was attractive only down to the level of the bar. Below that level, where the customers could not see her, a barmaid, he alleged, wore a sloppy old skirt and comfortable footwear. This detail, like others he had elaborated, was nevertheless omitted from the 'Sirens' chapter, presumably because it would have impaired Miss Douce's performance with her garter.

The question remains, why did he add many of these decorations? Why, for example, does Parnell's chess-playing brother appear and reappear? His resemblance to the dead man who had been Ireland's 'uncrowned king' makes him, in a small way, an incidental candidate for the role of the ghost of Old Hamlet, but this, surely, is only a distraction. The only candidate who concerns us, the father with whom Stephen must be 'atoned', is Bloom. If *Ulysses* is like a forest through which the reader finds his way, endowing the trees with strange resemblances to snakes and towers and human faces must look like an unnecessary complication. One answer might be that it makes the forest more interesting while the traveller is in it, but there is a deeper justification than that. To understand it fully, we must first study the use of symbolism in the novel. Provisionally, however, this much can be said. Living, as Joyce saw it, was like being immersed in an invisible medium. A story-line is like a current moving through that medium. If the story-line is a strong one, the reader's awareness of that medium is confined to a single movement, and an explicable, rational movement at that. A tenuous story-line, on the other hand, such as that of the meeting of Stephen with Bloom, permits a more comprehensive awareness of the medium the characters move in. It was for this reason that Joyce praised the inconsequential plots of Chekhov. 'All is muffled and subdued as it is in life, with innumerable currents and cross-currents flowing in and out, confusing the sharp outlines so loved by other dramatists.'

In Shakespeare's *Henry V*, Captain Fluellen takes Alexander the Great as the type of the great commander, and shows that his monarch is similarly a great commander, because he was born, like the prototype, in a mountainous country with rivers, and killed his best friend. In *Ulysses* Joyce takes a famous hero as the type of the all-round man, and demonstrates Bloom's resemblance to him by similar 'medieval' analogies. It should be noted that Fluellen was not led, in the first place, to consider Henry as a great commander by perceiving these analogies. He used the analogies to confirm what he already knew by experience. In the same way, Joyce does not expect the reader to be convinced of Bloom's moral stature by the analogies with the *Odyssey* which he works into his text. The analogies are there as a commentary on the behaviour of Bloom, which speaks for itself. The other systematic correspondences which were examined in the previous section all operate in this secondary way. The action is interesting without them and offers insights into human nature to the reader who ignores analogies. They serve only to reinforce the understanding of the action which the reader can arrive at simply by applying normal standards of judgement.

Much of the less systematic symbolism of *Ulysses* is also of this straightforward kind. It enables the author to gloss his own text. Thus, when he reads that the hackney cab in which Boylan rides away to his appointment with Molly is driven by 'Barton, James of number one Harmony Avenue', the reader can feel Joyce's elbow in his ribs. Even if the reader comes to learn that, according to *Thom's Directory*, a man with that name did live at that address in Dublin in 1904, he still realises that a plain fact has been employed to emphasise an obvious message. Joyce has used the bricks and mortar of Dublin to illustrate his fable just as God, in the view of medieval scholars, employed the world's flora and fauna to illustrate messages already made plain in the Bible.

The world can be regarded as a place in which we win and lose things. It can also simultaneously be regarded as an instructive exhibition. This was the medieval view. Not only the rainbow, but everything else God had created, was sent as a sign. The world was not only a field given to man for the fulfilment of his nature as a creature of God: it was also a book of symbols, open to the exercise of reason which enabled him to derive useful lessons from it, by making comparison. From the world he could learn, observing the ant, the uses of industry, just as from the Bible, reading the Song of Solomon, he could learn the true relationship of Christ with his bride, the Church.

The late-nineteenth-century symbolists also believed that the world could be treated as a book of symbols, and further that an artist might produce a book of symbols which would be a resumé of the world. The expectation of, and thence also the ambition to write, such a revelation was current when Joyce was a young man, and indeed Yeats and his friends had an expectation that it would be written in Ireland. Joyce was affected by this idea, and there is evidence that in his sillier moments he believed that in *Ulysses* he had produced a work of prophetic power. He was incorrigibly super-stitious. When he was working on *Finnegans Wake*, for example, he proposed that if he should fail to finish it the task should be entrusted to James Stephens, for the reason that the latter was born in the same place in the same year as he was, and, if further confirmation were needed, combined in his name the Christian names of Joyce himself and Joyce's fictional representative, Stephen. Accordingly it is not surprising that when a detail of *Ulysses* appeared to have foretold the fate of a real-life character the coincidence, to Joyce in one of his more irrational moments, appeared to be more than *mere* coincidence. The prophetic powers of a symbolist work, however, were not supposed to be of this sort. Symbolist truth was precisely not the kind of truth which experience can reveal or confirm but rather a hint, a suggestion not a statement, of influences which operate behind the veil at which common experience stops short. These suggestions were the opposite of categorical: they were am-biguous, because they dealt in hints and guesses, things seen through a glass darkly.

Intimations of this kind in a novel are more likely to be felt the less compelling and powerful the story interest. In the previous section we have already seen how Joyce praised Chekhov because, in his plays, the tenuous story-line afforded scope for a sense of 'innumerable currents and cross-currents flowing in and out'. In this observation he was, to a remarkable degree, repeating the defence made by the symbolist Maeterlinck, in a passage with which Joyce was certainly familiar. It occurs in *The Treasure of the Humble* (1897), a book in which Maeterlinck asserts: 'A transformation of silence—strange and inexplicable—is upon us, and the reign of the *positive sublime*, absolute to this day, seems destined to be overthrown.' The 'positive sublime', whose end Maeterlinck announces, is the sublimity of absolute, factual truth—the kind of truth believed in by the Realists. The new sublimity which Maeterlinck would substitute for it is not scientific, factual, and objective, but mysterious, vague and subjective.

I admire Othello, but he does not appear to me to live the august daily life of a Hamlet, who has the time to live, inasmuch as he does not act. Othello is admirably jealous. But is it not perhaps an ancient error to imagine that it is at the moments when this passion, or others of equal violence, possess us, that we live our truest lives? I have grown to believe that an old man, seated in his armchair, waiting patiently with his lamp beside him; giving unconscious ear to all the eternal laws that reign about his house, interpreting without comprehending, the silence of doors and windows and the glowering voice of the light, submitting with bent head to the presence of his soul and his destiny—an old man, who conceives not that all the powers of this world, like so many heedful servants, are mingling and keeping vigil in his room, who suspects not that the very sun itself is supporting in space the little table against which he leans, or that every star in heaven and every fibre of the soul are directly concerned in the movement of an eyelid which closes, or a thought that springs to birth—I have grown to believe that he, motionless as he is, does yet live in reality a deeper, more human and more universal life than the lover who strangles his mistress, the captain who conquers in battle or 'the husband who avenges his honour'.

The question to be considered now is whether *Ulysses* besides being 'medieval' is also a work in the new tradition heralded by Maeterlinck, a tradition of silent rather than of positive sublimity because it offers intimations of unutterable truths, rather than recognitions of the lessons of conscious experience. Certainly, in his relationship with Molly, Bloom is no Othello. It is more relevant, however, to begin this investigation by considering the case of the Hamlet figure—Stephen. Hamlet, says Maeterlinck, has time to live because he does not act, or to quote another symbolist, Mallarmé, 'il se promène, lisant au livre de lui-même'. The book which Stephen reads, as he walks through *Ulysses*, is none the less a world for being the book of himself. (He himself makes this clear, in the Library discussion.) Like the mystic Boehme, he regards the world as a repository of signatures he is there to read.

THE SYMBOLIC DOG   An animal symbol offers itself as a good starting-point. When Stephen is confronted with an animal symbol—the dog—his initial reading of it, when he encounters a dog on the shore in 'Proteus', is conventional enough to be termed 'medieval'. Dogs symbolise for him the menial mind, which fawns on superiors and snarls at equals. In particular he is reminded of Mulligan's hangers-on, the barking of whose applause is something he should despise. All this is sufficiently regular and predictable. There is also, however, a more personal reaction to the dog linked to a web of association so closely woven that unravelling it completely would involve examining all the situations in which Stephen plays a part.

Dogs dig things up—things which have been buried away. This image recurs. In 'Proteus' the dog on the sand 'dabbled and delved .... Something he buried there, his grandmother.' This links the dog with 'The fox burying his grandmother under a hollybush', the answer he gave to the riddle in the previous chapter. The dog thus symbolises Stephen's remorse for the part he played at his mother's death. It is the enemy within, gnawing at his breast. The 'agenbite of inwit' is a dog-bite. The genesis of this connection of the dog image with his mother's death—as also further ramifications of meaning—is tersely recalled by a phantom Mulligan in the course of Stephen's fantasies in 'Circe'. 'The mockery of it! Kinch killed her dogsbody bitchbody. She kicked the bucket. Our great sweet mother!' These exclamations refer back to the conversation between Stephen and Mulligan with which the novel opens. 'She kicked the bucket' is not Mulligan's phrase, but it catches exactly the deliberate insensitivity, learnt in the dissecting room, which he displays in that conversation on the subject of being 'beastly dead'. This insensitivity, however, has a theoretical underpinning of materialism. The body is all there is, and the body amounts to nothing. In the end it decomposes. We all emerge from the endless material flux, and eventually merge with it again. The sea, of course, is the symbol of that flux. She is our mother because it is from the flux that our bodies emerge. (The maternal and the material are etymologically linked, and evolutionary theory locates the origin of life in the ocean.)

Once matter is identified as female there is a basis for that misogyny expressed in 'bitchbody'. Again we see Stephen's kinship with Hamlet, who wished that his flesh, his maternal portion, would melt. Stephen's sense of the pathos of maternal love is contaminated by a sense, no less acute, of 'unclean loins'. The image of the dog thus fuses Stephen's remorse and his disgust over his mother's death, together, needless to say, with his appalled pity for her physical suffering—itself a further stimulus to revulsion against the body. In this cynical mood—and again etymology relevantly reminds us that the word cynic means canine—Mulligan's dismissive: 'It's all a mockery and beastly' seems justified. There are no final forms.

The connection of the dog with the sea, however, is more direct. It is not just etymology and inference that makes us connect a dog's life with meaningless flux, and flux with the sea. It was beside the sea that Stephen encountered the dog in 'Proteus', and the dog was no less protean than the sea. It resembled in turn a rabbit, a buck, a bear, a wolf, a calf, a pard and a panther. (In discussing this passage with Budgen, Joyce provided an etymological gloss: panther means all-beast.) Running about the strand it is brought up short when it encounters the carcass of another dog. This is symbolic enough, and Stephen's 'Ah, poor dogsbody', refers us to Hamlet's speculations over Yorick's skull, and the transformation Alexander's flesh might undergo to become loam to stop a beer-barrel. Stephen's comment on the dog's progress ending at the corpse—'eyes on the ground, moves to one great goal'—also converts the incident into an ironic comment on Mr Deasy's pronouncement in 'Nestor', that all history moves to one great goal, the manifestation of God. Here we have mockery of a kind highly congenial to Joyce. The dead dog is not merely a mockery of this idealism in its lowness, but also in its spelling. D-O-G is the opposite of G-O-D, a point formalised in the Black Mass celebrated by Mulligan and Haines in Stephen's fantasies in 'Circe'. Stephen does not share Mr Deasy's religious beliefs. Nevertheless, the phrase 'manifestation of God' represents the meaning of life for him, because he formulates his ideas in theological terms, and his aim in life is, as an artist, to redeem the senseless material flux of appearances by giving it conclusive form. That is what is meant for him by divine manifestation. The dog's progress thus mocks his artistic ambitions.

The protean dog, however, does not only mock art. It also demonstrates the possibility of art. The best way to establish this is to watch some of these transformations as Joyce effects them.

> Cocklepickers. They waded a little way in the water and, stooping, soused their bags, and, lifting them again, waded out. The dog yelped running to them, reared up and pawed them, dropping on all fours, again reared up at them with mute bearish fawning. Unheeded he kept by them as they came towards the drier sand, a rag of wolf's tongue redpanting from his jaws. His speckled body ambled ahead of them and then loped off at a calf's gallop. The carcass lay on his path. He stopped, sniffed, stalked round it, brother, nosing closer, went round it, sniffing rapidly like a dog all over the dead dog's bedraggled fell. Dog-skull, dogsniff, eyes on the ground, moves to one great goal. Ah, poor dogsbody. Here lies poor dogsbody's body.

> (58/52)

The animal is no less 'like a dog' when it is like a bear, a wolf, etc., than it is when it sniffs the carcass 'like a dog'. It is precisely through these transformations that the dog manifests its dogginess. Proteus will reveal the truth to the hero who hangs on to him, despite his transformations. There is a form behind the flux for art to reveal.

That the dog, in addition to the meanings already discussed, also symbolises the artist, is plain. The dog is an impersonator—a dramatist, a mummer like Stephen (according to Mulligan: 'Kinch, the loveliest mummer of them all'). A dogsbody is one who has no assigned function but can be called on to perform any role. It is the lowest position, which is why 'dogsbody' is Mulligan's patronising name for Stephen in 'Telemachus', but it is also a universal one. It points the way to the victory of art over flux effected by Shakespeare, not by the strength of a monolithic mind, but by 'myriad-mindedness'. Shakespeare too, in 'Scylla and Charybdis', is compared to a dog in his retirement in Stratford. 'He goes back, weary of the creation he has piled up to hide him from himself an old dog licking an old sore.'

The above discussion was extended. Even so, for the sake of simplicity, the ramifications of association which stem from the word and image 'dog' in *Ulysses* have been drastically cut back in it. Suffice it to recognise that the dog in *Ulysses* constitutes a symbol of extraordinary power, fusing impulses and fears whose origins and outlets are alike contradictory.

POTTED MEAT Bloom is blind to symbols. Even his writing on the sand in 'Nausicaa' suggests no echoes to his prosaic mind. Nevertheless he too is possessed by ambiguous images. As we learn from her soliloquy at the end of the book, Molly and Boylan concluded their sexual exertions with a feast of potted meat: blind though he may be to symbols, Bloom has no difficulty in reading this as a sign of sexual intercourse when he finds flakes of potted meat in the bed to which he at last finds his way, together with 'the imprint of a human form male, not his'. But potted meat is no less a symbol of Molly herself, whose use of a chamber-pot is a leading incident in the concluding stages of the novel. That Bloom himself is unconsciously affected by associations such as this is made clear by the way in which his mind is caught by an advertisement to which it

O'Connell Street, Dublin

obsessively returns in the course of the day. The reader, like Bloom, encounters it for the first time, in all innocence, in 'Lotuseaters', yet even there the implications of sexual intercourse are discernible.

> What is home without
> Plumtree's Potted Meat?
> Incomplete.
> With it an abode of bliss.

'Incomplete'. The word is like a knell. On all save one of the occasions it is used in *Ulysses* it carries this connotation, not as a reproach to Molly but as an indication of something lacking in Bloom. Thus in 'Ithaca' we learn of 'a period of 10 years, 5 months and 18 days during which carnal intercourse had been incomplete, without ejaculation of semen within the natural female organ'.

Sexual intercourse, however, is no guarantee of 'domestic bliss'. Bloom's failure in this particular respect is only one indication of a deeper and wider failure: he has lost the promise, the right to the abundance, the blossom and fruit, symbolised by 'Plumtree'. He has severed the shoot connecting him with previous generations, symbolised in terms of Judaism by the advertisement for Agendath Netaim's plantation company which he studies in 'Calypso'. He reads Agendath Netaim's advertisement, and thinking how the once promised land of Israel has reverted to barren desert, pictures it in terms of human sex.

> It lay there now. Now it could bear no more. Dead: an old woman's: the grey sunken cunt of the world.
> Desolation.
> Grey horror seared his flesh. Folding the page into his pocket he turned into Eccles Street, hurrying homeward. Cold oils slid along his veins, chilling his blood: age crusting him with a salt cloak.

(73/63)

In other words, he is turned into potted meat himself. (Remembering the snack she has shared with Boylan, Molly recalls with approval that it 'had a fine salty taste'.)

Potted meat, therefore, is associated in Bloom's mind with sex, with death, and with default. In the latter connection there is a witty reference, in 'Circe', to the fleshpots of Egypt, and an innocent use by Bloom in Lestrygonians of the phrase 'gone to pot'. As for death, as Bloom reflects in 'Hades', 'a corpse is meat gone bad'. From this it is an easy step for Bloom to consider Dignam's corpse in its coffin as tinned meat while he is choosing a sandwich at Davy Byrne's.

Ulysses putting out the eye of the Cyclops. Illustration for Joyce's Ulysses *by Henri Matisse.*

Sardines on the shelves. Almost taste them by looking. Sandwich? Ham and his descendants mustered and bred there. Potted meats. What is home without Plumtree's potted meat? Incomplete. What a stupid ad! Under the obituary notices they stuck it. All up a plumtree. Dignam's potted meat. Cannibals would with lemon and rice. White missionary too salty. Like pickled pork. Expect the chief consumes the parts of honour. Ought to be tough from exercise. His wives in a row to watch the. effect. *There was a right royal old nigger. Who ate or something the somethings of the reverend Mr MacTrigger.* With it an abode of bliss. Lord knows what concoction. Cauls mouldy tripes windpipes faked and minced up. Puzzle find the meat. Kosher. No meat and milk together. Hygiene that was what they call now.

(218/171)

It is notable how easily and naturally all three strands of association are interwoven in this passage—the corpse, sexual prowess, and the lost covenant.

By this ambiguity and fluidity such symbols—consciously examined in the mind of Stephen, free of all suspicion in the mind of Bloom—qualify for a Symbolist reading. In neither of the two cases considered, however, do the symbols appear to be objective properties of the world of Dublin. They appear rather to be products of the peculiar minds of the two characters concerned. For this reason they could well be considered as touches of psychological realism. Ambivalence is not characteristic only of Symbolist symbols: it is no less characteristic of the symbols Freud had identified and analysed in the mental operations of his patients.

LEITMOTIV. Another feature of the art of Symbolism which, confined to the mind of a single character, can also be viewed as a piece of psychological realism is the *leitmotiv*—a phrase or word repeated with suggestive frequency. By analogy with music this can be an element of composition. In psychology, however, it can be regarded as a telltale symptom, like Stephen's repeated 'agenbite of inwit' (remorse of conscience). No less revealing is the frequency with which Bloom employs the word 'phenomenon': the password of a man who believes that every event has a 'scientific' explanation. It is not so easy, however, to confine a particular word to a particular character. The word 'bitter' can be taken as a case in point. It is very much Stephen's word. It recalls his mother's death and the contradictions in his attitude to her, by way of the phrase from the song he sang to her which made her weep—'love's bitter mystery'—as also the bile she had spewed into the bowl by her sick-bed and thus also the salt sea, 'our grey sweet mother'. This combination of associations is established in 'Telemachus' and continued thereafter, as when in

'Proteus' he thinks of her as drowning in bitter waters without his trying to help her, or in 'Circe':

THE MOTHER: (*A green rill of bile trickling from a side of her mouth*) You sang that song to me. *Love's bitter mystery.*

The word is not however used only when it preys on Stephen's mind. It is used by Dubliners in bars, ordering 'bitters' or talking of 'bitter experience'. When they do so, however, their words mean more than they intend because Stephen's preoccupations now colour the word when someone else is using it.

Words and phrases also develop for the reader the same kind of special associations which they have for an individual character. For example, the word 'jingle' occurs twenty-two times. At first harnesses jingle in general. Then in 'Sirens' it is the harness of the cab bearing Boylan to the Ormond bar—a jaunty jingle. After his departure it is the same sound, but now Boylan is off to his assignation with Molly, and Bloom too hears it and knows what it means. The sound recurs, as Boylan is carried, sprawling, on his way. Bloom no longer hears it, but now for the reader who still hears it, there is an echo of Bloom's grief. Next the memory of the sound keeps breaking into Bloom's stream of consciousness as a sign of the sexual assertiveness of tenors and other males who make easy conquests. Boylan arrives at his destination, and the word becomes a sign of sexual intercourse, denoting as it has already done in 'Calypso' the noise of the jogged brass quoits on Molly's bed.

Leitmotiv, therefore, is not confined to the rendering of the inner life of the characters. It can also be the means of a direct communication from author to reader. Typical of this is the phrase 'a cry in the street'. Stephen repeats this phrase almost exactly. The repetition, however, is not a sign of obsession. It is an indication to the reader to compare the two occasions of its use. The words themselves mean nothing special to Stephen himself. The first occasion is Stephen's reply to Mr Deasy's pronouncement that all history moves towards one great goal, the manifestation of God. Indifferent to any such manifestation, Stephen declares Mr Deasy's God to be 'a shout in the street'.

His own God is the person met at the end of that long journey he describes in 'Scylla and Charybdis'. 'We walk through ourselves, meeting robbers, ghosts, giants, old men, young men, wives, widows, brothers-in-love. But always meeting ourselves.' When we recognise this underlying self, we achieve what Shakespeare achieved—Shakespeare of whom Alexandre Dumas said that, next to God, he had created most, and that the whole world of drama emanated from him just as the whole physical world had emanated from the sun. To become Shakespeare Stephen must recognise himself in Bloom, a realisation he is approaching when in his drunkenness in 'Circe', he asks himself.

> STEPHEN: (*Abruptly*) What went forth to the ends of the world to traverse not itself. God, the sun, Shakespeare, a commercial traveller, having itself traversed in reality itself, becomes that self. Wait a moment. Wait a second. Damn that fellow's noise in the street. Self which it itself was ineluctably preconditioned to become. *Ecco*!

Stephen is consciously quoting his own observations in the Library scene, when he speaks of the travelling subject traversing itself. His repetition—or near repetition—of 'shout in the street' from his conversation with Mr Deasy is, however, the chance result of an accidental interruption. He is not quoting himself there. The only person who picks up the repetitions is the reader, who is thus alerted to link Bloom, the sun, and Shakespeare with the true God whose manifestation is the function of art.

In the same way the book also contains symbols that operate only for the reader, unlike the dog symbol and the potted meat symbol, which are parts of the minds of Stephen and Bloom. Even these private symbols, it should be noted, tend to escape from the private worlds of these two characters. Bloom's potted meat is glanced at in 'Cyclops', where Joe Hynes says of a faithless wife: 'Get a queer old tailend of corned beef off that one, what?' In the phantasmagoria of 'Circe' it is not Stephen but Bloom who becomes a hunted fox, and it is he rather than Stephen in that chapter whose footsteps in Nighttown are dogged by a protean dog, which is at different times referred to as a spaniel, retriever, terrier, wolfdog, setter, mastiff, bulldog and greyhound. It is as if certain symbols, like certain ideas, attached themselves first to one character and thus to another in the course of the day.

Other symbols are common properties from the start. The understanding of these symbols is not part of the process of understanding the mind of a particular character but understanding the world which all the characters inhabit. The rose is a case in point. It is a female symbol, the common property of every female from the Blessed Virgin to Gerty MacDowell, its redness the colour of a bleeding heart and, also, of menstruation. 'Yes we are flowers all a womans body yes', Molly reflects, and the book supports her assertion. Miss Douce, at the approach of Boylan in 'Sirens'—'rose and closed her reading, rose of Castille. Fretted forlorn, dreamily rose.' Gerty MacDowell's 'rosebud mouth was a genuine Cupid's bow'. Even Stephen's mother, when her ghost comes to haunt him, is accompanied by 'an odour of wax and rosewood'. The *Rosevean*, with its three crosstrees, also associates this flower with 'love's bitter mystery'.

At the other end of the spectrum, however, the rose is expressive of that fertile flowering which characterises the land of promise which Bloom has lost, and the divine perfection Stephen expects of art. Molly's soliloquy produces a cataract of roses which overflows into both these masculine territories.

> I love flowers Id love to have the whole place swimming in roses God of heaven theres nothing like nature the wild mountains then the sea and the waves rushing then the beautiful country with fields of oats and wheat and all kinds of things and all the fine cattle going about that would do your heart good to see rivers and lakes and flowers all sorts of shapes and smells and colours springing up even out of the ditches primroses and violets nature it is as for them saying theres no God I wouldnt give a snap of my two fingers for all their learning why dont they go and create something I often asked him atheists or whatever they call themselves
>
> (931/703)

This flood of words seems entirely spontaneous and undirected, yet it continues to incorporate a whole collection of objects which the preceding chapters—dealing with other characters—have converted into symbols. Flowers, of course, include more than roses: they extend into Bloom's country, not forgetting his name, and his alias 'Henry Flower'. The mountains remind us of the scene on the Hill of Howth previously recalled by Bloom and about to be remembered by Molly. The sea and the waves belong to 'Proteus'. The crops are the sign of the Promised Land, as also the oxen, although these have developed additional associations in 'Nestor' and 'Oxen of the Sun'. The rivers and lakes too belong to a consistent water symbolism developed elsewhere in the book. 'God' is ubiquitous, at least as a word, throughout the novel. And 'why dont they go and create something' is a question applicable to both Stephen and to Bloom, although each has his special calling—Stephen to recreate, Bloom to procreate. This passage of inner monologue is therefore highly symbolic. It is also no less highly realistic.

This fusion of realism and symbolism is Joyce's peculiar gift. Nothing could be more characteristic of Molly than the fact that 'after the last time' she should have enjoyed her port and potted meat with Boylan. It demonstrates her appetite, her health and her indifference. Even in this detail, however, Joyce was at work setting up correspondences. Molly is the counterpart of Penelope in the *Odyssey*. Penelope wove a web. So do spiders, and female spiders, as Joyce reminded himself in his working notes, devour their mates after sexual intercourse. (In this case the husband, not the lover, is eaten.)

A QUESTION OF SERIOUSNESS   There is no single way of reading *Ulysses*, but for those who have recognised some of the symbols one way is certainly attended by a realisation that there is more meaning in the book than they first suspected, and a sense that still more meaning lies beneath the surface of apparent facts, still waiting for them to uncover it. This sense can develop from being a sense about the book to being a sense about the world depicted in the book. After all, it is not only the writing and the words used by the characters that form these links and correspondences which are simultaneously so irrelevant and so suggestive. Events, the bare facts, also have the same effect. The appearance of the *Rosevean* is as pat as a vision. The shout in the street was as good as a voice crying in the wilderness. Even Bloom's watch is psychic: it proves to have stopped exactly at the time when he was cuckolded. And at the eve of Stephen's departure from 7 Eccles Street the stars themselves blazon forth the connection of the artist with the citizen (who, being named Leopold, has Leo as his celestial counterpart), when the two men observe

A star precipitated with great apparent velocity across the firmament from Vega in the Lyre above the zenith beyond the stargroup of the Tress of Berenice towards the zodiacal sign of Leo.

(826/624)

What is the reader to make of these portents in a novel which adheres so meticulously to verisimilitude? Like the answer to many questions about *Ulysses*, the answer to this question will depend on the reader. Clearly Joyce is not suggesting that the presence of the *Rosevean* off Sandymount on the morning of 16 June 1904 was not sufficiently explained by the despatch of a cargo of bricks from Bridgwater to Dublin, or that a fault in the mechanism of Bloom's watch is not a sufficient explanation of the fact that his watch stopped that afternoon. The reader who trusts in Occam's razor, the scientific principle that those explanations are to be preferred which posit the minimum number of unobservable entities, will therefore regard the symbolic presentations of these coincidences as literary embellishment. The reader who prefers to make the most of a text may, on the other hand, reflect that when he looks back on the events of his own past life he sometimes glimpses a pattern transcending mere cause and effect. Coincidences, in such a view of things, are truly significant because they mark the intersections of the pattern of cause and effect with another deeper and more personal pattern of relationships, a pattern which he believes in, even though he could not justify his belief. It is a pattern of this sort that the Symbolists sought to unveil, and which Joyce offers to the reader in his intricately executed designs and correspondences. The designs are not intended to reproduce designs which operate in reality: it is not, for example, suggested that every hour of the day is in some way dominated by a specific organ of the body. Nor are the correspondences offered as infallible indicators: the precipitation of a star towards the zodiacal sign of Leo does not establish astrology as a science. What these features of the novel do, however, suggest is that there are more designs and correspondences on earth than are dreamt of in Bloom's philosophy.

The reader who is prepared to go so far with Joyce is helped by the sense of the ridiculous which remains with him even in his most mysterious moments. Perhaps the most effective of these is the last moment which the two heroes spend together, when standing side by side, making water in the garden, they contemplate the lighted bedroom window and the stars. In the sense given to the word by Maeterlinck, this moment is sublime. It is, however, also ridiculous. We have compared the process of reading *Ulysses* with a journey through a forest, and this comparison matches a classic Symbolist image of human life offered by Baudelaire:

> Nature is a temple where living pillars sometimes allow confused words to escape; there man passes through forests of symbols that glance at him familiarly.

Joyce presents a similar image, no less comic than it is impressive. It occurs when Bloom walks in the cemetery between the graves in 'Hades'.

> Mr Bloom walked unheeded along his grove by saddened angels, crosses, broken pillars, family vaults, stone hopes praying with upcast eyes, old Ireland's hearts and hands.
>
> (143/114)

Although Bloom ignores the angels, they accompany him because he is one of the chosen people. Elijah, in 'Circe', tells us who the chosen are in an exhortation.

> Have we cold feet about the cosmos? No. Be on the side of the angels. Be a prism. You have that something within, the higher self. You can rub shoulders with a Jesus, a Gautama, an Ingersoll.
>
> (625/473)

Again the words are comic. They are banal, ridiculous, and bathetic. Despite the open invitation to mockery, however, they also contain— in the phrases 'something within, the higher self'—one more formulation of a central theme of the novel. In the same way, despite the mock-heroic inflation, the conclusion of 'Cyclops' gives us the apotheosis of Bloom, complete with angels.

> And they beheld Him even Him, ben Bloom Elijah, amid clouds of angels ascend to the glory of the brightness at an angle of fortyfive degrees over Donohoe's in Little Green Street like a shot off a shovel.
>
> (449/343)

The enemy of the angelic host is Mulligan, whose mockery is not, like Joyce's, a way to salt sententiousness but mockery unalloyed, reducing everything to insignificance, the foe therefore of art. As Stephen reflects, when Mulligan displays his tricks in the opening pages:

> Idle mockery. The void awaits surely all them that weave the wind: a menace, a disarming and a worsting from those embattled angels of the church.

(25/27)

The object of Mulligan's mockery had been the Eucharist, here as in *A Portrait* a symbol of recreation. ('Transmuting the daily bread of experience into the radiant body of everlasting life' is Stephen's description of the artist's function in that novel.) It is also, as communion, a symbol of fellowship. The last of several versions of the form of the Mass in *Ulysses* occurs when Stephen and Bloom, in Eccles Street, drink cocoa—'Epps massproduct'—together. Stephen, however, does not break bread with Bloom. Bread he has, in 'Oxen of the Sun', relegated to those who live by bread alone. This exclusion is part and parcel of the revulsion which colours his attitude to material reality and until he can overcome it he cannot become an artist, for to quote his own words in that chapter: 'In woman's womb word is made flesh but in the spirit of the maker all flesh that passes becomes the word that shall not pass away.' It is the latter transformations which links the artistic process with the Eucharist. It is wrought upon the details of everyday life in *Ulysses*, to the extent that those details operate as symbols.

Style

It was said of Macaulay that he wrote in a style in which it was impossible to tell the truth, but this must be admitted of any style if by 'truth' the truth, the whole truth, and nothing but the truth is meant. Style is defined by its selection of words and structures. The more distinctive the style, the more it narrows the range of these choices. It filters the experience offered to the reader before it reaches him, restricting and colouring his perception. The style in which a book is written therefore expresses a particular kind of interest in the material it treats.

It might seem that this expressed interest must be the author's personal interest in his subject, and in many novels this is indeed the case. D.H. Lawrence, for example, is personally present in almost every line he writes, giving himself away generously to all comers, revealing in the choice and arrangement of his language a personal engagement to lively modes of thought and feeling which he offers us to share. It is not, however, inevitable that style must embody such a personal revelation. Thus, in *Dubliners* and *A Portrait* Joyce manifests a developing tendency to employ styles which do not express directly his own personal interest in the situation he has chosen to explore. In 'The Dead', for example, when he informs us that 'It was always a great affair, the Misses Morkan's annual dance' (199/173), this does not indicate that he shared or expected the reader to share the interest this sentence expresses, namely an interest in the party as a major social event. On the contrary his interest was in the effect upon the characters of a vision of life so limited that *they* could so regard it. The language he employs does not express directly Joyce's more removed kind of interest, but it provides material selected for that interest. It is not his language, but the language of his characters. He has borrowed his style from them, in order to express not himself but them.

INTERIOR MONOLOGUE   When *Ulysses* first appeared, the element of its style upon which critical attention was first concentrated was the use of interior monologue. This was a natural development of Joyce's earlier method of telling the story in the characters' own words. As Bloom and Stephen pursue their course through the earlier chapters —up to 'Wandering Rocks'—each character is continuously talking to himself, and the reader is presented with a rendering of this 'stream of consciousness' in a monologue. The most salient characteristic of such a monologue is that it is not directed continuously to any particular end. One train of thought switches, through associations which are neither logical nor conscious, to another. Moreover it is not always conducted at the same level of consciousness, so that the extent to which it is focussed on any particular subject will vary. In addition it will vary in the extent to which it is concerned with the character's immediate environment. Sometimes he will be wrapped in his own thoughts. At other times he will be interested in what is going on in front of him and, when this is the case, the monologue will be even more liable to chance breaks and interruptions.

For these reasons the interest it provides for cannot be an interest in a developing plot. Even the stream of consciousness of Macbeth before the murder of Duncan could not have been entirely concentrated on the crime which he was contemplating. As for Stephen and Bloom, they are not aware of the possibility that they will meet that day, let alone aiming at bringing their meeting about. The interest for which Joyce is providing in these chapters is not, therefore, an interest in the overall action of his novel. It is an interest in the minds of the two characters, with their different limitations and strengths, which will eventually go to make their meeting so significant.

This is not, of course, the only interest for which it provides, As we have seen, Joyce uses the looseness of interior monologue to weave leitmotivs and symbols into his text in a developing pattern. Then too, as memory forms a considerable part of the stream of consciousness it is also a means of providing the reader with detailed information about each character's past. Stephen, perhaps, the reader already knows, but before he sees the last of Bloom he has acquired sufficient information about this new character to compile his complete biography. The main interest of the monologue, however, and one to which it is naturally suited, is to show how the characters' minds work.

This is partly achieved by revealing the contents of those minds. It is, however, also revealed by style. The difference in education between Stephen and Bloom is registered by the difference between their vocabularies, their range of reference and the depth of their consideration. Their different temperaments reveal themselves no less dramatically. Compare, for example, the difference in sympathy, curiosity and observation manifest in the following two passages. In the first, Stephen has met his bedraggled sister in the street.

> She is drowning. Agenbite. Save her. Agenbite. All against us. She will drown me with her, eyes and hair. Lank coils of seaweed hair around me, my heart, my soul. Salt green death.
>
> (313/242)

The passage is rich with imagery derived from his meditation by the shore in 'Proteus', expressing his fear of being submerged in the meaningless flood of matter. If he comes to her help, he will lose his soul. His attitude is self-regarding, and the style expresses this.

The second passage is taken from Bloom's encounter with a figure no less sad, Mrs Breen, a friend of his youth now married to a lunatic.

> Opening her handbag, chipped leather, hatpin: ought to have a guard on those things. Stick it in a chap's eye in the tram. Rummaging. Open. Money. Please take one. Devils if they lose sixpence. Raise Cain. Husband barging. Where's the ten shillings I gave you on Monday? Are you feeding your little brother's family? Soiled handkerchief: medicinebottle. Pastille that was fell. What is she? ...
>
> (199/157)

There is a marked increase in speed and jerkiness of rhythm. Bloom is more observant and alert than Stephen, and together with this quality goes a different kind of interest, which leads him to consider the implication of what he sees in the light of his common knowledge of family life. He naturally puts himself in Mrs Breen's place. His attention is also less focussed than Stephen's. He digresses to consider the public danger of hatpins.

Interior monologue is convincing only if it does not give the reader the impression that it has been written for his benefit. This is one reason why it must seem undirected. Couched in the present tense, it gives the impression that there is no knowing what will come next. For the same reason, it must seem private. There is much that goes without saying, when one is talking to oneself. No doubt a recording of a stream of consciousness would be totally incoherent, and Joyce's rendering of it, in passages such as those just quoted, is more coherent than the real thing, just as dialogue in a play is more coherent than tape-recorded natural speech. Nevertheless by the substitution of phrases, exclamations, and telegraphese for complete sentences he does render this feature of a stream of consciousness convincingly. He also cunningly makes the interior monologue refer to features in the characters' lives which the reader is not immediately aware of, while the character takes them for granted. Thus, when Bloom sets out to buy a kidney for his breakfast he says to himself

Not there. In the trousers I left off. Must get it. Potato I have.
(67/59)

The reference to the potato is something the reader must wait a long time to understand. Joyce does not allow his concern for psychological realism, however, to cloud the reader's understanding too far. The immediately preceding sentence reads

On the door he felt in his pocket for the latchkey.

This sentence completely explains the first three observations.

This explanatory sentence, of course, is not part of Bloom's interior monologue, and it is important to realise that interior monologue does not monopolise the first half of the novel. Even when we are presented with the characters' own words, these often take the form of dialogue, not of monologue. The characters are not talking to themselves, but to other people. ('Aeolus' and 'Scylla and Charybdis', for example, are largely dialogue.) In addition, to set the scene solidly, or to explain what a character is talking to himself about, Joyce continually employs third-person narrative, as in the sentence just quoted. The style in which these narrative passages are written is often, as in *A Portrait*, a reflection of the consciousness of the character. As such, it blends so smoothly with the interior monologue that it can only be distinguished from it upon reflection. An example of this occurs in 'Proteus'.

The grainy sand had gone from under his feet. His boots trod again a damp crackling mast, razorshells, squeaking pebbles, that on the unnumbered pebbles beats, wood sieved by the shipworm, lost Armada. Unwholesome sandflats waited to suck his treading soles, breathing upward sewage breath. He coasted them, walking warily. A porter-bottle stood up, stogged to its waist, in the cakey sand dough. A sentinel: isle of dreadful thirst.
(50/46)

The vivid onomatopoeia with which this third-person narrative presents Stephen's sense impressions is not only Joyce's gift to the reader. It is also characteristic of Stephen's own interest in language. He is continually fusing words—as 'shipworm' in this passage, and invents phonetic equivalents for sounds. ('Listen: a fourworded wavespeech: seesoo, hrss, rsseeiss ooos'.) The narrative thus merges almost indistinguishably into the monologue, as it does at the end of this passage. 'Isle of dreadful thirst' has been strongly criticised for its emotional inflation. The criticism, however, should not be levied at Joyce: the text has slipped back to interior monologue, Stephen's own comment on what he sees. He is 'reading signatures', interpreting objects as symbols. (And in this case it is worth pointing out that his comment is not a romantic projection of private emotion, but a joke about Erin Isle's drink problem.)

A similar dramatic quality can be found in the narrative passages assigned to Bloom. Take the following

His heart astir he pushed in the door of the Burton restaurant. Stink gripped his trembling breath: pungent meatjuice, slop of greens. See the animals feed.

Men, men, men.

Perched on high stools by the bar, hats shoved back, at the tables calling for more bread no charge, swilling, wolfing gobfuls of sloppy food, their eyes bulging, wiping wetted moustaches. A pallid suetfaced young man polished his tumbler knife fork and spoon with his napkin. New set of microbes. A man with an infant's saucestained napkin tucked round him shovelled gurgling soup down his gullet. A man spitting back on his plate: halfmasticated gristle: no teeth to chewchewchew it. Chump chop from the grill. Bolting to get it over. Sad booser's eyes. Bitten off more than he can chew. Am I like that? See ourselves as others see us. Hungry man is an angry man. Working tooth and jaw. Don't! O! A bone! That last pagan king of Ireland Cormac in the schoolpoem choked himself at Sletty southward of the Boyne. Wonder what he was eating. Something galoptious. Saint Patrick converted him to Christianity. Couldn't swallow it all however.

– Roast beef and cabbage.

– One stew.

Smells of men. His gorge rose. Spaton sawdust, sweetish warmish cigarette smoke, reek of plug, spilt beer, men's beery piss, the stale of ferment.

Couldn't eat a morsel here. Fellow sharpening knife and fork, to eat all before him, old chap picking his tootles. Slight spasm, full, chewing the cud. Before and after. Grace after meals. Look on this picture then on that. Scoffing up stewgravy with sopping sippets of bread. Lick it off the plate, man! Get out of this.

(214/168)

Just as we can tell without effort that the last sentence is addressed by Bloom to himself, the one before it to a man wolfing his lunch, so also we can tell that certain sentences do not originate in Bloom at all, but are the work of a narrator—the first two sentences, for example, but not the third. The point of view of this narrator, however, is very close to that of the fictional character. The difference in language between them is not one of tone, despite Bloom's jokiness, except in so far as the more orthodox syntax of the narrative implies a more conscious attention to the reader's needs.

Nevertheless, there is here a wider gap than in the passage from 'Proteus' between the style of the narrative and that of the monologue. Bloom, like Stephen, is alive to the pleasures of language, but his manipulation of language takes a different form—of which the joke, 'Couldn't swallow it all however' is typical. The word 'astir', in the opening sentence, does not belong in his vocabulary. It is not, however, an idiosyncratic choice. It does not obtrude. Certain features, however, do obtrude, notably the attempt to give a verbal rendering of the acts of chewing and swallowing, which are in no way representative of Bloom's tricks with words. Here the style of the narrative is making its own distinct contribution to the text, as something quite separate from the style of the central character. The presentation of Bloom is, from the start, continuously subject to these intrusions. Bloom, for example would not have stopped to register the sound made by his cat in 'Calypso' as 'Mrkgnao'. The conventional 'miaow' would serve his turn, just as 'rippled' would have served to describe the movement of his bathwater, instead of the 'ripprippled' which the narrative supplies.

TECHNICS Considered as examples of stylistic intrusion, however, this onomatopoeia is merely the tip of an iceberg. Joyce's schemes of the novel included a list of 'technics' (Table 5, page 145). Some of these are not directed to the manner of writing displayed in the text. The Gilbert scheme, for example, allots 'catechism' both to 'Nestor' and to 'Ithaca', distinguishing them only by qualifying the former as personal and the latter as impersonal. This classification relates merely to the construction of the presentation, and suggests a resemblance which pays no attention to the extraordinary difference in style between the two chapters. Other entries, however, do relate to style as well as to construction. The technic of 'Lestrygonians', for example, is 'peristaltic prose'. Peristalsis is the wavelike, circular churning movement by means of which food is processed through the internal organs in the process of digestion. Joyce informed Budgen that he had spent a whole day on two sentences in this chapter, describing the emotion induced in Bloom as he looks into a shop-window displaying women's silk underclothing.

Perfume of embraces all him assailed. With hungered flesh

obscurely, he mutely craved to adore.

(214/168)

The selection of some of these words may seem precious, but upon examination it proves justified. 'Assailed' suggests the soft, silky nature of the assault, and 'hungered' (instead of 'hungry') implies the passive nature of the disturbance. What Joyce claimed to have spent the day on was not, however, the selection of these words but their arrangement, and here the idiosyncrasy is less easy to justify. It claims the reader's attention, but to what? The answer is that in its lack of active progression it enacts the automatic, undirected, mulling 'peristalsis' of the feeling, which although it is not paralysis is akin to it.

As such the language, while not a product—even a possible product—of Bloom's mind still renders it for the reader to inspect. The reader is not invited to consider the nature of the style for its own interest. The style is still providing for his interest in the character of Bloom.

The same defence cannot, however, be made of the division of 'Aeolus' into short sections, each of which carries its own headline in newspaper style. The technics assigned to this early chapter relate to rhetoric, and the chapter, as Joyce pointed out to Gilbert, exhibits a wide variety of rhetorical forms. This feature has its relevance to the wider interest of the chapter, although it distracts the reader's immediate interest from what is going on. The headlines can be justified in the same way, but their distracting effect is far more marked, and even adds a touch of mockery which seems pointless, at least as far as Bloom and Stephen are concerned, if not the journalists present.

The headlines were added to this chapter when Joyce was rewriting his novel for publication in book form, and they constitute an intrusion into the earlier part of the novel of procedures which came increasingly to preoccupy him in the second half. In the second half of the novel the reader's natural interest in Bloom and Stephen is badly provided for by the style, although that interest can survive the obstacles Joyce places in its way, to be finally satisfied. The style becomes increasingly bizarre, soliciting attention for its own sake. Slabs of language, sentences and phrases, were collected by Joyce in notebooks, to be inserted in due course in places that he found appropriate, marked in different coloured crayons to indicate their allocation. The resulting art, as Valéry Larbaud observed, was comparable with that of a worker in mosaic. It is certainly the opposite of the procedure of an explorer, following a stream of consciousness to its source, which is the method of the earlier chapters.

The chapters assembled in this industrious way, starting with 'Sirens', are all completely different from each other. All that they

have in common is their eccentricity, which is not invariably successful in engaging interest. There are passages of undeniable
boredom, others of unique entertainment and perspicacity. In 'Sirens'
the insidious mastery of song is presented, as affecting songs are sung
at the piano, by language which, besides featuring continual musical
references, is itself manipulated to produce musical effects.

> Miss Kennedy sauntered sadly from bright light, twining a
> loose hair behind an ear. Sauntering sadly, gold no more, she
> twisted twined a hair. Sadly she twined in sauntering gold hair
> behind a curving ear.
>
> (331/256)

It is churlishly pedantic to deny that this chapter carries the reading
of the entire action further, and that the stylistic innovations contribute to that effect. They widen the framework of the reader's
perception. This is also true of the satirical use of style in the next
chapter, 'Cyclops', where the Fenian bully is mocked by passages
which parody the flatulent forms of prose employed by the powers
that be or would be while the main action is narrated by an anonymous misanthropic barfly in his local idiom. Bloom is only magnified,
in the eyes of the reader, by the motiveless hostility which he inspires
in those present. Their style betrays them.

> – But it's no use, says he. Force, hatred, history, all that. That's
> not life for men and women, insult and hatred. And everybody
> knows that it's the very opposite of that that is really life.
> – What? says Alf.
> – Love, says Bloom. I mean the opposite of hatred. I must go
> now, says he to John Wyse. Just round to the court a moment
> to see if Martin is there. If he comes just say I'll be back in a second.
> Just a moment.
> Who's hindering you? And off he pops like greased lightning.
> – A new apostle to the gentiles, says the citizen. Universal love.
> – Well, says John Wyse, isn't that what we're told? Love your
> neighbours.
> – That chap? says the citizen. Beggar my neighbour is his
> motto. Love, Moya! He's a nice pattern of a Romeo and Juliet.

There follows a strange passage in which Joyce temporarily takes
over the narrative to give the venom of the company a concentrated
form which epitomises their contempt, after which, as if nothing
had happened, the barfly resumes his story.

> Love loves to love love. Nurse loves the new chemist. Constable
> 14A loves Mary Kelly. Gerty MacDowell loves the boy that has
> the bicycle. M. B. loves a fair gentleman. Li Chi Han lovey up
> kissy Cha Pu Chow. Jumbo, the elephant, loves Alice, the

elephant. Old Mr Verschoyle with the ear trumpet loves old Mrs Verschoyle with the turnedin eye. The man in the brown macintosh loves a lady who is dead. His Majesty the King loves Her Majesty the Queen. Mrs Norman W. Tupper loves officer Taylor. You love a certain person. And this person loves that other person because everybody loves somebody but God loves everybody.

– Well, Joe, says I, your very good health and song. More power, citizen.

(432/331)

Parody is also employed in 'Nausicaa', the next chapter. Here, as in Homer the perspicacity of a princess recognised a hero in the naked castaway Ulysses, the romanticism of Gerty induces her to see in Bloom one of the dark strangers who haunt the pages of the cheap fiction she reads. Much of the narrative is therefore conducted in the style of a cheap novelette, although with characteristic fluidity Joyce contrives to weave Gerty's own idiom among the literary cliches.

> Her hands were of finely veined alabaster with tapering fingers and as white as lemon juice and queen of ointments could make them though it was not true that she used to wear kid gloves in bed or take a milk footbath either. Bertha Supple told that once to Edy Boardman, a deliberate lie, when she was black out at daggers drawn with Gerty (the girl chums had of course their little tiffs from time to time like the rest of mortals) and she told her not let on whatever she did that it was her that told her or she'd never speak to her again.

(452/346)

It has been objected that this treatment is needlessly cruel in its mockery, but if the reader fails to feel sympathy for Gerty in this chapter (as Bloom quite finely does) the fault is probably his, rather than Joyce's. The same cannot, however, be said in defence of the effect of mockery produced by the parodies employed in 'Oxen of the Sun', the next chapter. This is the most notorious chapter in the book, because in it, on the pretext that a child is being born in the hospital where it occurs, Joyce offers nine successive sections of parody, recapitulating the history of English prose, to match the nine months of gestation. If the previous three chapters, by their styles, distracted the reader's attention from the personal interest of the actions in which the characters were engaged, this was only to refocus it on wider social and cultural implications. In this chapter, however, the parodies seem pointless. Certainly they do not support the theme of fecundity which it is intended to embody. On the contrary, the effect is one of mockery which undermines that theme.

Meanwhile the skill and patience of the physician had brought about a happy *accouchement*. It had been a weary weary while both for patient and doctor. All that surgical skill could do was done and the brave woman had manfully helped. She had. She had fought the good fight and now she was very very happy. Those who have passed on, who have gone before, are happy too as they gaze down and smile upon the touching scene. Reverently look at her as she reclines there with the motherlight in her eyes, that longing hunger for baby fingers (a pretty sight it is to see), in the first bloom of her new motherhood, breathing a silent prayer of thanksgiving to One above, the Universal Husband.

(550/417)

As the reader scorns the style, so he may scorn the message.

In the last four chapters attention is again focussed on the personalities of the characters. The first three of these chapters, however, do not resemble the first half of the novel, in which the reader's interest in those characters was first generated. In the case of 'Circe' it is obvious why this should be so. As it is concerned with material of which the characters are for the most part not conscious, it cannot be presented as their streams of consciousness. Instead it takes the form of a fantastic drama, returning at intervals to the events in the brothel, but mainly ignoring or holding the realistic action at a standstill, frozen, while a totally unrealistic and grotesque drama is enacted, expressing Stephen's and Bloom's deepest terrors and lusts, and involving a host of characters, living and dead, who are not physically present in the brothel at all. It might easily be said that Joyce allowed his inventiveness to run riot in this chapter, especially in connection with the hidden life of Bloom, but on the other hand it would be difficult to point to any detail which is not revealing. Bloom is spared nothing. It is not so much his palpitations that are disquieting as the way he wriggles. Joyce is relying on the reader's self-knowledge to restrain his condemnation. Certainly this chapter is not only a *tour-de-force*, opening up an entirely new literary method for later novelists, but also, in its context in *Ulysses*, an indispensable illumination.

By contrast 'Eumaeus', the next chapter, offers a fog of words. It is written in no style at all, because there is no principle governing the vocabulary or structure. The language is exhausted, tedious and ridden with clichés. What is worse it is confusing and unfocussed. Each sentence drags along until it comes to an inconclusive halt. As reading it produces weariness, it has been defended as a reflection of the two characters' state of mind, but this apology will not hold water. Bloom, for one, is excited by this opportunity for a heart-to-heart discussion with an intellectual, and keenly interested in the topics raised. Moreover an appreciative personal response is also developing in Stephen. By the end of the chapter, the two men are walking arm in arm. What this unfocussed style does produce is a sense of language as a medium, simply because it is such an imperfect medium itself. We still want to see what is happening, and Joyce forces us to peer through this fog to do so.

Again the style of the next chapter offers a total contrast. 'Ithaca' is unnaturally, clinically lucid and objective. It almost seems as if Joyce had adopted a style in which it *is* impossible to tell a lie. This effect is produced because so many of the questions, which it is concerned to answer, relate to such precise physical details as a catalogue of the books upon Bloom's shelves, or the effect upon the entire water supply of Dublin when he turns the tap on. Also included, however, are blankly worded reports of the characters' thoughts. We believe them too, because the focus is so entirely factual. The effect of the style is not confined to one of credibility, however. There is a continuous irony, resulting from the reader's interpreting the information he receives in a manner beyond the scope of the unsympathetic narrator. Thus, after Bloom has devised various plans to continue his aquaintance with Stephen, the question is asked:

> What rendered problematic for Bloom the realisation of these mutually selfexcluding propositions?
>
> The irreparability of the past: once at a performance of Albert Hengler's circus in the Rotunda, Rutland square, Dublin, an intuitive particoloured clown in quest of paternity had penetrated from the ring to a place in the auditorium where Bloom, solitary, was seated and had publicly declared to an exhilarated audience that he (Bloom) was his (the clown's) papa. The imprevidibility of the future: once in the summer of 1898 he (Bloom) had marked a florin (2s.) with three notches on the milled edge and tendered it in payment of an account due to and received by J. and T. Davy, family grocers, 1 Charlemont Mall, Grand Canal, for circulation on the waters of civic finance, for possible, circuitous or direct, return.

> Was the clown Bloom's son?
> No.

> Had Bloom's coin returned?
> Never.

(816/617)

Above all this, however, the style helps us to view the two men as minute parts in a universal system pursuing its inevitable course, an extension of the cosmic vision first expressed by the child Stephen, in *A Portrait*, when he wrote his name and universal address on the flyleaf of his geography book.

The final chapter, 'Penelope', marks a return to the stream of consciousness, but now this stream has only one bank. As Molly lies in bed, revolving past and future in her mind, external stimuli have almost, although not entirely, vanished. The resulting flow of associations is assisted by an absence of punctuation and logical connection, allowing it to pursue its own unimpeded current, plotted only by the recurrence of certain words, especially a reassuring but strictly illogical 'because' and the assured and welcoming 'yes' with which it starts and finishes. Despite its similarity with the opening chapters, this unlocalised chapter therefore does not constitute a simple return to realism. As Joyce indicated in his scheme (Table 2, p. 109), the action takes place out of time. It is not fixed, but floating.

A lack of fixity is also the key to the multiplicity of styles. It is meant to liberate the reader. The viewpoints of Stephen and Bloom, which shaped the initial chapters, were readily accepted by the reader because they were so like the reader's own view of reality. Both characters were moving in a world which he could recognise. Although the style was novel, he could quickly adjust himself to it, precisely because, once grasped, it proved so familiar in its effect. The function of the later styles is to deny him this comfortable conformity with his habitual sense of relevance and truth. The strain imposed upon him by adjusting to them is not just the result of their novelty. It is produced by the continual shifts in perspective which they enforce. This was Joyce's own explanation of his strange proceeding to an alarmed Miss Weaver. He wished to induce a sense of relativity, a realisation that no one viewpoint was adequate, because any way of seeing reality must also be a form of blindness to it. The various styles in the novel make provision for various sorts of interest, but in its entirety the novel also demonstrates that no one sort of interest can cope with everything there is to be interested in.

So far we have compared reading *Ulysses* with proceeding through a forest, but at this point the most useful comparison is that offered by Joyce himself in 'Proteus'. It is a protean book. We seize it to find out the nature of reality. Immediately it assumes a series of different shapes. The question to be answered is, if we hold on firmly to the end, does it tell us a final truth?

Table 5   Technics

TITLE	LINATI SCHEME	GILBERT SCHEME
I Telemachus	3- and 4-person dialogue Narration Soliloquy	Narrative (young)

2	Nestor	2-person dialogue Narration Soliloquy	Catechism (personal)
3	Proteus	Soliloquy	Monologue (male)
4	Calypso	2-person dialogue Soliloquy	Narrative (mature)
5	Lotuseaters	Dialogue Soliloquy Prayer	Narcissism
6	Hades	Narration Dialogue	Incubism
7	Aeolus	Deliberative oratory Forensic oratory Public oratory Tropes	Enthymemic
8	Lestrygonians	Peristaltic prose	Peristaltic
9	Scylla and Charybdis	Whirlpools	Dialectic
10	Wandering Rocks	Labyrinth moving between two banks	Labyrinth
11	Sirens	Fuga per canonem	Fuga per canonem
12	Cyclops	Alternating asymmetry	Gigantism
13	Nausicaa	Retrogressive progression	Tumescence–detumescence
14	Oxen of the Sun	Prose (embryo-foetus-birth)	Embryonic development
15	Circe	Vision animated to bursting point	Hallucination
16	Eumaeus	Relaxed prose	Narrative (old)
17	Ithaca	Dialogue Pacified style Fusion	Catechism (impersonal)
18	Penelope	Monologue Resigned style	Monologue (female)

Even now the outcry which greeted *Ulysses* upon publication has not entirely subsided. There are still public voices which would endorse the verdict of the *Sporting Times* reviewer who, in 1922, declared that the novel 'appears to have been written by a perverted lunatic who has made a speciality of the literature of the latrine'. Nor is it only on prudish grounds that the book has been condemned as harmful. There is a deeper objection. Joyce does not portray sex as a source of fulfilment. Bloom's sexual impulses constitute no source of joy, but rather a harassing predicament from which he seeks relief. The same attitude colours Joyce's treatment of other aspects of life. The world is not presented as an arena of fulfilment, but rather as a school of resignation. The best that we can hope for is to be pacified, as Bloom is pacified, by the recognition of necessity. This pessimistic view denies most human aspirations. A mature reader, whose respect for that patient character will have grown with his developing response, will not find Joyce's view of Bloom hostile or uncharitable. He must, however, agree that judged by generally accepted standards, if Bloom is to be regarded as Everyman, then Joyce's view of man is mean. The possibilities of life for Bloom are meagre. 'And so they are', would be quite simply the reply of Joyce, 'for you.'

His defence of *Ulysses* against the outcry it produced, was proudly to claim that it was true. If the book was not fit to read, he asserted, life was not fit to live. The main indictment which he had to answer related of course to his handling of sex. Regarding this, in a letter to Stanislaus while *Ulysses* was being written he announced:

> Anyway, my opinion is that if I put down a bucket into my own soul's well, sexual department, I draw up Griffith's and Ibsen's and Skeffington's and Bernard Vaughan's and St Aloysius' and Shelley's and Renan's water along with my own. And I am going to do that in my novel (inter alia) and plank the bucket down before the shades and substances above mentioned to see how they like it: and if they don't like it I can't help them. I am nauseated by their lying drivel about pure men and pure women and spiritual love and love for ever: blatant lying in the face of truth.

It was not, however, only about sex that society, in his view, insisted that writers must tell lies. He aimed to let fresh air in all round. Therefore nothing could have pleased him more than Bennett's report: 'James Joyce sticks at nothing, literally. He forbids himself no word. He says everything—everything. The code is smashed to bits.' As he saw it, the code must be smashed in order to give men a chance of such happiness as life had to offer. If, judged by the standards society imposed, his picture of life was disgusting, this only went to prove that those standards should be abandoned, because his picture, although unflattering, was true. His exposure of what he regarded as the actual condition of humanity was not however an indictment of humanity. For him the discrepancy between ideals and facts was a source of entertainment, in which his laugh was on the side of the sinners, not against them. It was against the falsehoods which they were expected to conform with. Human life need not be a nightmare, once history—that false account of mankind which men are taught from birth—had been stowed in a dustbin.

Accepting all this, however, we must ask into what sort of new world, awakening from the nightmare of history, Joyce invites us to emerge.

The aesthetic views of Stephen Dedalus entitle us to expect a picture of that world. Like Shakespeare, by achieving self-knowledge Joyce should be presenting us with a picture in which he shows us 'in the world without as actual what was in his world within as possible', a work of art in which the details are all radiant with some inner meaning, which makes sense of life. Viewed in the light of this expectation, *Ulysses* is disappointing. It lacks the integrity which Stephen Dedalus required of a work of art—and this, too, is a major scandal, a critical scandal. In any given place, so much is implied in the text that it cannot all be taken in at once. Similarly, considered in totality, the parts will not add up. 'Wholeness, harmony and radiance' are conspicuous by their absence. If *Ulysses* is like a forest we cannot see the forest for the trees.

The book is not, however, intended to be a realisation of Stephen's aspirations. If *Ulysses* lacks integrity, this lack itself is part of the design. As R. M. Adams observes: 'the meaningless is deeply inter-woven with the meaningful in the texture of the novel'. Thus Hely's sandwich-board men thread their way in and out of view from chapter to chapter, and the man in the macintosh makes inexplicable appearances. These invented details are inserted to add to the book's solid reality by the sheer contingency of their presence in it. Other features of the book can indeed be explained but only by research into obscure facts which would otherwise be completely inaccessible and which the reader cannot be supposed to know. In the words of Ellmann:

> Joyce's surface naturalism in *Ulysses* has many intricate supports and one of the most interesting is the blurred margin. He introduces much material which he does not intend to explain, so that his book, like life, gives the impression of having many threads that one cannot follow. For example, on the way to the funeral, the mourners catch sight of Reuben J. Dodd, and Mr Dedalus says,

'The devil break the hasp of his neck.' This reaction seems a little excessive unless we know that Dodd had lent money to Joyce's father . . .

(*James Joyce*, Oxford University Press)

These unexplained insertions deliberately disobey Stephen's requirement that all parts of a work of art should be perceived to cohere in a unified whole. A novel which met this requirement might be beautiful but, by the same token, in Joyce's view, it would falsify reality. Joyce had no intention of replacing the nightmare of history with another kind of dream. Accordingly the view of the world and its inhabitants which he presents is one of partial chaos. Both Stephen and Bloom are moving through 'the incertitude of the void'.

Stephen cannot stomach such a view. He seeks a meaning: his aim is to move 'from the known to the unknown'. Moving in the opposite direction—from the uncomfortable mysterious to the comfortably mundane, Bloom can digest chaos. He is too busily engaged in life to take a general view of it, and when he feels tempted in that direction (in 'Calypso') pulls himself up with the reminder: 'Well, I am here now.' His wisdom is that which Voltaire taught to Candide and Johnson to Rasselas. He gets on with the job of everyday living. As a moral exemplar it might, however, seem that he leaves much to be desired. As Peake reminds us:

> Onto Bloom are heaped all the attributes and conditions which our society most despises. He is a cuckold and a resigned one at that; he is in will, if not in deed, unfaithful, but resorts to masturbation rather than adultery; he has masochistic tendencies and other unacceptable sexual inclinations; he is often, even generally, lacking in spirit, and physically timid; he writes suggestive letters under a pseudonym; he is feebly ingratiating both to his dominant wife and to his contemptuous fellow citizens; his head is filled with ridiculous fancies, notions and hopes; socially, financially, maritally he is considered a failure; his bearing is such that newsboys mock it; racially he is an outcast, a renegade from his forefathers' race and religion, an unwelcome and unbelieving recruit to the race and religion of those who despise and humiliate him.

(*James Joyce: the Citizen and the Artist*, Arnold)

All this is true. It can only be said that any example we can hope to follow can only be one which leaves a lot to be desired. Additionally it can be claimed that Bloom's example has a lot to recommend it. He has Christian virtues—succouring the needy and helping his neighbour. He has the classic Aristotelian virtues of moderation, temperance and prudence, and the Stoic virtue of resignation.

Above all, what he has is vitality, which is why he ultimately wins the preference of Molly. This endorsement might not seem to amount to very much. She is piggish and vulgar, and although she also possesses more endearing qualities, moral discrimination is not one of them. Nevertheless, just as her faults do not in the end deny her the role of Penelope, so also she fulfils the role of Earth goddess which Joyce assigned to her, the vital force that keeps us going despite our failures. She loves life and ignores death. Bloom is her true husband because he lives to live another day.

Life, as Bloom lives it, is more than mere existence. He is continuously responsive, and can put himself in the place of others, as he puts himself imaginatively in the cat's place when we first see him, feeding it milk, regarding it 'curiously, kindly'. The phrase also describes Joyce's viewpoint, at least while he had his pen in hand. There are other parallels. *Polytropos* is Homer's epithet for *Ulysses*: 'a man of many resources'. Bloom is full of schemes, just as *Ulysses* deploys a multitude of literacy devices. Above all, perhaps, like Bloom Joyce continually finds things funny (a word found frequently in Bloom's vocabulary and Molly's, never in Stephen's).

It is sometimes claimed for Joyce that in *Ulysses* he placed the whole world between the covers of a book. In terms of a complete report, this claim does not bear examination. The novel hardly begins to offer even a complete picture of Dublin. The characters all belong to one narrow section of society, and their concerns are small. Nor can the claim be sustained on a metaphorical level. The impressive lists of symbols, arts and organs are not matched by an organised presentation of life in all its aspects. What Joyce did achieve, however, was a book which is very *like* life—full of meanings, but hard to understand, to be approached as Bloom would approach a room full of brutes—tentatively but not without hope. Despite all the critics and interpreters, in the end, like Bloom, we have to find our own way through it.

" SHAKESPEARE AND COMPANY "

— SYLVIA BEACH —

12, RUE DE L'ODÉON

PARIS (VIᵉ)

May

with a half a glare of his picky ham unde
the sky of his parallel brows.

my soamheis brother

am stophere

walk while you have the night
for the morn cometh wherein
every post shall sleep.

walk while you have the night
for morn. light breakfast bringer,
morroweth wherein every post
shall fall for sleep.

A sheet of working notes for Finnegans Wake, *in the author's hand*

5 Finnegans Wake

Surface and structure

Most people with an interest in modern literature have at least an inkling of the kind of thing they might find in *Finnegans Wake*, derived from some ingenious pun they have heard quoted. 'Young and easily freudened' is a general favourite. Approaching the text in hope of more entertainment of this sort they will not be entirely disappointed. Sticking their thumbs into Joyce's 'mess of mottage', they will pull out many a 'current pun'—'the hanging garments of Marylebone', for example—or a 'quashed quotato', such as: 'Lord heap miseries upon us yet entwine our arts with laughters low!' There are also memorable Celtic patterns of linked sounds, like: 'It's something fails us. First we feel. Then we fall.'

Such superficial plucking of the text does not, however, constitute reading it. We can enjoy these extracts without relating them to their context. There has never been another book whose context was so dense with implications. Yet when we attempt to make coherent sense of whole sentences, not to mention paragraphs, chapters, or the book in its entirety, we find the process less immediately rewarding and far more laborious. In each case the structure seems to have been specially devised to baffle comprehension. The sentences are often of enormous length, constructed clause within clause with each clause apparently an irrelevant digression, so that before he reaches the end of the sentence the reader has lost his way. Moreover, an unusually large part of the text is composed of exclamations, questions and lists, not to mention intermittent concoctions, each one hundred letters in length, representing claps of thunder.

If the reader found this difficult path strewn with nuggets of amusing word-play, he might find his labour more acceptable, but this is not what he finds. The word-play, at a first reading, seems more of an obsession than a means of expression. Varying in intensity, but never ceasing, for the most part it does not amuse. The reader soon realises that it is not Joyce's purpose to divert him with puns. Indeed the words are subjected to such dislocations that they are rarely acceptable as puns. They are strained to accommodate their double meanings, composite words deliberately knocked together, rather than felicitously significant verbal coincidences. Moreover, they make eccentric demands on the reader's knowledge. Some of their components have been taken not from English but from a wide selection of foreign tongues, including pidgin and Esperanto. Other elements contributing to their composition are the names of innumerable historical and fictitious personages, as also place names, with which even a highly literate person may not be acquainted. While several useful studies offer to help him to identify the resulting allusions, the reader is likely to be soon daunted, and demand to know why he should continue to apply to a recent work of fiction the skills which are normally required only in the deciphering of some exotic hieroglyph.

The answer is that the narrative of *Finnegans Wake* has a unique motivation. It is usual for a narrative to feature a set of distinct characters, involved in a series of distinct episodes, culminating in a definite conclusion. Such a narrative structure is the expression of a sense of life as an onward process, in which we either progress or regress. The sense of life embodied in *Finnegans Wake*, on the contrary, is of a process in which neither progress nor regress is possible. Life is a merry-go-round, in which the same characters and the same episodes come round again and again, borne on the same structure. For this reason they must be seen to coalesce. The words must suggest each other no less than they differ. The different characters must be recognisably the same. The circular structure must exhibit itself in the parts of the book no less than in its overall construction, whose own circularity is clinched by the way it opens half-way through a sentence, the beginning of which is the unfinished sentence with which it ends. Leaving aside for the moment the question whether the resulting achievement justifies the unorthodoxy of the material and its treatment, it must at least be granted that the unorthodoxy serves a purpose. The words, the characters, the episodes and the structures are all designed to coalesce.

The characters are defined not by their qualities but rather by their functions. There is a fixed pattern of relationships, which determines a set of roles. This pattern receives a stable embodiment in terms of family relationships, namely a mother and father, their twin sons and their daughter. The whole of human history, myth and ritual is presented in terms of this constant framework, which is localised in Chapelizod. Here we find the father, Humphrey Chimpden Earwicker, who keeps an inn. As a precarious representative of authority, he represents all father figures, as well as certain imposing geographical features which symbolise authority. His name is legion. His initials HCE stand also for 'Here Comes Everybody', and he is incarnated in a host of other characters, especially those, like Adam, or the Master-Builder, or even Humpty Dumpty, who suffered great falls and therefore stand—or lie—in need of resurrection. The eponymous Finnegan himself is such a character. He is the hero of a ballad who was killed as a result of a fall from a building on which he was at work as a hod-carrier, and whose corpse was resurrected when it was accidently splashed with whisky at the resulting wake.

HCE's wife, Anna Livia, is similarly a host of mutable but life-enhancing heroines as also a multitude of rivers, especially the Liffey. Their two sons, Shaun and Shem, represent all male oppositions such as Esau and Jacob, Brutus and Cassius, Abel and Cain, the ant and the grasshopper, De Valera and James Joyce—the one always a conformist, the other a rebel. Issy, the daughter with her dangerous charm, recalls in her person a string of *femmes fatales.*

Only their roles, however, are fixed. Even within this recognisable family the characters themselves coalesce. Issy's inevitable growth is towards motherhood. Anna Livia in her youth was herself a temptress. The son in due course will topple and replace the father. The mother, as her thoughts in old age return lovingly to her dead father, reverts to daughterhood. By a complementary process, the daughter has become the centre of the ageing father's affections. Even the characters involved in the basic family unit, therefore, are indistinct.

Nevertheless, this coalescence is the result of a change in their rôles. The rôles themselves are constant, and involve a series of episodes, some within the family and others involving the family's relationship with society at large, as Earwicker, being an inn-keeper, is also a public figure. These episodes are of more than one kind. There is a whole set of dynamic situations inherent in the given rôles. But the set is nevertheless finite—confrontation, reconciliation, seduction, trial and accusation, fall and resurrection. Fall and resurrection is the basic pattern. It is, of course, a circular pattern.

An example of this use of basic rôles is the story of 'The Prank-quean', which can easily and pleasurably be read as an introduction to the novel, as it is self-contained and entertaining. It occurs in the first chapter, pages 21 to 23. It is one of the episodes of confrontation and reconciliation but also incorporates a trial by riddle. This story reads like a fairy tale. Jarl van Hoother lives in a tower with his twin sons, Tristopher and Hilary, and a daughter, 'the dummy'. A mischievous fairy, the prankquean, appears three times within his gates. The first time, after asking Jarl a riddle which he cannot answer, she runs off with Tristopher. The second time, having returned Tristopher, and again asking a similar riddle, she kidnaps Hilary. The third time she brings Hilary back but is prevented from doing further mischief by the emission of a thunderous sound by Jarl van Hoother and the closing of the gate. This also results in her being caught in the home with the rest of the family and they all have tea (which Joyce told Miss Weaver in one of his letters was a fitting end for any story).

This story features all the roles. Jarl van Hoother is a version of

Family group in Paris in the 1920s. James and Giorgio Joyce standing, Lucia and Nora Joyce seated.

HCE, the not totally effective but also not totally negligible father figure. His Dutch name associates him with foreign rule, just as Earwicker himself is of Norse descent. Anna Livia features as the Prankquean, a source of instability, finally domesticated. The dummy is the dumb belle Issy, whose temptations are manifest in the story by the way in which, when she is left alone with one of her brothers, they misbehave together. Tristopher and Hilary represent the two twins. Their opposition is represented in their names, suggesting sorrow and joy.

Consideration of the twins leads to examination of the way in which not only characters but also structures repeat themselves. One of the structural principles of the book as a whole is provided by the philosophy of Giordano Bruno, whose motto was: 'In tristitia hilaris, hilaritate tristis' (Joyful in sorrow, sorrowful in grief). This is the principle of the complementarity, and ultimate unity, of opposites. In the course of the story each twin is converted by the prankquean, during his kidnapping, into his opposite. The sad Tristopher becomes a 'luderman' (i.e. a playboy). The gay Hilary becomes a 'tristian' (i.e. a believer in grief). This conversion, it should be noted, is registered by the inversion of their names. Tristopher becomes 'Toughtertrees', and Hilary becomes 'Larryhill'. Because they are twins yet also enemies, Shem and Shaun are the principal vehicles for Bruno's theory throughout the book. The theory, as illustrated in their relationship, is not only a factor in the structure of individual episodes and sections, but also of a continuous movement throughout the book. At first locked together in combat they are separated to be united in the middle of the novel in a composite son who challenges and overthrows the father figure—as Tristan, for example, winning Iseult from the aged Mark of Cornwall. Thereafter they again separate to be brought together again towards the end. The overall structure of their relationship is thus a figure eight.

The main structure of the novel, however, is cyclical, and derived from the philosophy of the eighteenth-century Italian philosopher, Giambattista Vico. The thunderous sound which accompanies Jarl van Hoother's re-establishment of order in his household is one of the one-hundred-letter thunder words already mentioned as a recurrent feature of the text. According to Vico it was a thunder-clap which initiated each of the successive cycles of human history. Interpreted as a threat from Heaven, it frightened mankind into abandoning the state of anarchy in which men had been living. A religiously regulated way of life ensued, to be followed in due course by an aristocratic period, in which order was arbitrarily enforced by heroic leaders. This in its turn gave way to a period of rational civic law, which again in its turn dissolved into a state of chaos, from which another clap of thunder eventually recalled mankind once more to order, and another cycle.

This Viconian scheme provides a sequence composed of three substantial stages followed by a dissolution. The overall structure of the novel follows the same sequence, with three main books followed by a final short one in which the characters collapse. The same structure is repeated in the chapters and episodes contained within the main structure. Thus, for example, the story of the prankquean consists of her three arrivals at the father's door, and ends with the collapse of that pattern of adventures into a new and inconsistent situation which will, in its turn, initiate a new series of confrontations. (We do not feel that, just because she is now resident with him, the prankquean will cease to provoke the vulnerable Jarl van Hoother.)

The characters, episodes and structure of the Prankquean story are thus all designed to coalesce with other corresponding features in the rest of the book. So also is the language. Take, for example, the word 'rain' which is used, apparently perversely, instead of 'ran'. This substitution hardly justifies itself locally as a significant pun. When the prankquean flees, we are told that 'she rain, rain, rain'. When she returns, the first time she 'started to rain', and the second time she 'started raining'. The reason for this is that throughout the novel the female principle is associated with water, including 'making water'. Thus we are told that when the riddling prankquean first appeared at Jarl van Hoother's stronghold, she 'made her wit'. The most persistent form taken by this association is with rivers, and in particular with the Liffey. Rivers, like people, run. Indeed 'riverrun' is the first word in the book. But rivers, as the last pages of the book insist, are part of a cyclical process whereby water from the sea rises to form clouds which precipitate water as rain in the hills, whence it flows back to the sea as a river. Rain is thus associated with the river's youth and the youth of women. Moreover in the household the woman also *reigns*. A prankquean must be regal. ('Let her rain now', says the ageing Anna Livia, thinking of her daughter, who, for good measure, is elsewhere referred to as 'the young reine'.)

This is not to suggest that structure, characters and language operate only to enforce the reader's sense of repetition and coalescence. They also serve to differentiate the separate parts of the novel. Vico's three stages are used to give a distinctive background— religious, heroic and civic respectively—to each of the three main books. The fields of allusions and references vary from chapter to chapter. The texture of the language itself varies in density. It is not consistent throughout. But these are only minor functions. Everything in the novel contributes overwhelmingly to a sense of fluctuating sameness.

Depth

A television screen converts a bombardment of particles into a picture. Joyce used this process as an explanation of his method in *Finnegans Wake*—an interesting example of his Bloom-like interest in new developments in science and technology. The unassisted reader, however, is more likely to find himself in the position of a new-born infant, bombarded with sense data in a blooming and buzzing confusion which it has not yet learned to convert into the sight of its mother's face and the sound of her voice. Even when equipped with a knowledge of the patterns which guided Joyce in disposing his particles of language, the reader often finds himself at a loss to recognise them. For Joyce himself the pattern was clear. After some initial experiments, he developed a solid sense of the work as a whole, expressing itself microcosmically in its parts, and macrocosmically in its total structure. In the words of A. Walton Litz, 'he held the incredibly complex form of the *Wake* in his mind in a single image, and could move from one section to another with complete freedom' (*The Art of James Joyce*). He worked from notebooks packed with verbal fragments, each with its allotted place— or at least area—in the design, indicated, as in the case of the material of *Ulysses*, by a coded colour sign. For the reader to make out Joyce's design in the finished product, however, is a different matter.

The outlines sketched in the previous sections do not feature so boldly in the text. In any case, they are only the most salient of a multitude of interlocking schemes. The cycle of fall and resurrection, for example, is also represented in terms of various myths of rebirth, upon which the text draws freely, as also upon the accompanying rituals. Various schemes that, with minor variations, incorporate a sequential pattern similar to Vico's are also drawn upon for contributions. For example, from Hinduism and Theosophy Joyce borrows an alternative cycle of four ages, which can readily be adjusted to the Viconian cycle of three plus one. He also draws upon the Hindu sacred syllable AUM, whose three syllables demarcate a cycle in the breathing of a yogi. A, the out-breath, represents Brahma, the creator; U, the pause after the out-breath, represents Vishnu, the preserver, who keeps things in place for a season; M, the in-breath, represents Shiva, the destroyer, who annihilates them, taking them back to the creator. An unmarked interval follows, in which the breath is retained before the cycle starts again. Here again, therefore, we have the form of a Viconian cycle. Another natural cycle is the passage of twenty-four hours, from sunrise to sunrise. This too is incorporated in the time scheme of the book, but, because schemes interlock so readily, other time schemes are also applicable—the cycle of a week, and the cycle of a liturgical year ending at dawn on Easter Day immediately before the Resurrection.

This multiplicity of schemes makes for confusion. There is, however, a more formidable obstruction to the clear perception of any general outlines, namely the words. The coalescence in single words of various meanings—none of which is prohibited by its context—inevitably impedes unequivocal recognition of plain sense. 'Who is who when everybody is somebody else' is the heading given by Adaline Glasheen to a tabulated list of characters in her *Census of Finnegans Wake*. It is not only that the personages involved in the text are so many that her book is as big as a biographical dictionary. Even when they have been located, they cannot always be decisively pinned down as versions of the father, or of this twin or that, so that their place in the basic pattern still remains doubtful. Students of Joyce tend to tackle these and kindred problems by applying themselves to Joyce's sources, work-books, early drafts, letters and recorded observations. In other words, they treat them more as historical than as critical questions, as if despairing of the text itself. Or if the text itself is applied to, it is used more as archaeological evidence than as literature. Finding that four stones which he has unearthed, when connected by straight lines, produce a rectangle, an archaeologist may argue that he has located a building. So Clive Hart, in *Structure and Motif in 'Finnegans Wake'*, contends that one of the forms in which the opposition of the two twins is expressed is spatial: one twin moves around the world in a West–East direction, the other South–North. These different directions have their significance in Irish history: voluntary emigration to America, compulsory transportation to Australia. The evidence, however, is buried in the form of scattered place names, intermittently referred to in the text.

Not that this makes the theory implausible. On the contrary, another comparison contained in the novel to explain its nature is that of an archaeological dig. The point is that with a text of this description the reader is involved in a question even more vital than 'Who is who?', namely 'What are they all doing, and why?' For example, the outline of the story of the Prankquean given in the previous section is not something the reader who turns to it will find staring him in the face. It is overgrown with puzzling details, whose eventual elucidation will not serve to make things any simpler. Thus the prankquean is referred to as 'her grace o'malice'; the phrase is perhaps suggestive in itself, and the word 'grace' is noticeably recurrent throughout the novel, sometimes recalling this episode. Three hundred pages later, for example, we read how a character 'fell from grace so madly'. The echo in this later phrase of 'grace o'malice' does not seem fortuitous when we learn of the existence of a sixteenth-century woman pirate, Grace O'Malley, who kidnapped the little son of the earl of Howth from Howth Castle, to teach him a lesson in manners. (Jarl van Hoother's title 'van Hoother', of course, gives him the lordship of Howth.) Thus details reach out to one another and connections proliferate throughout the novel, obscuring the main structure like ivy.

To continue with this particular tendril, sometimes the reference depends upon the external support of a well known phrase, like 'Grace Abounding', which is well suited to the Prankquean. 'Goodness gracious' enables Joyce to describe the 'bedroom eyes' of the temptress—'gooseys gazious'—and also to associate her with divinity by transforming 'goodness' into 'goddess'. Other allusions are internal, as when reminscences of HCE include 'the O'Moyly gracies . . . playing him pranks'. The theological concept of divine grace is, of course, intrinsic to the theme of resurrection of the fallen man which is central to the book, and 'Anna' means 'grace', so that Grace O'Malley is an incarnation of Anna Livia. The remission of sin is 'Grace's Mamnesty', a phrase which requires us to take note that one term used to refer to the novel is 'mamafesta'. Countless connections of this kind range throughout the text, establishing paths which criss-cross to confuse any attempt to trace a main route through it. There are so many intersections. Indeed, every word is a point of intersection.

Wyndham Lewis has a useful recollection of a conversation with Joyce.

> We were talking once, I remember, when I first got to know him, about the cathedral at Rouen; its heavily encumbered façade. I had said I did not like it, rather as Indian or Indonesian sacred buildings are a fussy multiplication of accents, demonstrating a belief in the virtue of quantity, I said. All such quantitative expression I have at all times found boring, I pointed out. I continued to talk against Gothic altogether, and its 'scholasticism in stone': the dissolving of the solid shell—the spatial intemperance, the nervous multiplication of detail. Joyce listened and then remarked that he, on the contrary, liked this multiplication of detail, adding that he himself, as a matter of fact, in words, did something of that sort . . .
>
> (*Rude Assignment*, Hutchinson 1950)

Lewis objects to a work like Rouen cathedral because it swarms with such detail that it is impossible to see its form. This comparison is a useful one, but it is not a fair one. If we could take in the whole of *Finnegans Wake* at one time like a façade, seeing all its details simultaneously, and how they fit—the way in which Litz suggests that Joyce himself saw his entire work as 'a single image'—then the details might be seen to be something more than elaboration. They might be seen to be consistently linked by traceable motifs, to compose an integrated whole. The problem facing the reader is precisely the impossibility of perceiving *Finnegans Wake* in this spatial manner. He has to read it sentence by sentence, one after another. His perception of the text is subject to the modality of time. Reading the text is an exercise in memory.

Of course this is true of any work of literature. Reading a detective novel, for example, we have to remember who the characters are, what evidence they have given of their motives, where they were at given times, and so on. In the case of a work in which internal symbols are employed—as in *Ulysses*—we have to remember much more than that, recalling, for example, when we meet a dog in the story, the previous occasions on which a dog appeared. In the case of *Finnegans Wake*, this task becomes impossible. We have to remember not only the appearance of images but the appearance of individual words, and, individual though the words unquestionably are, this cannot be done (although the reader will find Clive Hart's *Concordance* helpful).

Nevertheless, memory is the means whereby we do overcome the tyranny of time. Thanks to memory we can escape the 'ineluctable modality', which is the subject of Stephen's meditations in 'Proteus'. We are no longer constrained to perceive together only those objects which present themselves together. In memory we can also perceive together objects which originally presented themselves at intervals. In his *Time and Western Man* (Chatto and Windus, 1927), Lewis grouped Joyce with those writers whom he condemned for undermining western civilisation by dissolving solid shapes in a temporal flux. Accordingly Lewis features in *Finnegans Wake* as an incarnation of Shaun, the conformist opponent of his rebellious twin brother, Shem the Penman. The most noteworthy of the encounters between these two, which has direct reference to Lewis, occurs in Joyce's version of the fable of the grasshopper and the ant. (In view of our interest in Grace O'Malley, it is worth recording here that 'grasshopper' is rendered in the fable as 'gracehopper'.) In Joyce's version the ant champions space against time as well as prudence against improvidence. Although subject to criticism, the grasshopper makes a point on its own behalf in the course of their exchanges.

> Your genus its worldwide, your spacest sublime!
> But, Holy Saltmartin, why can't you beat time?

While making inordinate demands upon the reader's memory, *Finnegans Wake* also offers him a unique opportunity to do just that —to beat time (i.e. defeat it).

The text affords this opportunity because it operates a pattern modelled upon the deepest mechanism of the mind, a pattern which, although it is verbal, is illogical. The first principle of formal logic is the Law of Identity, which postulates that everything is what it is, and not another thing. Of course, not all our discourse is strictly logical. In a sense we break the Law of Identity every time we use a metaphor. The more we do this, the more our use of language approximates to what Freud called 'the primary processes' of the mind. These processes, as Freud describes them, correspond with the basic literary devices of 'metaphor' (i.e. substituting one object for another which resembles it) and 'metonymy' (i.e. denoting one object by another with which it is associated). In symbolism these devices were carried as far as language seemed capable of taking them, until Joyce wrote *Finnegans Wake*.

According to Freud, the primary processes of the mind dispense with language and use images directly. They are thus much freer to fuse one meaning with another, because, although we use metaphor or metonymy we are still subject to the Law of Identity in respect of our use of words. However freely we allow ourselves to consider one object as another, we still persist in considering each word we use as being itself and not another word. This, manifestly, is not the case with words devised by Joyce for use in *Finnegans Wake*. In this connection it is notable that there was one use which, according to Freud, the primary processes did make of language. This is that use which operates by ignoring the Law of Identity, namely the pun. A pun occurs when two words accidentally collide. (A 'collideroscope' is another of Joyce's descriptions of *Finnegans Wake*.) Thus, thanks to a pun, a dreamer the subject of whose dream is a match, meaning a marriage, may dream of a match in a box of matches. The pun, Joyce declared, is mightier than the word. As we have noted, his words are rarely pure puns. They are composite words. Their function is nevertheless identical with that of the pun. They serve to produce a coalescence of logically unrelated meanings.

All this, it may be objected, is very well, but we have already admitted that the only person who could grasp these connections in their entirety was Joyce himself the author—in this resembling in a unique manner God the Creator, with whom the youthful Stephen compared him in *A Portrait of the Artist*. However widely the reader calls upon the assistance of commentators he cannot remember it all. As he reads the most he can achieve is hints of recognition, glimmerings of allusion. *Finnegans Wake* is a dream indeed. Even for the most alert of readers, like Bottom's dream it has no bottom. But this, precisely, is its value. The reader perceives it as Strether, in Henry James's *The Ambassadors*, saw Paris.

It hung before him this morning, the vast bright Babylon, like some huge iridescent object, a jewel brilliant and hard in which parts were not to be discriminated nor differences comfortably marked. It twinkled and trembled and melted together, and what seemed all surface one moment seemed all depth the next.

There is even a moral to be learnt from this interesting vision. It is not be found in the works of Vico or Bruno. As Joyce explained in a letter to Miss Weaver, although he personally found their ideas congenial, in his book he was only 'using them for all they [were] worth.' What they were worth was to supply a framework for his glittering bauble. In the book itself he offers clearer explanations. One of them reads as follows.

in this scherzarade of one's thousand one nightinesses that sword of certainty which would indentifide the body never falls . . .

Taken in one sense this is simply a statement about the text, pointing out the impossibility of being certain of the meaning of its words, but it can also be read as a truth about life which the text enacts as it is read. Scheherazade narrated the stories of *The Thousand and One Nights* to postpone her execution. The suggestion is that this is how we live too, telling ourselves a sequence of vague stories which are all about the self-same naughtiness. The stories therefore all have the same meaning, as charades offer clues to a word whose identity they conceal. Our inability to spell out the word constitutes our reprieve, in so far as the state of suspense in which Damocles existed in Hades can be so regarded: it was also a punishment. Such is the intrinsically doubtful consolation Joyce, in his mature scepticism, has to offer us. We can never be certain of the meaning of life, and as long as our uncertainty lasts we escape the calamity of being identified. His word is 'indentifide', which serves to define the identification. If we substitute a faith (fides) for our hesitancy (a key word in *Finnegans Wake*), its summons (indent) will put an end to us in the very moment that it relieves us of suspense. The moral is simple. While there's doubt there's hope.

6 The modernity of Joyce

No single work has exercised more influence on the development of the novel in the twentieth century than *Ulysses*. This influence operated in more than one direction. One of these was to reinforce the tradition of realism which it so painstakingly exemplified in its documentation of everyday life in Dublin, and so outrageously in its defiance of proprieties. Writers with a strong sense of social responsibility were encouraged by Joyce's example to persevere with novels in which narrative interest was subordinate to accurate reporting. One such was James T. Farrell, whose Studs Lonigan trilogy (1932–35) recorded the mean minutiae of a depressed existence no less painstakingly and far more painfully than *Ulysses* does. Another American trilogy—*USA* (1937) by John Dos Passos— in its 'Camera-eye' interludes even adapts some of Joyce's stylistic innovations to these traditional uses.

In general, however, Joyce's innovations were adopted by novelists in revolt against the constraints of the tradition of realism, which they regarded as incapable of rendering human experience in its full depth. Their emphasis on the subjectivity of experience naturally led them to adopt interior monologue. As Joyce himself insisted, interior monologue was not his invention, and had first been employed by a Symbolist of the previous generation, Emile Dujardin. Nor was he the first writer in the history of the novel to employ multiple perspective, symbolism, or a mythological framework. Nevertheless it was largely due to the impact of *Ulysses*, which made use of all these methods, that novelists began to experiment with them in the twenties and thirties.

Virginia Woolf, the most celebrated exponent of interior monologue, found *Ulysses* offensive but was also fascinated by it. Its influence upon her writing is unquestionable. She had already read the early serialised chapters of Joyce's work in 1918, before she began work upon her first distinctive novel, *Jacob's Room* (1922). *Mrs Dalloway* (1925), the first of her novels to make continuous use of interior monologue, also bears a structural resemblance to *Ulysses*, dealing as it does with the casual experiences of two unconnected characters, living through the same day in the same vividly presented city.

It was a poet, not a novelist, who first acclaimed Joyce's device of imposing a traditional myth upon a rendering of contemporary experience. This, T.S. Eliot declared, had 'the importance of a scientific discovery'. The modern writer's problem was that there was no currently accepted scheme which he could use to organise the chaos of modern life and give it shape. Myths, however, though no longer believed in were still current among the literate, thus offering an eternal pattern in which to arrange the fragments of experience which were all that we had left: He himself applied this method in *The Waste Land* (1922). In the novel the same influence is manifest in the work of the Austrian novelist Hermann Broch. In his trilogy *The Sleepwalkers* (1928–31) a set of characters are seen, all unwittingly, to be governed in their lives by a timeless pattern which manifests itself in the novel through leitmotivs and symbols.

The use of a mythological pattern in a novel need not, however, imply a belief that it corresponds to a force which is causally at work in everyday life. As we have seen, it is unlikely that Joyce himself believed in the factual existence of such mechanisms. His procedure was similar to that of Thomas Mann in *Doctor Faustus* (1947), where the myth serves as a comment on the story by offering an equivalent. In general the use of myth became a trick of the trade, serving as a substitute for plot. By 1963 John Updike could even offer to assist interpreters by appending a 'Mythological Index' to his novel *The Centaur*—no less a sign of Joyce's influence if it is taken as a joke than if it is taken seriously.

Symbolism of course was a well-established feature of imaginative literature long before Joyce began to write. His innovation, with which he was already experimenting in *Dubliners*, was the fusion of symbolism with realism. Probably the cinema has done more than Joyce to train readers to interpret everyday objects as symbols. It was, however, from Joyce that many novelists acquired this device— notably Malcolm Lowry, whose *Under the Volcano* (1947) employs features of the Mexican landscape as symbols for features of the hero's consciousness. This novel also is shot through with repeated phrases and other recurrent items used as leitmotivs.

Perhaps Joyce's most fundamental experiment in *Ulysses* was in the use of multiple perspectives. The reader sees the action from various points of view, none of which solicits his wholehearted endorsement. Pre-eminent among the next generation of novels which inherited this relativism was William Faulkner's *The Sound and the Fury* (1929), of which R.M. Adams remarks (in *After Joyce*, Oxford University Press, 1977): 'Faulkner's masterpiece isn't . . . in any sense a Joycean imitation, though it's clearly a book which, without the example of Joyce, would not have taken anything like its present form.' When it comes to the question of imitating *Ulysses*, however, the first thing to be said is that none of Joyce's successors attempted to compose a work of anything like the same complexity. His structure was used as a quarry, but remains as unique today as it was on the day it was first published.

The influence of *Ulysses* was not, however, exhausted in the example it afforded to novelists aiming at a break with realism. It also exhibits a feature which anticipated, and has therefore influenced, a more recent and far more subversive development. This development is the diversion of the reader's attention away from the story by concentrating it upon the way in which the novel is written. The theory which underlies this apparent perversity is a distrust of language arising from a concern with truth. Even an attempt to narrate events which actually occurred is doomed to end in fiction, because language inevitably falsifies experience. The novel is an ideal instrument to make this clear, if the novelist is prepared to advertise instead of concealing the artificial nature of his work. From this point of view Laurence Sterne (a writer from whom Joyce himself claimed descent) appears to be the model novelist, never allowing his reader to lose sight of the fact that he is holding a book in his hand, and continually reminding him that there is all the difference in the world between living a life and telling the story of one.

This post-war movement has had little effect upon British novelists. The reader of Anthony Powell or Kingsley Amis, for example, finds his attention held by the events they portray, not by the manner in which they portray them, although in the work of Iris Murdoch and John Fowles we do detect a refusal to entertain our sense of reality to the full. The sense that what we are reading is palpable fiction is, however, more deliberately entertained abroad. In America, for example, the infinitely complicated plot of Thomas Pynchon's *V* (1961), and the elaborate pastiche and parody of John Barth's *The Sot-weed Factor* (1960) defy the reader to suspend his disbelief no matter how willing he may be to do so. Perhaps the best example of this kind of fiction is Vladimir Nabokov's *Pale Fire* (1962), where the attention is continually engaged by distracting word-games and odd correspondences. Footnotes and comments on an autobiographical poem by one fictitious character are supplied by another, whose own reminiscences sound fictitious even in the context of the fiction. The work of the Argentinian Jorge Luis Borges operates in the same way, forcing the reader to abandon and question his sense of reality.

One result of this development has been a belated interest in the work of the Irish novelist Flann O'Brien, a devoted admirer of Joyce, who approved of him in return. In his *At Swim-Two-Birds* (1939) O'Brien observes: 'A satisfactory novel should be a self-evident sham to which the reader could regulate at will the degree of his credulity.' Joyce marked this passage in his copy of the book, and certainly *Finnegans Wake* fully meets its requirements. Nobody could read it as if it were a window on the world. Its stained glass is not designed to be seen through, but rather to be appreciated for its own sake. Just as a piece of pure music does not engage the listener with its resemblance to a storm at sea or a Persian market, so Joyce's last work does not engage the reader with a view of family life or the battle of Balaclava, although both items are objects of reference in it. The reader is engaged instead by the puzzle and pattern of its language.

Although the band of *Finnegans Wake's* admirers is continuously growing, no novelist has yet attempted to adopt its innovations. It cannot therefore be regarded as a direct influence on the recent development under discussion. *Ulysses*, however, is undoubtedly such an influence, especially its second half, which is written in a variety of styles calculated not to make the reader feel that he is reading the truth but rather to despair (quite rightly) of ever reading it. Thick screens of verbiage obscure the reader's view of the behaviour of the character. His attention is continuously claimed not by the events narrated in the novel but rather by the obtrusive manner of the writing. This feature of Joyce's novel has both contributed to the approach to fiction exemplified by novelists like Nabokov, and also earned increased appreciation with the development of that approach. Those critics who regard literature as a medium to make us more conscious of the restraints imposed on consciousness by language were, after all, anticipated by the youthful Stephen Dedalus when, in the opening years of the twentieth century, he informed Davin that language was one of the nets which had been spread to ensnare his soul.

Unlike his successors, however, Joyce does not link this linguistic intrusion with a diminution of credibility. Despite the obtrusive style, the reader of the later chapters of *Ulysses* still believes in the reality of the narrated events. The earlier chapters establish our personal interest in Bloom and Stephen on such a solid foundation that the later, flimsier artifice, while trying our belief still fails to shake it—except possibly in the 'Oxen of the Sun' chapter. In this connection it is worth noting that Joyce never takes steps to undermine the consistency of his narrative, as do some of his successors—Samuel Beckett, for example, in *Molloy* (1950). Here we have an account of his adventures, written by one of the characters, which ends at the point where he started to write it, quoting its own opening words, and declaring them to be false. The narrative thus undermines its own credibility. Certain minor contradictions and impossibilities have been detected in *Ulysses*, and it has been suggested that they are attempts by Joyce to produce a similar effect. If so, however, they are strangely inept for they are almost imperceptible. How many readers have noted with surprise that Bloom's chest measurement is given as a mere twenty-eight inches? Such discrepancies are the product of carelessness, not art. What is remarkable about *Ulysses* is the continuous effort made right through to the end to ensure conformity with material facts. Joyce may have had one foot well forward with the avant-garde, but he kept his other foot solidly planted in the camp of old-fashioned truth-to-life. The function of the bizarre writing is to supply an unfamiliar perspective on a very solid image of reality.

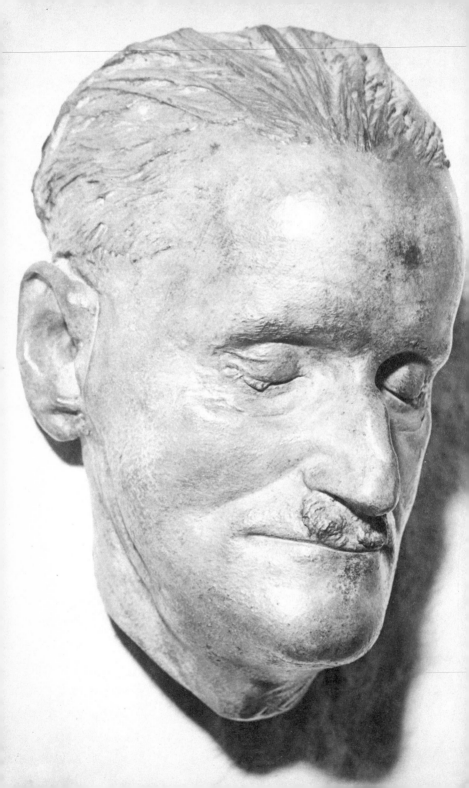

In performing this function they anticipate yet another recent development of the novel, the work of a group of French writers associated with what is simply known as 'The New Novel'. Their ambition, like Joyce's, is to awaken us from the nightmare of history. Humanity, as they like Joyce see it, is imprisoned in an old old story which impairs its vision. We see things the way we have been trained to see them, and cannot imagine there is any other way. To free us from this imprisonment novelists like Alain Robbe-Grillet, Michel Butor and Claude Simon offer us remarkably detailed, concrete representations of events involving human beings but bereft of normal human interest. They acknowledge Joyce as a major pre-cursor, and many sections of *Ulysses*, especially the 'Ithaca' chapter, anticipate their methods. The effect of Joyce's non-human perspec-tives is, however, markedly different from theirs. His break with tradition is comparatively superficial.

According to Robbe-Grillet, human nature is a myth. From the cradle to the grave we are told tales about creatures called men, rather as we are told tales about fairies and dragons, except that in the case of men we are informed by the story-tellers that these beings actually exist and indeed that we ourselves belong to the species. In point of fact, however, there are no such creatures. Consequently when they have stories to tell about creatures like us the New Novelists feel called upon to make it abundantly clear that they are not offering their readers yet another lying fairy-tale about mythical beings. And indeed a novel like Robbe-Grillet's *Jealousy* (1957) has no more resemblance to other novels than it has to a fairy-tale. The myth of human nature, which teaches us to believe in the existence of typical characters with conventional hopes and fears, is banished from it.

This is certainly not the case with Joyce. We have only to consider Joyce's sense of humour—a feature notably absent from the 'New Novel'—to see how traditional his view of human nature is. It depends upon myths, in a way very similar to that in which music-hall jokes depend upon them. 'Gilbert the Filbert' sounds like a typical Joycean minor character. Much of the entertainment which he has to offer us is based, quite simply, on the affectionate recognition of stock types. Obviously true of *Finnegans Wake*, this statement also holds good for *Ulysses*, where it is by drawing on long-established folklore that Joyce establishes a character with a name like 'Nosey Flynn'. And this is not true only of minor characters. The major characters are filled in with enormous detail, but this detail does not modify the simple lines on which they are constructed. Joyce springs no psychological surprises on us, as Proust and Dostoevsky do. We recognise the kind of people we have to deal with in his books as soon as we meet them, and do not have to alter our first impressions

Joyce's death mask

in the light of subsequent developments, interested though we are to find out what will become of them.

Wyndham Lewis complained that all Joyce's characters were stereotyped. In a sense this is true. Even Stephen Dedalus conforms to an established type. It was not by providing new insights into human nature that Joyce proved his genius, in this respect, but by demonstrating the unsuspected range of comprehension offered by commonplace wisdom, expansively applied. Jung admiringly confessed that he had learnt much about female psychology from Molly Bloom's soliloquy, yet there is nothing in the twists and turns of Molly's mind to surprise the common reader. Only Joyce would invent—or record—such a copious supply of responses. No sooner does he encounter them, however, than the reader recognises them as characteristic. The characters reveal no unsuspected depths. Not the least of the achievements of *Ulysses* is this demonstration of how illuminating common sense can be. The function of art, according to Joyce's youthful aesthetic, was to enable us to contemplate what we have actually got and find it satisfactory. In due course he forged in the smithy of his soul the uncreated conscience of the twentieth-century city-dweller, and found him to be a 'competent citizen', working his way 'from the unknown to the known', undaunted by what Stephen calls 'those big words that make us so unhappy'.

The motto of the City of Dublin is *Obedientia civium urbis felicitas* (the obedience of the citizens constitutes the happiness of the city). Variously transformed it haunts the pages of *Finnegans Wake*, where *obedientia* is rendered as 'hearsomeness', 'obesity', 'boxaneness', 'obeisance', and 'ubideintia' (i.e. 'where-godliness'). If we read it as all adding up to conformity we can almost take Dublin's motto as an expression of Joyce's improbable moral. For, as *Finnegans Wake* points out, U and I are both to be found in Dublin. Indeed, everybody lives there.

Milton Hebald's sculpture over Joyce's grave in Zürich

Part Three
Reference Section

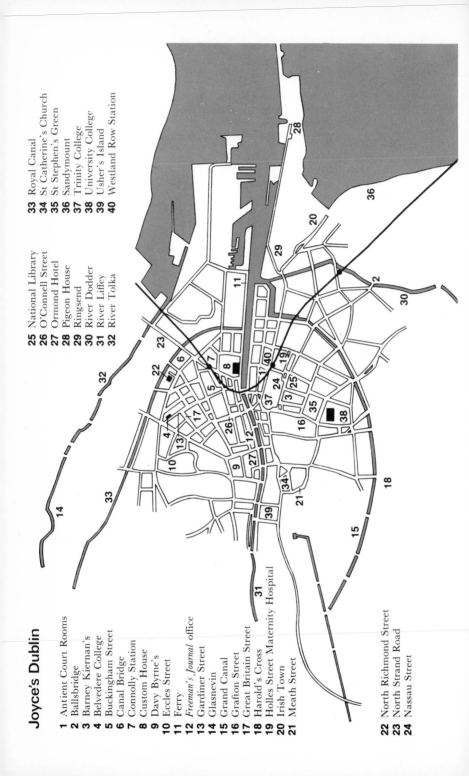

Joyce's Dublin

1 Antient Court Rooms
2 Ballsbridge
3 Barney Kiernan's
4 Belvedere College
5 Buckingham Street
6 Canal Bridge
7 Connolly Station
8 Custom House
9 Davy Byrne's
10 Eccles Street
11 Ferry
12 *Freeman's Journal* office
13 Gardiner Street
14 Glasnevin
15 Grand Canal
16 Grafton Street
17 Great Britain Street
18 Harold's Cross
19 Holles Street Maternity Hospital
20 Irish Town
21 Meath Street

22 North Richmond Street
23 North Strand Road
24 Nassau Street

25 National Library
26 O'Connell Street
27 Ormond Hotel
28 Pigeon House
29 Ringsend
30 River Dodder
31 River Liffey
32 River Tolka

33 Royal Canal
34 St Catherine's Church
35 St Stephen's Green
36 Sandymount
37 Trinity College
38 University College
39 Usher's Island
40 Westland Row Station

Topographical

James Joyce was not a man to leave his mark upon a place. He lived in too many places for any of them to qualify as a centre of literary pilgrimage, like Haworth Parsonage, or—to mention a comparison he would himself have welcomed—Shakespeare's birthplace. The nearest thing to such a landmark to be found on his track through life is the Martello tower at Sandycove. In point of fact, however, Joyce lived there for only a few days, and it is celebrated for the part it played in his fiction rather than in his life.

If Joyce, however, did not leave his mark on places, they left their mark on him. In this connection it is easy to underestimate the effect upon his mind of his residence on the Continent, where almost all his work was written. Trieste, Rome, Zürich and Paris all played their parts in relaxing and enriching his attitudes. The attitude which mattered aesthetically, however, was his attitude to the city he had left behind, and it is therefore in Dublin that the places of significant interest to a student of Joyce's work are to be found.

Finnegans Wake—or at least the dream within it—ranges all over the world, but the central hero of the dream is located in Chapelizod, just outside the city. As for the rest of Joyce's work, it is astonishing how much of the scene is set in central Dublin. Parallel with Joyce's own childhood, *A Portrait* starts outside the city, with scenes at Clongowes Wood Academy, and the homes in Rathgar, Bray and Blackrock which were a feature of John Joyce's more prosperous days. Thereafter, however, apart from the visit to Cork, the scene of action is the small area represented in the map on page 174 (although it would have to be extended eastward a little to take in the Bull Wall). All but two of the stories in *Dubliners* are similarly located, as is also the entire action of *Ulysses* in which Bloom takes part.

Larger scale maps—such as are provided with *A Topographical Guide to James Joyce's 'Ulysses'* by Clive Hart and Leo Knuth (*A Wake Newslitter*, 1975)—reveal Joyce's punctilious observance of the restraints of space and time. This is most striking in 'Wandering Rocks', which correlates the movements of various groups and individuals over a precise area, giving the overall impression of an animated map. Many stories in *Dubliners* share in this characteristic. If the characters are walking through the streets we are told exactly where they have come from and where they are going, and, as they make their way we can see the route by which they are getting there. 'If that fellow was dropped in the Sahara', John Joyce said of his eldest son, 'he'd sit, be God, and make a map of it.'

This does not, however, mean that the reader can go and view for himself the scenes where Joyce pictured his stories taking place. After some eighty years, during which Dublin became the capital of an independent republic, much has disappeared or changed. Among the disappearances, in addition to the horse-drawn tram upon whose step the youthful Stephen hesitated to embrace E— C—, must be numbered the Nelson Pillar and the Pigeon House, together with a great deal of the eighteenth-century domestic architecture which, in various states of repair, must have formed the background as Joyce recalled it.

The only events in *Ulysses* located outside this area are Stephen's memories of Paris and Molly's of Gibraltar. The latter was a city which he had to construct imaginatively, but Stephen's memories matched Joyce's own. The pilgrim treading Joyce's Parisian footsteps, however, might well prefer to follow him in his later and longer sojourn—not by tracing his family's restless moves from one lodging to another, but by sitting down to a good meal, ordered without regard to cost in an expensive restaurant, as Joyce enjoyed inviting guests to do. As Sylvia Beach recalls:

> The head-waiter would read to him the items on the bill of fare so that he would be spared the trouble of getting out several pairs of glasses and perhaps a magnifying glass. Joyce pretended to take an interest in fine dishes, but food meant nothing to him, unless it was something to do with his work. He urged his family and the friends who might be dining with him to choose the best food on the menu. He liked to have them eat a hearty meal and persuaded them to try such and such a wine. He himself ate scarcely anything, and was satisfied with the most ordinary white wine just as long as there was plenty of it. As he never drank a drop all day long, he was pretty thirsty by dinnertime. The waiter kept his glass filled. Joyce, would have sat there with his family and friends and his white wine till all hours if at certain moments Nora hadn't decided it was time to go...
>
> Wherever Joyce went, he was received like royalty, such was his personal charm, his consideration for others. When he started on his way downstairs to the men's room, several waiters came hurrying to escort him. His blindness drew people to him a great deal. (*Shakespeare and Company*, Faber 1959, p. 203.)

Although after the war there was a scheme to remove his remains from Zürich to Dublin, it came to nothing and perhaps peaceful and multi-lingual Zürich is their more appropriate resting-place. Accordingly it is to Zürich that the pilgrim must go to catch a last glimpse of an elegant 'gracehopper', seated in a pose characteristically loose-limbed and easy, not in the least monumental (p. 170).

Short biographies

Innumerable individuals whom Joyce knew during his early years contributed features to his fictitious characters. The interest of their lives to a Joyce reader is not, however, such as can be met by summary biographies, as it all lies in details. For example his clever but disreputable fellow-student Vincent Cosgrave, the original of Lynch in *A Portrait* and *Ulysses*, 'was committed to idleness and rancorous ill success' (Ellmann). Besides trying to convince Joyce that he had been having an affair with Nora at the time when Joyce and Nora fell in love, he failed to come to his friend's assistance when he was assaulted in the street (unlike Bloom, at the end of 'Circe'). He thus earned the name of 'Lynch', Lynch being a mayor of Galway who had hanged his own son.

For these and similar revealing details the reader is referred to Ellmann's life of Joyce and to *Surface and Symbol: The Consistency of James Joyce's 'Ulysses'* by R. M. Adams.

It is an interesting comment on the condition of Ireland in Joyce's youth that Byrne, the original of Cranly, emigrated to America and Skeffington, the original of McCann, met a violent death at the hands of the British when he tried to stop looting by soldiers during the Easter Rising. Clancy, the original of Davin, was murdered by Black and Tans when he was Mayor of Limerick, and Cosgrave committed suicide.

SYLVIA BEACH, 1887–1962. When she was fourteen, Sylvia Beach's father, a Presbyterian pastor, took his family to Paris where he had a temporary appointment looking after American students who were living there. The city made a due impression. She returned there in 1917 for a stay which even the German occupation of the city twenty-three years later failed to shorten. Shortly after her arrival her pursuit of everything that was new in literature led her to the bookshop of a radically modern young Frenchwoman, Adrienne Monnier, who herself admired things American. 'I was disguised in a Spanish cloak and hat, but Adrienne knew at once that I was American.' They became life-long friends, and in due course Sylvia Beach set up her own bookshop, Shakespeare and Company, just round the corner from her friend's, at 12 rue de l'Odéon.

Her shop was a hive of literary activity, the scene of frequent readings and organised discussions, with a lending library attached for those who wanted to keep in touch with the latest thing in literature. In particular it naturally attracted literary pilgrims from America, and served as a centre for the distinguised band of American

expatriate writers then working in Paris. Combined with Adrienne Monnier's contacts with the French literary world, her resources and influence, although materially slender, were formidable. The day when she suggested to Joyce that, in the absence of any other publisher, she might publish *Ulysses* for him was a milestone on his road to international fame.

Their subsequent relations were typical of Joyce's dealings with his Paris friends. He made continuous demands upon her services, and her advice. Attention, time and purse (in the form of advances) were willingly placed at his disposal. Believing in his genius, she was proud to be of help to him, and the association naturally enhanced her status. The bond however was subject to increasing strains, and weakened in the later years, especially when the American ban on *Ulysses* was lifted, and publication started in the USA.

Sylvia Beach remained in Paris throughout the German occupation, except for a six months' period of internment. Her own shop was eventually forced to close, but Adrienne Monnier stayed open, selling the clandestine publications of the underground Éditions de Minuit (which after the war were to sponsor the works of Samuel Beckett and the 'New Novel'). Sylvia Beach's memoirs, *Shakespeare and Company*, end comically but gracefully with the Liberation, in a scene featuring Ernest Hemingway arriving with his company to clear the rue de l'Odéon of snipers on his way to 'liberate the cellar at the Ritz'.

SAMUEL BECKETT, 1906–   . Born near Dublin into a Protestant family, Beckett studied at Trinity College and was then awarded a fellowship at the École Normale Supérieure in Paris, where he soon became a member of Joyce's intimate circle of helpers. Apart from a year as Assistant in French at his old college in Dublin—a post he resigned because he found academic life uncongenial—he spent the remaining years before the war mainly in London and Paris, writing unorthodox fiction and poetry which went virtually unrecognised. When war broke out he happened to be in neutral Ireland, but promptly returned to Paris where in due course he joined the Resistance. The last two years of the war he spent as a fugitive from the Gestapo, in Vichy France, where he joined the maquis when the Germans moved in.

In the years immediately following the war he experienced an extraordinary burst of creativity, writing, at first in conditions of considerable poverty, a series of novels and plays which won him international acclaim, culminating in the award of the Nobel Prize in 1970. By that time, however, his output had become scanty, and what there was of it lacked the ironic gaiety which, in the work of his middle period, balances his sterilising sense that there is 'nothing

Joyce and Sylvia Beach, standing in the doorway of Shakespeare & Co.

to express'. His presentation of absurdity has become increasingly desperate and stark, in direct contrast with that of Joyce, whose presentation of absurdity became increasingly elaborate and comic as he grew older. The sacramental sense of the creation which he had acquired as a Catholic did not leave Joyce when he had jettisoned his belief, whereas Beckett's Protestant directness forbade him to celebrate a universe in which he could see no meaning.

As a writer Beckett followed Joyce's example of exile, as also his preoccupation with technique and heroic devotion to his individual intention. He found himself as a writer, however, only when he had abandoned his early Joycean exuberance of language: as against the copiousness of the mature Joyce he deploys a style which really does manifest the quality Joyce attributed to the style of *Dubliners*— 'scrupulous meanness'.

FRANK BUDGEN, 1882–1971. One of the incidental pleasures of the study of Joyce is that of making the acquaintance of this robust and genial man who was too good a friend of Joyce to stand too much of his nonsense, yet subtle and appreciative enough for Joyce to respect as well as trust. Liberally self-educated, he had roughed it in his youth, and been a sailor before proceeding to Paris, in 1910, to learn to paint.

In 1914 he moved to Zürich, where he spent the war years working for the Ministry of Information and developing his art. In due course he met Joyce there, and became his appreciative critic and boon companion. After the war, when Joyce went to Paris, Budgen returned to England. Here he lived until his death, continuing with his painting as long as his eyesight permitted. His book *James Joyce and the Making of 'Ulysses'* is an indispensable commentary on the novel Joyce discussed with him, chapter by chapter, in the course of writing it. He also wrote an early introductory essay on *Finnegans Wake* which is still useful.

EDOUARD DUJARDIN, 1861–1949. Writer and editor, intimate of Mallarmé, an artist devoted to the inner life, Dujardin was a well-known literary figure in the Paris of his youth, where he espoused the twin causes of Wagner and Symbolism. He was best known for his aesthetic theories and his free-verse poems. Little attention was paid to his novel, *Les Lauriers sont coupés* (1887), although it was praised by a few, including his friend George Moore. In due course his other writings too fell out of fashion, and by 1920 he was only a figure in literary history, whose physical survival went unnoticed.

Suddenly, and successfully, *Les Lauriers sont coupés* was republished in 1924. It is the first novel ever written in which the entire action is registered in the mind of a single character, simultaneously with its occurrence, in the form of interior monologue. Joyce, who had acquired a copy during his 1902 stay in Paris, had informed Valéry Larbaud of his indebtedness to Dujardin, and this was the result. The old man was honoured and fêted, summoned, as he himself remarked, like Lazarus from the grave, by the new literary lion. He even wrote a book about his discovery.

His novel itself does not interest those whose curiosity moves them to read it, but according to Melvin Friedman (*Stream of Consciousness: a Study in Literary Method*, Yale University Press 1955): 'The germ of nearly all the techniques used after him, in the modern novel, is found in *Les Lauriers sont coupés*: the monologues of reminiscence and anticipation in Virginia Woolf, the passages of sensory impression in Dorothy Richardson, the rites of selfidentification performed by Proust's narrator and by Joyce's autobiographical hero, and the varying internal rhythms of the episodes of *Ulysses*.' In the light of this, Joyce's acknowledgement requires no justification, but it is illuminating to note that at the time it was attributed to a desire to deny his debt to psycho-analysis.

T. S. ELIOT, 1888–1965. With the support of Ezra Pound, T. S. Eliot quickly became an important literary influence in England, where he settled in exile in 1915 to become a naturalised citizen in due course. Unlike the other original *Egoist* writers, he continued to exercise his influence, not only as a major poet and critic but also as an editor and publisher, to support Joyce's reputation to the end— and even beyond it, when he wrote a letter protesting at *The Times*'s wartime dismissal of Joyce, upon his death, as a coterie author. For his part, while he found it hard to believe that *The Waste Land* was a major poem, the living Joyce valued this association.

Eliot, on his side, owed much to Joyce. He was the first critic to hail the mythical framework of *Ulysses* as the offer of a new perspective to the modern writer, and duly adopted this new method in his own work. Even in its detail *The Waste Land* reveals the influence of *Ulysses*—in such features as the dog which digs up the buried past and also the drowned sailor suffering a sea change.

His vision of the sordid city also runs parallel with that of Joyce, but in the opposite direction. The squalor that Joyce contemplated with relish filled Eliot with disgust. For Eliot's vision of 'the boredom, the horror and the glory' of life Joyce substituted one of vitality, acceptance and absurdity. Eliot might have been referring to *Finnegans Wake* in the lines—

> The lengthened shadow of a man
> Is history, said Emerson
> Who had not seen the silhouette
> Of Sweeney straddled in the sun.

For Eliot the squalid fact of Sweeney provides an ironic comment on Emerson's exaltation of a human being. In *Finnegans Wake* Joyce presents the lengthened shadow of just such a man to celebrate his humanity even while he ridicules his silhouette.

OLIVER ST JOHN GOGARTY, 1878–1957. In *It Isn't This Time of Year at All: an unpremeditated autobiography*, Gogarty declared. 'As "I am a part of all that I have met", you can judge me on the principle of "show me your company and I'll tell you who you are".' While Joyce would not have accepted this as a general principle, he would certainly have applied it to Gogarty, who was an essentially public character. For Joyce this meant that he must be a fraud, who took his lead from his audience. For Gogarty it meant that he was a good fellow, which was how he portrayed himself in several volumes of reminiscence. The less agreeable portrait presented in *Ulysses*, where he features as Buck Mulligan, infuriated him. 'That bloody Joyce whom I kept in my youth has written a book you can read on all the lavatory walls in Dublin.'

In fact the difference is not so much between two views of Gogarty as between two viewpoints. Joyce would have agreed that Gogarty was what he thought he was—a man of the world and a man of action. The latter point is granted unequivocally, when Stephen (in 'Proteus') acknowledges that he would not himself have the courage to save a man from drowning as Mulligan had—and Gogarty did. Gogarty also showed courage during 'the Troubles' when, as an outspoken opponent of Sinn Fein, he was the target of several shootings and the victim of a kidnapping from which he escaped by his own efforts. Eventually he was forced to lie low in England for a year, and, upon his return, eschewed party politics, although he was a senator from 1922 to 1936. He was also a noted sportsman, not to mention a leading surgeon and physician and a wit.

What Joyce would not have recognised was Gogarty's claim to be a poet. Many distinguished men of letters, however, respected him in this rôle, including W. B. Yeats who was a personal friend. His approach to literature, like that of Mulligan, was hellenist, and consequently his hostility to Joyce was guided by more than personal resentment. He deplored any art in which, in his words. 'discord (took) the place of harmony, disruption the place of unity'. As for *Finnegans Wake*, according to Gogarty it was a case of Joyce reduced to talking to himself in his sleep, because nobody else would listen to him any more.

EUGÈNE JOLAS, 1894–1952. Jolas was born a cosmopolitan. Torn between the claims of French and German, he would scarcely have had a native language even if he had been born in his parents' native Lorraine, but, as they were immigrants in America at that time, English also had a bid. When he was two, the family returned to Europe, and he grew up cherishing a romantic view of the New World. Returning there, at the age of sixteen, he found it to be the home not, as he had believed, of spiritual enlargement, but rather of mechanical enslavement. Highly literate, he worked his way up from menial jobs to journalism, but found no satisfaction in the achievement. News reporters, he decided, were not, as they themselves liked to think, 'mythmakers in the individual chaos'. They were working for the triumph of the machine.

Journalism did, however, offer him a chance to become a mythmaker himself. Returning to Europe, he replaced Ford Madox Ford as literary editor of the Paris *Tribune*, in which capacity he made it his business to acquaint Americans with the latest developments of art in Europe, and Paris in particular. In due course he intensified this activity by starting the periodical *transition*, whose title indicates his *avant-garde* intentions. He wanted to introduce his readers to current artistic stirrings before they had become established movements. In this it must be granted that he succeeded, as the list of contributors to *transition* makes clear. *Finnegans Wake*, appearing in instalments as *Work in Progress* as Joyce advanced with it, provided an element of continuity, but there was a host of other names which have since become famous. Nor did Jolas confine his attention to Paris, although Paris alone, at that time, supplied an interesting selection of writers and painters from many countries. He published indigenous Americans and also East Europeans, including the Russians Blok and Esenin.

Behind this fruitful editorial activity lay a theory of art. It was fortunate that this theory was a woolly one: its woolliness enabled him to welcome any iconoclast as an ally. The vagueness and unsubstantial optimism of his thinking, however, have attracted much critical contempt. In general he was proclaiming a revolution which by freeing the human mind from conventional blinkers— especially those imposed by language—would, he believed, enable mankind to understand the nature of reality for the first time. The Surrealists came nearest to embodying his aspirations. Joyce, for his part, although he appreciated the services of Jolas, who remained his loyal friend, was careful not to identify himself with this 'Revolution of the Word'.

transition never made a profit, and the last number had already appeared when war broke out in 1939. In 1940 Jolas, and his wife Maria, returned to America. Although he returned to Europe after the war, eventually settling in Paris, the scene had changed, and he relinquished the title *transition* to a newer movement.

JOHN S. JOYCE, 1849–1931. The only son of a flashy, generous father who died when he was still young, John Joyce inherited property and talents which would have proved a more than modest competence had he been less reckless and excitable. His youth abounded in vain attempts—to join the French army in the Franco-Prussian War, to join the Fenians in the national struggle, to train for a professional singing career. His brief career in business, as secretary to a distilling company, was suddenly cut short when the company went bankrupt. This failure was due to no fault of his, and indeed he was thanked by the shareholders for his efforts on their behalf in the crisis.

His next easy employment was probably what unfitted him for self-supporting effort for the rest of his life. For services to the Liberal Party (which was sympathetic to Home Rule) he received a well-paid, undemanding post in the office of the Collector of Rates for Dublin. 'I was cock of the walk that day,' he mused later, remembering election day, 'and I will never forget it.' At this stage in his life, despite his marriage and the acquisition of a multiplying family, his salary added to the income from his property (to which some loans upon that property were already joined) enabled him to live in the style he found so congenial, displaying his prowess as a singer, oarsman, drinker and conversationalist. As a small child his eldest surviving son, James, enjoyed the attentions of a nurse-maid, and was sent to a prestigious school.

Already, however, he was living slightly above his income rather than below it. The margin widened enormously and suddenly when, owing to the reorganisation of local government, his post was abolished. For the rest of his life his income was the return—continually diminishing as he realised his capital—upon the property his father had left him, together with an inadequate pension and the meagre rewards of the chance employment placed in his way by charitable acquaintances. Required to state his father's occupation when he entered university, James Joyce wrote, 'entering competitions'.

By all accepted standards his life was a failure, and he behaved like one. He was not only irresponsible and selfish but sometimes also vicious and malevolent in his treatment of his family. Stanislaus, whose Dublin diary affords remorseless glimpses of his father in decline, declared that he was one of the deserving poor—i.e. those who deserved to be poor. Perhaps the most repelling incident was his outburst when, coming home drunk during his wife's last illness, he shouted at her to get her dying over with. It takes a great deal, in such a context, to accept the quiet answer he gave to the indignant Stanislaus on that occasion: 'You don't understand, boy.' James Joyce did understand, however, because he admired his father's wasted gifts—his voice, his wit, and also the strong, incongruous rationality which manifested itself in some of his recorded judgements if not in his behaviour. Thus, cursing at the weather one wet day he was reproached by a pious friend: 'Hush John! Do you not know that God could drown the world?' 'He could', came the reply, 'if he wanted to make a bloody fool of himself.'

He had a special affection for his eldest son, and was proud of his success. 'He was the silliest man I ever knew, and yet cruelly shrewd', Joyce commented when he died. 'He thought and talked of me up to his last breath. I was very fond of him always, being a sinner myself, and even liked his faults.'

STANISLAUS JOYCE, 1884–1955. The first thirty years of Stanislaus Joyce were devoted to his brother James, in whose genius he had an unwavering confidence from boyhood, although he deeply disapproved of his behaviour. 'One must judge him by his moments of exaltation, not by his hours of abasement', he reminded himself in his youthful diary. It is easy to smile at his primness at a safe remove from Joyce's irresponsibility and selfishness, but Stanislaus certainly earned the right to criticise by the devotion with which he placed his purse and his time at his brother's disposal during the years they spent together as teachers in Trieste, before the outbreak of war in 1914.

Their separation at that time, caused by Stanislaus's internment by the Austrian authorities, proved permanent, apart from Joyce's brief return from Zürich to Trieste after the war, and a couple of subsequent brief meetings. It was caused by factors deeper than the accident of residence. *Ulysses* constituted a departure from the inspiring role he had mapped out for his brother. He was nothing if not serious, and his conception of seriousness, though always honest, was remarkably priggish. As *Finnegans Wake* began to appear in serial form his disapproval turned into contemptuous dismissal. The work on which Joyce spent his enormous energies for the best part of twenty years was, in his opinion, 'a drivelling rigmarole'. Nevertheless the two brothers remained in touch, and still felt some responsibility for each other. The last missive Joyce wrote was a postcard to Stanislaus, giving him the names of people in Italy who might be of use to him in the difficult position in which he found himself as a British subject now Italy had entered the Second World War.

An outspoken man with strong, narrow principles, Stanislaus had a way of provoking trouble, as when in his youth he refused to perform his Easter religious observance. In the same way, unlike his brother, he was interned by the Austrian authorities during the First World War on account of his open hostility. Similarly, during the Fascist régime, he was temporarily deprived of his professorship at Trieste. (On this occasion James Joyce again marshalled his Italian friends in his brother's support.) Temperamentally he was the opposite of his brother, who cast him in the antagonist role—the ant versus the grasshopper—in *Finnegans Wake*, where his features merge with those of other authoritarian personalities such as Wyndham Lewis and De Valera. Another portrait of his self-sufficiency is presented in the character of Mr Duffy in 'A Painful Case'. The portrait of Stanisluas as Maurice, in *Stephen Hero*, is more affectionate.

He died in 1955 on 16 June—'Bloomsday'.

VALÉRY LARBAUD, 1881-1957. Born with a silver spoon in his mouth, Larbaud was a sickly child, who early learned the pleasures of imagination. His first literary work was published when he was only sixteen. Another source of pleasure to him was the unfamiliar. He travelled widely in Europe and North Africa, and, in a series of books, created a fictitious equivalent of himself, a hedonistic South American millionaire named A. O. Barnabooth, who escaped the threat of boredom by indulging his curiosity in a vagabond but well-appointed way of life. In 1935 he fell ill and was stricken dumb as well as paralysed. Nevertheless, he continued to write essays and critical articles.

As might be expected, his sympathies were cosmopolitan, and he had an unusually wide knowledge of literatures in languages other than French. (The books in his library of 12,000 volumes were bound in their national colours.) Much of his writing took the form of translations from several languages, but especially English. He regarded it as his special task to acquaint French readers with new literary experiences offered in other tongues, and enjoyed a special reputation in that field.

It was therefore a great step for Joyce when, even before *Ulysses* was fully completed, they met and Larbaud became his devoted admirer. (Joyce, as Larbaud later remarked, could talk about nothing and still seem a genius.) He helped to launch the publication of *Ulysses* with a lecture, well staged at her bookshop by Sylvia Beach, and in due course he assisted with the translation of the novel into French. He also invented the term 'interior monologue', and was quick to adopt this new narrative method in a work of his own, with due acknowledgements to Joyce, who remained his friend until his death.

WYNDHAM LEWIS, 1884-1957. Lewis, who was no less distinguished as a painter than as a writer, studied at the Slade School and then spent the early years of the century in Paris, where he developed an avant-garde enthusiasm for form. Returning to London in 1909 he became an associate of Ezra Pound with whom he founded the Vorticist Movement. His paintings, which were revolutionary in their vision, brought him more fame than his writing, although much of the latter was outrageously polemical, galvanised by aggressive comparisons and truculent exaggerations.

He also wrote stories and novels, *Tarr* (1918) being published by the Egoist Press. His approach to fiction, and satirical fiction in particular, was innovatory. Dispensing with the terms in which human behaviour is conventionally explained, he described characters in action much as the behaviour of birds might be described by an ornithologist of genius who scrupulously eschewed the fallacy of comparing them with men.

Nevertheless by the outbreak of the Second World War his name no longer ranked with those of Eliot, Pound and Joyce with whom he was still proud to be associated, despite his public airing of their differences. This relative neglect was doubtless due in part to the arrogant and ill-judged invective that he discharged in all directions, most of them unpopular. There was, however, a more valid reason for his failure: he dissipated his enormous energy in ill-considered squibs. Perhaps he lacked the patience and humility required for major artistic achievement. Nevertheless his work is still alive because it still creates offence together with some enthusiasm, for he was one of the first to adopt many of the current concerns of thoughtful novelists and cultural critics.

Joyce took very seriously the criticism of *Ulysses* in *Time and Western Man* (1927) in which, among other memorable observations, his novel was described as 'an Aladdin's cave of incredible bric-à-brac'. It was the first attack to be made on him by a critic who understood his importance. His revenge was to cast Lewis in the role of Shaun in *Finnegans Wake*, which makes use of many of Lewis's remarks. This identification was unjust, in that Lewis even more than Joyce was an enemy of the people. But Joyce was right to see in him his opposite. Where Joyce was ambiguous and subtle, Lewis was dogmatic and simple. Joyce explored himself mockingly: Lewis asserted himself truculently. Joyce's ridicule is sympathetic, whereas that of Lewis is contemptuous. Joyce's art is fluid and aural, while Lewis strove for fixed visual shapes. Joyce prized innocuous forms of life, Lewis, dangerous ones. Where Lewis resembled Joyce was in his sharp sense of the ridiculous—and in the struggle with blindness which darkened the last years of his life.

GEORGE MOORE, 1852–1933. Born into a Catholic family of the Irish landed gentry, George Moore was educated in England, and spent his early manhood as a leisured dilettante in Paris, where he frequented artistic circles and became familiar with recent developments in painting and literature. As a result, when he took up a literary career, his work showed French influences, especially those of Zola and (in description) the Impressionist painters. Besides espousing the realist's edifying aim of telling his readers the facts of contemporary life he also took pleasure in shocking them.

His characteristic blend of pessimism, conceit and mischief made him an unsuitable associate for the writers of the Irish Movement, with which he cultivated an active relationship during its early days. Despite his admiration for Yeats, he soon became bored with the make-believe. The twilit atmosphere which made peasants appear like sages did not suit his sceptical eyesight. In due course he returned to England to publish three volumes of fictionalised memoirs— *Hail and Farewell* (1911)—which presented an entertaining, memorable but unreliable account of his recent adventures in the land of his birth.

In *Ulysses*, during the Library discussion, it appears that a literary party is to be held that evening at his house, where Mulligan is welcome but Stephen is not. This is typical of his relations with Joyce at the time when the novel is supposed to occur: he was not impressed by the young man's poems, and had nothing else to judge him by. Later, however, he acknowledged Joyce's powers. Consulted about a grant from the Civil List for Joyce, during his Zürich period, he confessed his envy in respect of 'The Dead'. Joyce similarly paid him the tribute of a cautious respect, but their relations were never cordial.

In many respects Moore was Joyce's precursor—in his preference of European to Irish antecedents, his cult of prose style, his readiness to outrage social and sexual prejudices, his rejection of the Irish Movement's mythology, his denunciation of the repressive role of Catholicism and the stunting of individualism in Ireland, not to mention his development of fictionalised autobiography and his readiness to put his acquaintances into his books. Perhaps the greatest difference between them was that between Joyce's copiousness and Moore's parsimony. His writing is characterised by an absence of relish, a wary celibacy. He distrusted productivity— hence Joyce's title for him of 'lecturer on French Letters to the youth of Ireland'. (The chief policy Moore recommended to Ireland was birth control.)

EZRA POUND, 1885–1972. Ezra Pound was born in Idaho, and educated at the University of Pennsylvania and Hamilton College. After a short period teaching, he left America for Europe in 1907 not to return, except for brief visits, until he was brought back as a prisoner in 1945 as a result of his support for the Fascist cause during the war. Immediately after his release from a mental hospital— for he was found insane instead of being prosecuted—he returned to Italy where he spent his last years. Like Joyce he was thus a self-appointed exile.

From 1907 until 1920 he spent most of his time in London, where he was the centre of literary innovation. His enthusiastic adaptations and translations of classic poems from other languages opened up new lines of development for English poetry. At the same time he was deeply involved in the revolutionary aesthetic theories of

Vorticism and Imagism. Through his influence with publishers he gave generous practical encouragement to new writers, of whom T. S. Eliot and James Joyce were the most notable.

From 1920, when he moved to Paris and thence later to Italy, Pound's sympathies moved away from Joyce. The later chapters of *Ulysses* had already dismayed him by their acrobatic style, and he found nothing to interest him in *Finnegans Wake*. The role for which he had cast his protégé was that of the English Flaubert, and he could not recognise a different achievement.

There was, moreover, a deep division of sensibility between the two men. Where Pound looked for strong heroes, Joyce found weak ones. Pound's social attitude was authoritarian and directive, Joyce's permissive and tolerant. The character of Bloom might be regarded as Joyce's answer to Pound's regrettable sneer, in his *Cantos*, at 'the warmth of family feeling, among the Jews of Central Europe.

GEORGE RUSSELL, 1867–1935. Born a Protestant, in poor circumstances, Russell studied painting after leaving school, and remained an occasional painter for the rest of his life, but is better known as a writer. At first as a hard-worked, ill-paid clerk and also librarian for the Dublin Lodge of the Theosophical Society, the only creative work for which he could find time was the writing of poetry. In this way he became known to W. B. Yeats, who secured him the post of village organiser for the Irish co-operative movement. Later he became editor of the *Irish Homestead*, organ of that movement, a position in which he played a considerable rôle in Irish intellectual and political life.

The first story of *Dubliners*, 'The Sisters', was published in Russell's paper, to be followed by two more. In general, however, Russell distrusted Joyce and Joyce despised Russell, although it was through the good offices of Russell that he first made himself known to the established literary world of Dublin. Conscientious and benevolent, Russell did many things to help Joyce, but less than for some other young people. For his part, Joyce was interested in Theosophy and Asian mysticism, which were Russell's main concern, but could not respect a spiritual innovator who was so subservient to proprieties. Together with Gogarty he played a practical joke on Russell's Hermetic Society, involving the use of women's underwear. It seems to have come as a relief to Russell when Joyce ran off with Nora Barnacle and, throwing forbearance aside without scruple he could inform Stanislaus, 'Your brother is a perfect little cad'. (Nevertheless, on the point of leaving, Joyce raised a loan from him which he acknowledged in Ulysses with the letters 'A.E.I.O.U'.)

'AE' was his pen-name, taken from the word 'aeon'. By this word he meant the process whereby, having departed from God in being individualised, a soul returned to God. In general his spiritual doctrine was one which, largely self-educated, he had concocted for himself from various esoteric or transcendental sources. The main aim of his life was not artistic creation but to tread the spiritual path. His ideal of perfection was not colourful. Abstinence played a great part in it. So, however, did honesty, and this involved him in controversy.

It was characteristic of Ireland at the turn of the century that his mysticism should have involved him in the national movement. Like Yeats, and many others, he believed that a world cataclysm was at hand which would be initiated by the appearance of a new messiah (complete with a sacred text) in Ireland. Firm in his principles, when the violence did come he did not shrink from it—not that he took part, but that he recognised it as something intrinsic to his hopes. The outcome, however, disappointed him. In an Ireland which, as he saw it, independence had merely made safe for materialistic commerce, he found himself increasingly out of place, and he died in England.

His later relations with Joyce were honourable and well-intentioned, and, in 1927, he was one of the 167 distinguished writers who protested against the pirating of a version of *Ulysses* (altered without authorisation) in the USA.

ETTORE SCHMITZ (Italo Svevo), 1861–1928. Born in Trieste, of German Jewish descent but Italian in his sympathies, Ettore Schmitz contributed elements to the character of Bloom, but was far more intellectually aware of the civilised scepticism inherent in his social role. He cultivated a deliberately bourgeois scepticism. When they met in 1906 he and Joyce quickly understood each other, and became intimate.

Schmitz had engaged Joyce to teach him English, a language he had a commercial use for as a banker, but, under the pseudonym Italo Svevo he had also, many years before, written two unsuccessful novels, one of which, *As a Man Grows Older* (1898), Joyce greatly admired. No doubt the fact that the book was written in an impure, non-literary Italian dialect assisted, rather than impeded, Joyce's appreciation, just as it had contributed to the novel's failure to find Italian readers.

When *Ulysses* made Joyce a power in the literary world he took care to praise his friend's work to Valéry Larbaud, who confirmed his judgement. 'Svevo' was translated, and eventually recognised even in Italy. Meanwhile he had written a third pessimistically funny novel, *The Confessions of Zeno*, the most famous feature of which is the opening chapter, where the hero's combined desire and refusal to be cured of his smoking habit comically and cunningly signifies a basic human ambiguity. Schmitz died as a result of a car crash, but not before enjoying one more cigarette which, he promised his wife who survived him, was really going to be his last.

Signora Schmitz made her own contribution to Joyce's work, who gave her name Livia to Anna Livia Plurabelle in *Finnegans Wake*, also endowing his heroine with her original's abundant auburn hair. In Dublin, he explained, the waters of the Liffey receive a reddish tinge from the effluents from the dye-works.

HARRIET SHAW WEAVER, 1876–1961. The long life of Miss Weaver continuously displayed that utter devotion to the task in hand which Joyce brought to his art. The dutiful daughter of pious and philanthropic parents, she spent her time in the service of others. Starting as a Sunday-school teacher and then as a social welfare worker, she grew away from the domestic religious background under the influence of thinkers like John Stuart Mill, to become an altruistic rationalist, but still preserved her deep family feeling. Strong personal loyalties, above all to James Joyce, characterised all her dealings.

Inheriting considerable wealth, she regarded her money as a trust to be exercised for the public benefit. In 1913 she became the chief financial support and business manager of *The New Freewoman*, a journal espousing the cause of women's rights, but also involved in a wider championship of 'philosophic individualism'. It quickly developed into a purely literary publication. Ezra Pound acted as adviser, and Richard Aldington and T. S. Eliot were in turn assistant editors. Miss Weaver herself became editor in 1914, and remained so until the demise of the journal in 1924. During that time she had assisted many distinguished writers in their first steps to recognition.

Prominent among these writers was Joyce, whose *A Portrait of the Artist as a Young Man* first appeared in *The Egoist* in serial form. Miss Weaver found it superbly truthful and beautiful, and when she learned of the hand-to-mouth existence of its author she decided to use her wealth to release him from financial cares. This task lasted as long as Joyce had life. Chronically incapable of living within his income, he repeatedly dipped into the considerable sums she kept settling upon him, instead of contenting himself with the interest. Nevertheless her respect for him never wavered, and she saw him through every crisis, although before the end relations between them had been marred by an unjustified coldness on his part, so that at times she only learned of his needs through an intermediary.

To a sympathetic observer the story of their relationship reveals the strain under which Joyce lived for the last fifteen years of his life, no less than his undeniable egoism. Indeed it might have seemed that two such different characters—he disciplined only in his art, she, for her part, intensely and even comically proper—were destined to disagree. At first, however, although never intimate

they seemed curiously well matched, because with all save a few chosen companions Joyce employed a formal reserve of manner to equal that of Miss Weaver. He was also naturally grateful, and feeling she had a special claim to his work he regularly sent her manuscripts and proofs of *Finnegans Wake* as it progressed, as well as discussing it with her.

After some years, however, her frankness compelled her to reveal to him her fear that he was wasting his genius on the production of a curiosity of literature. Her sense of responsibility also made it impossible to conceal her alarm at his drinking and her concern at his improvidence. Most wounding of all, although she more than once undertook the arduous and thankless task of looking after his daughter Lucia, she was frankly unable to support his insistence that the girl was entirely sane. As a result, although her affectionate devotion never wavered, Joyce came to regard Miss Weaver with distrust and suspicion, as somebody who was prejudiced against him. Nevertheless, he still counted upon her assistance in his various difficulties. When he came to die, it fell to her to pay the funeral expenses and act as literary executrix.

Meanwhile, in 1936 she joined the Communist Party. Humility was her most unfailing characteristic. Just as she never failed to render Joyce small tiresome services like making reservations and checking references, so, as a communist, she rejoiced in marching, handing out leaflets, secretarial duties and working in a bookshop. She remained a loyal communist until her death, and was to be seen in her eighties, selling the *Daily Worker* in the streets of Oxford. She was also always available for consultation by Joyce scholars, who still derive unique advantage from the papers she collected.

W. B. YEATS, 1865–1939. Belonging to an earlier generation, W. B. Yeats nevertheless offers interesting similarities with Joyce. Perhaps the most revealing one is that although he won early acclaim in Ireland, and was the central figure of the Literary Revival, an admirer of Irish traditions, and honoured as a senator—in all of which he was Joyce's opposite—he nevertheless died abroad after several years' absence, if not in exile, at least having learnt the truth of Joyce's warning to him in *The Day of the Rabblement*: 'the artist, though he may employ the crowd, is very careful to isolate himself'. Like Joyce he had also come to respect 'the place of excrement', and to develop in his art an Irish relish of indecorum. His writing, like Joyce's, although less ostentatiously, displays idiosyncratic reading and draws on a fund of personal memories. He was also another constructor of schemes. It is characteristic of Joyce that he was one of the few admirers, when it appeared in 1925, of

Harriet Shaw Weaver

A Vision, in which Yeats simultaneously explained the history of mankind and the development of the individual human soul in terms of a reciprocating mechanism operated, in lunar phases, by two intersecting cones.

Quite possibly Yeats never devoted to Joyce's major work the attention required to appreciate it, and at first, when all Joyce had to his credit was his poems, he was irritated by the young Ibsenite's unwarranted pretensions. His efforts to help Joyce in his early days deserve all the more credit. On the occasion of Joyce's first departure abroad he put him into contact with journals and editors, to help him to earn something by book reviews. Ten years later it was Yeats who drew the attention of Ezra Pound to Joyce's poem 'I Hear an Army', thus at last opening the way to publication. During the war he used his influence to procure official recognition of Joyce's talent by a welcome grant from the Royal Literary Fund, followed by a grant from the Civil List. He admired *A Portrait*, and recognised that *Ulysses* was 'an entirely new thing'. This novelty, however, was something alien to him, a disintegration of what should remain whole, which he defined (in the first edition of *A Vision*) as the common characteristic of Joyce, Eliot, Pound and Pirandello.

Joyce shared this sense of a fundamental difference, and was not shy of publicly expressing it in his early days, as in *The Day of the Rabblement* and *The Holy Office*. He was also jealous of Yeats, which sharpened his tongue in private criticism. Thus, designating Ibsen and himself as intellectual strikers, he accused Yeats (in a letter to Stanislaus) of being an intellectual blackleg. Nevertheless he never lost the early admiration for Yeats's work which showed itself most convincingly in the way he helped to soothe his younger brother George, and also his mother, in their last days, by singing to them a poem of Yeats—'Who Goes with Fergus?' In 1939, when he heard of the death of Yeats, he was not content merely to acknowledge the many kindnesses he had received from him, but, astonishingly, added that Yeats was the better writer.

Bibliography

Works

1907 *Chamber Music*, Jonathan Cape, 1971.
1914 *Dubliners*, ed. R. Scholes, Jonathan Cape, 1971.
(1907) *Stephen Hero*, ed. T. Spencer, Jonathan Cape, 1969.
(1914) *Giacomo Joyce*, ed. R. Ellmann, Faber, 1968.
1916 *A Portrait of the Artist as a Young Man*, ed. C. G. Anderson,
   Jonathan Cape, 1968.
1918 *Exiles*, ed. P. Colum, Jonathan Cape, 1968.
1922 *Ulysses* (A definitive text is still awaited), Bodley Head, 1960.
1927 *Pomes Penyeach*, Faber, 1968. (This edition also includes *The Holy
   Office* and *Gas From A Burner*.)
1939 *Finnegans Wake*, Faber, 1964.
   Aesthetic Writings, ed. E. Mason and R. Ellmann, Faber, 1959.

Concordances

The peculiar significance of linguistic detail in Joyce's work makes
concordances more useful than is normally the case with prose.
Unfortunately the concordances refer to the pagination of American
editions which does not usually coincide with that of British editions.

G. LANE, *Word Index to James Joyce's 'Dubliners'*, Haskell, 1972.
C. G. ANDERSON, *Word Index to James Joyce's 'Stephen Hero'*, Norwood
   Editions, 1958.
L. HANCOCK, *Word Index to James Joyce's 'Portrait of the Artist'*, Univer-
   sity of Illinois, 1967.
M. L. HANLEY, *Word Index to James Joyce's 'Ulysses'*, University of
   Wisconsin, 1951.
C. HART, *A Concordance to 'Finnegans Wake'*, Appal, 1963.

Biography

A selection of Joyce's letters, edited by Stuart Gilbert, was published
in 1957. This early collection now forms the first volume of a three-
volume collection, edited by R. Ellmann (Faber, 1966), which is
accordingly not arranged in overall chronological order. A selection
including important letters missing from the collected edition (also
edited by R. Ellmann) was published in 1975 (Faber).
A vivid, if prejudiced, picture of Joyce's youth is painted by Stanislaus
Joyce in *My Brother's Keeper* (Faber, 1958). The indispensable work

for a student of Joyce's life is R. Ellmann's *James Joyce* (Oxford, 1959). Two books by Patricia Hutchins, *James Joyce's Dublin* (Methuen, 1959) and *James Joyce's World* (Methuen, 1957), trace his footsteps at home and abroad respectively, describing the places where he lived and relating some associated incidents. C. G. Anderson's *James Joyce and his World* (Thames & Hudson, 1967) contains a large and interesting selection of illustrations.

Background

SYLVIA BEACH, *Shakespeare and Company*, Faber, 1960.
R. ELLMANN, *Eminent Domain*, Oxford, 1967.
R. ELLMANN, *The Consciousness of Joyce*, Faber, 1977.
H. HOWARTH, *The Irish Writers*, Rockliff, 1959.
H. KENNER, *The Pound Era*, Faber, 1972.
WYNDHAM LEWIS, *Blasting and Bombardiering*, Calder, 1967.
D. MCMILLAN, *transition, The History of a Literary Era*, Calder, 1975.
V. MERCIER, *The Irish Comic Tradition*, Galaxy, 1962.
K. SULLIVAN, *Joyce Among the Jesuits*, Columbia University, 1958.
E. WILSON, *Axel's Castle*, Collins, 1962.

General criticism

The studies listed in this and the following three sections represent only a minute fraction of the available criticism, which is added to every year by new studies. As a result of Joyce's attachment to allusion, symbol and specific devices, much criticism of his work tends to be pedantic. No work which might be conclusively objected to on these grounds has been included, although several useful books have been omitted to make the list manageable. Although studies of individual works are separately listed, the reader should remember that some of the best introductory criticism of particular works is contained in the general studies. For example, the reader of *Ulysses* cannot do better than to start with the lengthy treatment of that novel in C. H. Peake's *James Joyce: the Citizen and the Artist*, and Matthew Hodgart's *James Joyce: a Student's Guide* provides the most useful companion to the reader embarking on *Finnegans Wake*.

Helpful early criticism of Joyce is contained in *James Joyce: Two Decades of Criticism*, ed. Seon Givens, (Vanguard Press, 1963), and a wide selection of reviews and other criticism published in Joyce's own lifetime is assembled in *James Joyce: The Critical Heritage*, ed. R. H. Deming (Routledge & Kegan Paul, 1970). Criticism which had appeared up to its date of publication is summarised and discussed in *James Joyce: The Man, The Work, The Reputation* by M. Magalaner and R. Kain (University of New York, 1956). Some idea of critical developments in the following decade can be gathered from the essays collected in *James Joyce Today*, ed. T. F. Staley (University of Indiana, 1969).

Two useful studies of particular aspects of Joyce's work are *Song in the Work of James Joyce*, by M. J. C. Hodgart and M. P. Worthington (Columbia, 1959), and A. W. Litz's *The Art of James Joyce* (Galaxy, 1964). The latter examines the methods by which Joyce composed and revised his major work. W. Noon's *Joyce And Aquinas* (Yale, 1957) is similarly specific.

A GOLDMAN, *The Joyce Paradox*, Routledge & Kegan Paul, 1966.

M. J. C. HODGART, *James Joyce: a Student's Guide*, Routledge & Kegan Paul, 1978.

H. KENNER, *Dublin's Joyce*, Peter Smith, 1955.

H. LEVIN, *James Joyce*, Faber, 1944.

C. MACCABE, *James Joyce and Revolution of the World*, Macmilliam, 1978.

C. H. PEAKE, *James Joyce: the Citizen and the Artist*, Arnold, 1977.

W. Y. TINDALL, *James Joyce: His Way of Interpreting the Modern World*, Scribners, 1950.

Early work

M. BEJA (ed.), *James Joyce's 'Dubliners' and 'A Portrait' (Casebook)* Macmillan, 1978.

T. E. CONNOLLY (ed.), *Joyce's Portrait: Criticism and Critiques*, Peter Owen, 1964.

C. HART (ed.), *James Joyce's 'Dubliners': Critical Essays*, Faber, 1969.

E. L. EPSTEIN, *The Ordeal of Stephen Dedalus*, Arcturus, 1973.

R. S. RYF, *A New Approach to Joyce*, University of California, 1964.

R. SCHOLES and R. KAIN (eds.), *The Workshop of Dedalus*, N. W. University, 1965.

T. F. STALEY and B. BENSTOCK (eds.), *Approaches to Joyce's 'Portrait'*, University of Pittsburgh, 1976.

Ulysses

The reader approaching *Ulysses* for the first time will be grateful for H. Blamires's attempt to supply a page-by-page summary of the action in *The Bloomsday Book*, (Methuen, 1966). He will also be saved some irritation by keeping at his elbow. Thornton's *Allusions in 'Ulysses'* (University of North Carolina, 1968).

R. M. ADAMS, *Surface and Symbol*, Oxford, 1962.

FRANK BUDGEN, *James Joyce and the Making of 'Ulysses'*, Oxford, 1972.

R. ELLMANN, *Ulysses on the Liffey*, Faber, 1973.

M. FRENCH, *The Book as World*, Harvard University Press, 1976.

S. GILBERT, *James Joyce's 'Ulysses'*, Faber, 1952.

s. l. GOLDBERG, *The Classical Temper*, Chatto and Windus, 1961.

m. GRODEN, *Ulysses in Progress*, Princeton University Press, 1977.

c. HART, *James Joyce's 'Ulysses'*, Sydney University Press, 1968.

c. HART, and d. HAYMAN (eds), *James Joyce's 'Ulysses': Critical Essays*, University of California, 1978. •

r. m. KAIN, *Fabulous Voyager*, University of Chicago, 1959.

j. h. MADDOX, *Joyce's 'Ulysses' and the Assault upon Character*, Harvester, 1978.

w. j. SCHUTTE, *Joyce and Shakespeare*, Yale Studies, 1957.

t. f. STALEY and b. BENSTOCK (eds), *Approaches to 'Ulysses'*, University of Pittsburgh, 1971.

w. b. STANFORD, *The Ulysses Theme*, Blackwell, 1954.

Finnegans Wake

The nature of *Finnegans Wake* is such that a reader will look in vain for a thread to lead him through it. Nevertheless he will receive the comforting illusion of one from *A Skeleton Key to Finnegans Wake* by J. Campbell and H. M. Robinson (Faber, 1947). This brave early attempt was made in advance of the detailed study to which the text has been subjected subsequently. More reliable but less specific guidance is offered in *A Conceptual Guide to Finnegans Wake* (Pennsylvania State University, 1974), edited by M. H. Begnal and F. Senn, in which a series of critics deal with the book chapter by chapter. W. Y. Tindall's *A Reader's Guide to Finnegans Wake* makes an anthusiastic personal attempt to render the same service, and offers explanations of a multitude of details while ignoring a host of others (Thames & Hudson, 1969).

Help with allusions and much more besides is available in J. S. Atherton's *The Books at the Wake* (Faber, 1959). Adaline Glashleen's *Third Census of Finnegans Wake* (University of California, 1977) is a suggestive work of reference.

The structure of the book is examined in C. Hart's *Structure and Motif in 'Finnegans Wake'* (Faber, 1962), and R. McHugh's *The Sigla of Finnegans Wake* (Arnold, 1976). One of the notebooks from which Joyce worked in composing his novel is published in T. E. Connolly's *Scribbledehobble* (North Western University Press, 1961).

An early, but still the most cogent, expression of reservations about the whole enterprise will be found in F. R. Leavis's 'James Joyce and "The Revolution of the Word"', *Scrutiny* II, 1933.

Acknowledgements

We are grateful to the following for permission to reproduce copyright material:

Faber and Faber and Harcourt Brace Jovanovich Inc for extracts from the poems 'Whispers of Immortality' by T.S. Eliot, 'The Love Song of Alfred J. Prufrock' by T.S. Eliot and 'The Waste Land' by T.S. Eliot from *Collected Poems 1909–1962*; Faber and Faber and New Directions (New York) for the poem 'The Return' by Ezra Pound from *Collected Shorter Poems* © 1926 by Ezra Pound, reprinted by permission of New Directions; The Society of Authors as the Literary representative of the Estate of James Joyce, The Bodley Head and Random House Inc for extracts from *Ulysses* by James Joyce. Copyright 1914, 1918 by Margaret Caroline Anderson and renewed 1942, 1946 by Nora Joseph Joyce. Reprinted by permission of Random House Inc; The Society of Authors as the Literary representative of the Estate of James Joyce and Jonathan Cape on behalf of the executors of the James Joyce Estate for extracts from *Stephen Hero* by James Joyce; The Society of Authors as the Literary representative of the Estate of James Joyce, Jonathan Cape, on behalf of the executors of the James Joyce Estate and Viking Press Inc for an extract from 'Chamber Music XXXV' in *The Portable James Joyce* with an introduction and notes by Harry Levin, copyright © renewed George Joyce and Lucia Joyce 1967 Reprinted by permission of Viking Penguin Inc; extracts from *Dubliners* by James Joyce, originally published by B.W. Huebsch in 1916 copyright © 1967 by the Estate of James Joyce. Reprinted by permission of Viking Penguin Inc; and extracts from *A Portrait of the Artist as a Young Man* by James Joyce copyright 1916 by B.W. Huebsch, 1944 by Nora Joyce copyright © 1964 by the Estate of James Joyce. Reprinted by permission of Viking Penguin Inc; The Society of Authors as the Literary representative of the Estate of James Joyce, Faber and Faber Ltd and The Viking Press Inc for extracts from *The Critical Writings of James Joyce* edited by Ellsworth Mason and Richard Ellmann copyright © 1959 by Harriet Weaver and F. Lionel Monro Administrators of the Estate of James Joyce. Reprinted by permission of Viking Penguin Inc; extracts from *Selected Letters of James Joyce* edited by Richard Ellmann copyright © 1957, 1966 by The Viking Press Inc. Copyright © 1966, 1975 by F. Lionel Monro as administrator of the Estate of James Joyce. Reprinted by permission of Viking Penguin Inc; and extracts from *The Letters of James Joyce Vol 2* edited by Richard Ellmann Copyright © 1966 by F. Lionel Monro as Administrator of the Estate of James Joyce.

Reprinted by permission of Viking Penguin Inc; The Society of Authors as the Literary representative of the Estate of James Joyce and Viking Press Inc for an extract from the poem 'Gas From a Burner' by James Joyce from *The Portable James Joyce* copyright © renewed The Viking Press Inc 1974, 1975 Reprinted by permission of Viking Penguin Inc.

We are grateful to the following for permission to reproduce photographs:

Beinecke Rare Book and Manuscript Library, Yale University, page 25; Calder and Boyars Ltd from *Blasting and Bombadiering* by Wyndham Lewis, page xii *right*; Croessmann Collection, Morris Library, Southern Illinois University at Carbondale, pages 86, 99, and 154; Richard Ellmann, Oxford, pages 55 and 56; Irish Times Library, page 97; James Joyce Museum, pages xii *left*, 18, 24, 127, 168, and 170 (photos: Irish Tourist Board), 18 *inset* and 192 (photos: John Morris); National Library of Ireland, pages 66, 67, and 125; Swiss National Tourist Office, page ii; Trustees of the Estate of James Joyce 1980, pages 92 and 151 (photos: James Joyce Museum/ Irish Tourist Board).

The painting *Bartender Reading a Letter* by Jack B Yeats is reproduced on the cover by kind permission of the artist's daughter, Annie Yeats (photo: Theo Waddington Gallery).

Whilst we have made every effort, we are unable to trace the copyright owner of the photograph reproduced on page 178 (provided by *Tuttolibri*, published by La Stampa, Turin) and would appreciate any information which would enable us to do so.

Index

Index to Joyce's Works